THIRTY MILES FROM PARADISE

THIRTY MILES FROM PARADISE

BOBBY LENNOX
with Graham McColl

headline

First published in 2007 by
HEADLINE PUBLISHING GROUP

1

Cataloguing in Publication Data is available from the British Library

ISBN 978 0 7553 1493 5

Career statistics compiled by Jack Rollin

Typeset in Garamond by Avon DataSet Ltd,
Bidford-on-Avon, Warwickshire

Printed and bound in Great Britain by
Mackays of Chatham plc, Chatham, Kent

HEADLINE PUBLISHING GROUP
A division of Hachette Livre UK Ltd
338 Euston Road
London NW1 3BH

www.headline.co.uk
www.hodderheadline.com

To Kathryn, my wife
and Gill, Garry and Jeff, my children.

CONTENTS

ACKNOWLEDGEMENTS

The strength and support of my family has been at the core of everything I have achieved in football and in life. Initially, that support came from Bobby, my father, Agnes, my mother, and Andrew and Eric, my brothers; then, in later years, from Kathryn, my wife, through 40 wonderful years of marriage. Gill, Gary and Jeff, my children, gave me great pleasure and joy through watching them grow up.

I would also like to thank the Lisbon Lions, a special group of people who shared with me in Celtic's greatest day and many other days on and off the football pitch.

Thanks also to Graham McColl for his commitment and craft in helping me with this book.

Finally, special thanks to everyone at Headline.

CHAPTER 1

HOME ADVANTAGE

Stamford Bridge in the late 1950s was an awesome sight and I was entranced as I stood on the pitch at Chelsea Football Club. Vast terraces stretched upwards on three sides of the ground and a set of six towering floodlights, newly installed and unique in top-flight British football, took the breath away. This was the kind of backdrop for football that I had dreamed about all of my short life and it was now within my grasp. As I stood on that pitch, though, feeling the first chills of autumn, I knew that the delights of the Kings Road, Chelsea FC and London life could not compare with the three towns that had dominated almost every waking moment of my early life and created horizons beyond which I felt little need to explore. The delights of London spluttered and fizzled like a soggy firework when set against the security I felt in my native Saltcoats and in Ardrossan and Stevenston, Saltcoats' two intertwined neighbouring towns on the Ayrshire coast. Chelsea were just one of a host of clubs that had shown a firm interest in my footballing talents once I had reached my mid-teens but, although I was desperate for a football career, every club's attempts to sign me had been thwarted by my love of my home environment. Chelsea, I knew, would be no different.

Colour and happiness had flooded my life ever since I had entered the world on 30 August 1943 in a small tenement house on Quay Street, Saltcoats, about 100 yards from the harbour. Woolworths was just around the corner, as was Patrick's, the toyshop, establishments that were uppermost in my infant thoughts. The 'shows', with their roundabouts, dodgem cars and games stalls, were always across the road during the summertime. I would also frequently be found wandering around down at the harbour, which was the main attraction for the young children of the area. It was a busy wee harbour, crowded with boats of all sizes, shapes and hues. As a three- and four-year-old, picking my way across the first stepping stones of life, the gaudy charms of that seaside scene, with the limpid greens, blues and reds of the boats bobbing in the harbour, afforded me a bright window on the world and soothed my soul. It lost none of its charm for me as I grew into boyhood and then adulthood.

Saltcoats in summer offered a holiday town's host of quirky, extra opportunities for innocent fun, such as splashing around in the outdoor bathing pool every day and using the beach for all sorts of childish games. The seafront would be populated by characters trying to make a quick buck from holidaymakers, but some among the natives, including my cousin Tommy Hughes and me, were equally susceptible to their approaches. Wandering up the street on summer days we two would regularly have our pictures taken by one of the jobbing photographers who offered to take a souvenir snap – for a price of course. My mother must have been sick of me coming back to the house to beg for the money to meet the cost of capturing yet another 'classic' seafront moment, not as a reminder of an annual holiday but of a mere stroll down our town's familiar streets. I had hundreds of them.

Thousands of visitors flooded into Saltcoats every summer during the boom years of the 1940s and 1950s, and when the trains came in they would be greeted by the Saltcoats boys standing with their barrows and bogeys, ready to haul people's suitcases to their guest-houses and hotels in exchange for a few bob. During the Glasgow Fair holiday fortnight, in July, the town would be mobbed. Everybody from Glasgow visited Saltcoats on holiday at some stage. The pubs and shops would be busier during the summer and people would turn their houses into bed and breakfast accommodation. It all meant that there was money constantly coming into the town, which was no bad thing, of course.

Life was not without the occasional touch of harsh reality, though, such as the day when my curiosity got the better of me around age seven and I wandered too close to the harbour's edge. Boats were launched via a slipway and I had one hand on the ledge there while trying to scoop a jellyfish out of the water with the other one. The jellyfish was of a non-stinging variety I hasten to add. I wasn't that daft. I lost my balance when my hand slipped, and I toppled into the water – a serious business for a non-swimmer. I can still recall gurgling water as I began to slip under the surface. Fortunately, two or three of the other boys managed to get a hold of me and dragged me out. They saved my life. It's a funny thing but although we were never away from the water when I was a child, I hate boats. Put me on the deck of any floating craft and you'll soon have a seasick sailor on your hands.

That seaside idyll meant that I was divorced from the bleak, industrial, city environment that shaped so many other young footballers of that era, but in Ayrshire football was still inseparably entwined in the existences of almost all youngsters. The game was especially inescapable for me. Andrew and Eric, my two brothers, were both accomplished amateur players and because they were considerably older than I was, I idolised them and everything they did, especially their feats in football. Andrew, who was 14 years old when I was born, played left-back, and Eric, who was nine, was good enough to play centre-forward for the Scotland Under-15 team. The biggest and most subtle influence on me, though, was my father, Bobby. Together, they sent me careering down a footballing path.

My dad was football-daft, loved the game, but I never saw him play and never even heard him talk about having played. He was a bookmaker's assistant so he was unable to attend matches on a Saturday but when I was small, when we lived in Quay Street during my earliest days, he would take me along to attend a lot of Junior games during the week. We'd maybe go to watch Irvine Victoria playing on a Monday night, Irvine Meadow on a Wednesday night and Ardeer Thistle on a Friday night – nor were we lone eccentrics in this pursuit. Junior clubs in the postwar decade were benefitting enormously from a huge jump in attendances. Few people had their own cars or television sets, so for colourful entertainment they would go to watch these most local of clubs. The grounds were always busy. You would actually have to queue at the turnstiles even if you arrived in good time for the match. Almost as soon as I was walking, my father, accompanied by three or four of his cronies, would take his wee boy along, and I would listen to Bobby senior talking away about football to his friends. It was his main subject of conversation.

Bookmaking was illegal during that postwar era, so my father did not work out of a set of premises. He would, instead, stand on the corner of Hirst Place in Saltcoats and people would approach him surreptitiously if they wished to place a bet. That favoured spot of his was within 20 yards of the sea and, as he waited there, the waves would sometimes come battering in and he'd have to take refuge at the mouth of a close, with water lapping at his feet. He would be 'lifted' by the police every so often, taken to the police station and fined and warned.

In those days, a policeman would tell my dad one day, 'Bobby, I'm going to take you into the police station tomorrow.' My father would respond, 'Right, see you then.' Next day they would both be as good as their words. The police had to make their presence felt occasionally, just to show they were remaining on top of things.

I think my dad quite enjoyed his work. He would have a flutter from time to time, but little enjoyment of gambling rubbed off on me. I have never had an urge to bet. My father had not always worked in the bookmaking business. He also worked in the shipyard in Ardrossan and he helped to build the sea wall at Saltcoats – something of which he would often, amusingly, remind me when we were on the seafront. He was a good worker and provided well for his family.

When I was four years old, we moved from Quay Street to Kinnier Road, farther up the town from the harbour, where we set ourselves up in a very well-presented council house. Moving there gave me even more opportunities to learn how to play football. We now lived only around 100 yards from a massive public park, so as often as I wished – which was a lot – I could spring on to its lush turf and roam free with a football at my feet. If I needed some variety, I could visit another park, which had a set of football pitches, although that was a bit farther away – all of 500 yards. I spent most of my free time down in those two parks, and I always had the ball with me. Almost every boy in the neighbourhood was the same. Half an hour after school, my friends and I would already have had our tea and, along with dozens of other boys, we would be out playing football until darkness cast its cloak over our games. Even from when I was extremely small, I took great delight in scoring goals. My dad never really prodded me or encouraged me to practise my game, but his deep love of football must have had a huge influence on me trying to improve as a player. Other guys' fathers would go out into the park and play with them but my dad never did that, principally because he was an older father. He was 44 when I was born. I went everywhere else with my dad and had great fun with him and, partly because of the nature of his work, I probably saw more of him than most boys did of their fathers.

All that practice meant that I must have developed into quite a good wee player because I was picked for the school team when I was eight – the only boy in my class to be given that honour. On the day on which I was due to make my debut, Mr McCann, the headmaster at St Mary's, my primary school, handed me my strip and told me that the bigger boys in the team would come to my class at half past three to collect me and take me to the match, which was to be played in Ardrossan. Such scenarios are really intense at that age – playing for the school team is the real thing and gives you a feeling of exclusivity. By twenty past three I was getting really nervous, sitting in the class waiting for those ten- and eleven-year-olds, all of whom seemed like giants to me.

Each passing minute weighed more and more heavily on me until I could take no more and at twenty-five to four, five minutes after the big boys had been supposed to collect me, I said to the teacher, 'Miss, I need to go home.' She reminded me that the boys were due to take me to the match. I said, 'Miss, I've got to go home. I'm not feeling well.' She told me to go to the headmaster, which I did and, handing back the strip, I told him I was going home because the boys hadn't come to collect me. He told me I could take a bus and get to the game that way but I insisted that I was going home. The excitement, the nervousness and the anticipation of the match had overwhelmed me so much that when the boys hadn't turned up, something inside me had made me determined never to go through that again.

The bigger boys had simply forgotten to collect me but the entire experience had a huge effect on me. Next time I was selected for the school team, I insisted I was not going to play and that led Mr McCann to contact my parents. My father told me that it was fine with him if I didn't want to play. Again, he didn't put pressure on me to forge my way forward in football.

The giving up of my place in the school team, even before I had kicked a ball, hurt me less than a more direct and hard-hitting repercussion from that episode. I had been in the habit of dashing home for lunch, which my mother always had out on the table, then dashing out again for a lunchtime kick-about with my school-mates. After absenting myself from duty with the school team, Mr McCann told me that, as punishment, I could no longer play with my pals at lunchtime and would, instead, be confined to a watching role. My mum intervened, telling Mr McCann that this was unfair and vindictive, and before long I was back playing with the boys at lunchtimes. I never did, in my remaining years at primary school, kick a ball for the school team.

There was, despite that hiccup, no diminution in my obsession with football, both as participant and spectator, and not only at the Junior matches that had initially enthralled me with their small-scale spectacle. The first time I ventured to see Celtic was in their match against Arsenal, the champions of England, in the first round of the Coronation Cup, an eight-team tournament held in May 1953 to celebrate the coronation of Queen Elizabeth II and featuring top Scottish and English clubs. My dad took me up to Hampden Park in Glasgow to see the game and, together with some of his friends, we travelled all the way there and back in style, by taxi – at least that was how it seemed to my impressionable nine-year-old mind. We were actually taken in someone's car but it was so rare for someone to own a car at that time that I assumed we must have been in a taxi. The grandeur of the occasion made a serious impression on me. We were among a crowd of 60,000 who saw Bobby Collins give Celtic a 1–0 victory, scoring direct from a corner. The following evening we were back in Glasgow to see Glasgow Rangers play Manchester United. My dad was a Celtic man but he was, just as much, a football man. He'd sometimes come in on a Saturday and say, 'The racing's been cancelled today but there's a match on at Ibrox and if we get a train we can be there.' So off we'd go to Saltcoats station to catch the train up to Glasgow. He loved the football so much that seeing a match, the best match he could see, was his greatest priority, even though Celtic was the team he favoured.

I was reasonably able at school and even sat for the Dux medal at St Mary's, although whether I ever had any chance of getting it, I don't know. There was no big build-up to the exam. We had been queuing up to go to class after lunch one day – football was part of our PE class that afternoon – when the names were read out of those who were to sit for the Dux exam. They had selected the top three pupils in each of the four classes. I was surprised to be included – I thought plenty of other boys in the school were cleverer than I was – but the teachers must have seen something in me. I still wasn't too happy about it – I was furious that I was going to miss my football that afternoon. That was an early indication of my priorities in life.

I passed the 11-plus, an examination taken by all children in their final year of primary school and a test that was feared greatly because it could determine, even at that early stage of your life, what would happen to you as an adult. If you failed it, you went to a school that concentrated on technical subjects and that meant you would almost certainly become a manual worker. If you passed, you would go to a school where they focused on academic subjects and that meant you had a strong chance of becoming a white-collar worker. My passing the 11-plus meant I moved on to St Michael's College in Irvine, rather than St Peter's, the technical school. It was a big thing for me to go to St Michael's because going to St Peter's would have meant that I had failed – and I didn't like failure. The education I received at St Michael's helped set me up for life and made me a more rounded person.

As my youthful years passed, very enjoyably, I went from being ahead of my time as a young footballer to slipping behind my football-playing pals. As we moved from primary to secondary school, they were spending their Saturday mornings playing organised, 11-a-side football, but I refused to do so. The blight of the experience I had suffered as an eight-year-old meant that I would not even consider playing for St Michael's. I remained hugely enthusiastic about the game – I was still in the park with my ball, morning, noon and night – but that early episode had left me with a mental block in terms of playing for an organised team.

One Saturday morning when I was 12 years old, I wandered down to a local playing field in Auchenharvie Park, which is situated between Saltcoats and Stevenston, to watch some of my friends participating in a match between Saltcoats Scouts and a team called St John's. It turned out that the Scouts were a man short and when I strolled up, having calculated that I would be arriving just as the game was kicking off, as was my wont to avoid getting roped in to play, Mr Nolan, a lovely man who ran the Scouts team, said to me, 'There's a strip, Bobby – on you go, quick, go and play left-half.' I had no time to get nervous or worry, no time even to think about refusing. The game had only just begun and I simply did as he asked me. Without ceremony, I was suddenly on a football park and playing for a team. I just put the strip on and played. It's strange when you can pinpoint one single day that has changed your life forever. One request from one person, and the fact that I listened, set me on a course that was to provide the most thrilling football life imaginable. It was a Saturday in September 1955. I did well and Frank Quinn, a great man who ran St John's, asked me to play for them on the following Saturday. I agreed and before long I was co-opted into the St Michael's school team and that was me off and rolling. I had really wanted to play in a proper team all along but had just been unable to bring myself to do it.

A couple of teachers at St Michael's, Mr Leishman and Mr McGuire, helped me with my game, and Mr Quinn and Mr Nolan were frequently on hand to provide me with advice. It seemed perfectly natural at the time but the attentions of so many mentors indicates, when you look at it in perspective, that they must have seen that I had something extra. After I had begun playing regularly for St Michael's I was told to enter the Ayrshire trials, which were being held at the playing fields in Irvine. This would prove to be yet another tripwire, over which I would inevitably stumble.

There were guys coming from Largs, Cumnock, from all over, to take part in these trials, the Possibles versus the Probables. Just three St Michael's boys were involved and I can vividly recall walking out of school and down to the playing fields, to be greeted by a sea of strange faces in our dressing room. The teacher who was supervising the trial read out the two teams and I discovered that my two fellow St Michael's pupils were on the opposing side. That brought on my phobia again and the teacher had no sooner finished reading out the teams than I blurted out, 'That's me. I need to go home. I'm not playing. I can't play. I'll need to go home.' With that, I left the dressing room. The teacher followed me out and told me that I should stay because, although this was a trial, which supposedly I had to get through, there was no doubt that I would be in the Ayrshire team and that, from there, I would also be going forward to the Scottish international trials. His attempts at persuasiveness cut no ice with me.

I was on my way home and there was no stopping me. It was inevitable that I'd go when picked in a team of strangers. I was so relieved to leave the dressing room but I was still embarrassed at how stupid the situation was, and it emphasised to me that if I was going to play the game seriously, I'd need to overcome this complex.

When I arrived home, Dad asked me how I had got on, only for me to tell him I hadn't played. His response was a resigned chuckle at a recurrence of my obtuse behaviour. My father didn't always have to go to see the Marx Brothers at the cinema if he wanted to find farce, but he would never berate me or show any anger at my actions. It was characteristic of him to be civilised and considered in his reaction to events because he was a real gentleman. I thought he was the nicest guy in the world. He was always well dressed, with a coat, a three-piece suit, cap and well-polished black shoes. He was also a generous man. He'd watch local boys' teams play tournaments and he'd slip sixpence here and sixpence there to the kids, especially to those from families who maybe didn't have too much. Mind you, there was no chance of me getting slipped a coin by Dad at a match because I refused to let him watch me. I was a shy boy, so I had said to my mum and dad that if they ever came near a game in which I was playing, I would just walk off the park. They never were visible at any of my matches but at Auchenharvie Park the pitches are actually in the midst of a forest. That was perfect for my dad because, unbeknown to me until two or three years later, he would come down there, stand behind a tree and watch me playing. I'd go home and he'd ask, 'How did you get on today? What was the score?' He'd know already because he'd been at the game.

Eric and Andrew were out and about a lot when I was young, so on the whole the house was nice and quiet during my early years. I liked that but it didn't stop me doing all I could to liven it up. If it was raining, I would play in the hallway, endlessly heading my ball against the wall. On dull, wet days I would be practising there all day. It must have driven my parents daft but not once did they tell me to stop or to put the ball down. They were protective of me, my parents. At dusk, every day, I was told strictly that it was time for me to get indoors. I could argue as long as I liked that other children were being allowed to remain outside but it would have no effect. I'd be pulled in to draw or sketch or trace. I also had hundreds and hundreds of comics to read. My dad brought one in every day. When he got his paper, he'd buy me a comic. I read the classic comics and ones themed on such stories as Robinson Crusoe and Ivanhoe, but I also loved the cowboy comics featuring Kit Carson.

I was probably spoilt. I had a big model fort, with lots of soldiers, and I also had lots of Dinky cars. I wouldn't say it was the case that if I wanted something I got it but I had plenty of toys, books and comics. It may have been this protective, quiet environment, with older parents, that made me a shy young boy. My father was also a fairly shy person and I think I maybe inherited his nature. As for my brothers, they were extremely supportive of me. Andrew, who was a motor mechanic, got married when I was still at primary school and left the house. I shared a room with Eric, who was a plumber. I really looked up to them and they were good role models. They let me go everywhere with them – I thought they were stars.

I had a great childhood. I didn't experience any real hardships. If there were any in my family when I was young, either I don't remember them or I was shielded from them. I don't think my dad ever made a lot of money but he made enough to keep us happy. During the winter, he would finish work as soon as it was dark and the racing was over for the day, and every Monday and Thursday, my mother, father and I would head for one of the three picture-houses in

Saltcoats. We'd always be there for the first house, at five o'clock, to see films such as *Old Mother Reilly* or the Marx Brothers' frenetic comedies. We also saw *The Robe*, starring Richard Burton, Jean Simmons and Victor Mature. That was the first epic American picture to use CinemaScope, the new and dramatic widescreen technique. We would be among the first to see any new film that came on at the pictures. One thing that I remember is that you couldn't get too many sweets when you went to the cinema because such luxuries were still rationed and required coupons. I wouldn't consider that a hardship, though.

School had been great for me, and created a good environment for playing regular football once I'd got over my fear, but by the time I was 15, I was desperate to leave. An academic career was not for me, despite having passed my 11-plus. I was very hopeful of becoming a professional footballer and any other job was going to be of a stopgap nature. The one in my mind was maybe to become a motor mechanic but nobody in the area needed apprentices for that trade at the time. My fear of playing organised football had by then evaporated simply through the sheer pleasure and camaraderie of playing the game for a team. I was lucky enough to take every upward step in company with boys I already knew, which counterbalanced the fear of being confronted with unfamiliar faces in the dressing room. That security of being among friends made it easier to get used to meeting new team-mates.

My first job, after finishing with school, was 'on the milk' – I became a milk boy. I enjoyed it. Every morning I was up and out at six o'clock to meet the milk van and begin our round. At that time, milk boys got just two days' holiday a year – Christmas Day and New Year's Day – and on the day before Christmas you had to make two runs. It was a five-hour round, delivering the milk out of a converted furniture van. Jock, the driver, kept the van moving forward constantly. We milk boys would drop out of the back, deliver the milk to a doorstep, then race back to catch up the van, which would have advanced slightly farther down the street, jump up and grab the next delivery of milk. Doing that for five hours every morning didn't do me any harm in building up stamina, strength and all-round fitness. The round finished close to where my best friend, Joseph Murray, lived and on a Saturday, after I was done, I'd head there. Mrs Murray would have a big plate of pudding ready for us. After that, I would go directly to the football field for my game, wherever I was playing that afternoon.

During my mid-teens, I began playing for a local parish club called Star of the Sea. They were the obvious team to join because my brothers and cousins played for them, so I found myself playing in the same amateur team as Andrew and Eric. Our first match was against Auchenharvie Rovers and, beforehand, Eric told me that whatever happened in the match, I wouldn't have a problem. He would look after me, and my safety was assured because Curly Monan, one of my cousins, was at left-back while Pat Lawler, another cousin, was in goal. Additionally, all of the other guys in the team were friends of ours. Eric told me that if there was any hassle, they'd help me out. Andrew, on the other hand, took a different tack. He told Eric that if there was any rough stuff I was to handle it myself because I was now in a man's game, playing with men, and had to learn to toughen up and stand up for myself. Five minutes into the game, one of the opposition players crashed into me and left me in a heap. Eric was three yards away and, bearing in mind Andrew's words, didn't intervene. Andrew, however, appeared to have forgotten his own advice – he ran 70 yards to have a punch at the guy.

I loved playing for Star of the Sea because they played with nets between the posts. As a small boy I had frequently gone to watch them play, largely because, before kick-off and at half-time, I could wander on to the pitch with my ball, stand on the six-yard line and thump the ball into the net again and again. I loved to hear the sweet swish of the ball smacking into the net and to see the ripple that it caused. Through playing for Star of the Sea I was picked for an Ayrshire amateur representative side and we went to play a Glasgow select, winning 1–0. I scored the goal. That was a big thing and apparently a Rangers scout, who had been at the game, started asking questions about me. Once he got the answers, he lost interest quite quickly.

Throughout my teens, I remained a keen spectator. As a youngster, my mum and dad were reluctant to let me go to Glasgow, unsupervised, to watch Celtic play but they'd permit me to go to watch Kilmarnock, as it wasn't far away and the bus from Saltcoats stopped quite near Rugby Park. I'd be lying if I said I turned into an avid Killie fan, mind you. It was more than a bit quirky, I know, but I always supported the away team every time I went to see Kilmarnock play, whether the opposition happened to be Hearts, Hibs, Clyde or any other club. Don't ask me why. I didn't shout for the opposition – I wouldn't have shouted at the football. I wasn't desperate to shout and was more interested in absorbing the action. It didn't bother me to see the home side getting beaten, though, because I went there to see the teams that came to Rugby Park as much as anything else. Of course, if the visiting team happened to be Rangers, I'd be hoping for a draw! Going to those matches and being part of a large crowd – that's what life seemed to be all about.

The first time I was allowed to go to Celtic Park was in August 1957, when I was nearly 14. A couple of pals and I went to see Celtic and Airdrieonians contest a League Cup match. We had great seats in the stand, there were 38,000 inside the ground and Bertie Peacock scored the winning goal in a 3–2 victory for Celtic. I was also in the schoolboys' enclosure at Hampden Park in April 1958 to see Bobby Charlton make his debut for England against Scotland and score from a Tom Finney cutback – Bobby nearly took the net away with his shot. England won 4–0 that day. A few years later I was at Hampden to see Denis Law, then at Torino, playing for an Italian League Select in a 1–1 draw against a Scottish League Select. He was a glamorous player, almost godlike in comparison to the rest of the players. Watching those greats, I never thought that the level at which they were playing was within reach for me. I had long been determined to make it as a football player and had no doubts that I had the potential to do so, but I never imagined that I could reach the greatest heights in the game.

I was loving my football and happy with life, but I couldn't continue to work as a milk boy for ever and as my 17th birthday approached, my mum and dad were quite worried about me. They urged me frequently to get a trade and told me that they would like me to become a motor mechanic or an electrician or something similar but, for me, this was immaterial. I was convinced that it was only a matter of time before a senior professional football club would sign me. My parents, aware of the realities and ravages of life, were rightly concerned that I was setting too much store by my dreams.

Most of the local Junior clubs had been requesting me to sign for them since I had started playing for Star of the Sea, including Ardeer Recreation, a club from Stevenston that was run by the industrial giant ICI. One evening, George Gillon, Ardeer Rec's representative, a guy who had scored a goal for Celtic against Rangers during the Second World War, came to our house to seek my signature. My mother, in one of the few moments in her life when she actually piped up, said, 'If you give him a job, he'll maybe play for your team.' George did the necessary and before I knew it, I was combining Junior football with a job in ICI's box-making factory. My parents thought that if I got into ICI, the company would possibly provide me with a much-prized apprenticeship for a trade but it didn't work out like that – the company would only take on so many apprentices at a time and fortunately, as I saw it, I wasn't one of them.

Once I started playing Junior football, I was quite happy for my dad to come along to watch me play but I would never have wanted my mother to be there. My mum, Agnes, was a small woman, around five feet in height and, although she was supportive of my brothers and me in everything we did, she would have freaked out watching us play football, with all the hard, physical contact that the game involves. One year, in the mid-1950s, we went on holiday to Aberdeen and took in an early season match between Aberdeen and Queen of the South, in which Graham Leggat, the Scotland international, scored a memorable goal for Aberdeen. It was one of the rare occasions on which my mum came to the football and as we sat in the stand she was jumping up and down and going completely doolally with nerves at all these guys crashing into one another. If it had been me whom she had been watching, it would have been far too much for her – her boys, to her, were the greatest and she would not have been able to stand seeing us on the end of some of the fearsome tackles that were dished out, especially at Junior level.

She was a great mother to us. A housewife all her days – as were most women in that era – she had to carry out a daily shop for her family every morning and that, along with all the cooking, cleaning, ironing, sewing, darning, washing and scrubbing involved in running a household with a young family, made for a full-time job. Everything had to be bought fresh on a daily basis in those pre-refrigerator days. The closest thing she had to convenience food was groceries from a horse and cart that used to trawl our streets. My mum was always there for us, always had everything ready for us. She was the star in our house.

Neither of my parents were great ones for constantly giving me advice or trying to prod me in any particular direction – apart from wanting me to get an apprenticeship – but, funnily enough, they both had some input in my choice of Junior club. These clubs provided an important step upwards and towards senior football. They were a healthy source of talent for Scottish League clubs and on match days Junior grounds were infested with scouts. While my mother had steered me firmly towards Ardeer Rec, my father had advised me to steer clear of Saltcoats Victoria. That must have been a hard thing for him to do because he was a dedicated fan of theirs – he had been at the match in 1925 when they won the Scottish Junior Cup for the only time in their history – but he told me that it might not be such a good idea to join Saltcoats Vics because, as the local boy, I might get more stick than the other players. That was true. After a defeat, the players from Glasgow and elsewhere would go home but I would have to spend the week in Saltcoats, answering any criticism.

Toiling at ICI was another occupation that did my footballing ambitions no harm. It strengthened my resolve to become a football player for the simple reason that it was a terrible occupation. Its mindless drudgery pushed me to do all I could to get out of that factory. I was part of a production line – my job was to use a mallet to knock pieces of cardboard into shape and then join the pieces together to make boxes – but I couldn't keep up with the guy who was at the stage before me at the conveyor belt so I had to work through my tea-breaks to try to catch up with my tasks.

Thousands of people from the three towns of Ardrossan, Stevenston and Saltcoats worked at ICI. It was the largest employer in the area and almost everyone with whom I had been at school spent some time working there. I think at one point they had a workforce of around 10,000. Rows and rows of buses, plus the ICI train, would be sitting awaiting the workforce at the end of each day's toil. The most exciting part of the day would be wondering whether your bus could get out of the gates before the train came along or whether you'd be delayed as it trundled along over the railway crossing, carrying its band of exhausted workers, while your bus stood stationary waiting for it to pass. If that was the high point, you can imagine the thrills the rest of the day held.

It had been impossible to escape the impact of ICI even as a blissfully happy schoolboy in Saltcoats. Every so often, as you were going about your business, you would hear a bang and then you knew that somebody had either been badly hurt or killed at the ICI factory. One of the major products that they manufactured was dynamite. You'd be in Saltcoats, hear that bang and see people drawn out of their houses and gathering in shop doorways to look up at an ominous cloud of smoke, floating across the sky.

Away from my workaday existence, my footballing hopes were kindled constantly. Several professional clubs were taking an interest in me, including Blackpool, who had long been established in England's top division. Stanley Matthews was still playing for them at the time. I went down on trial for a week and a half, along with Joe Murray, my pal from Ardeer Rec, but we never kicked a ball. The place was snowed in for the entire time we were there.

At Chelsea, I was on trial for four days. London was the last place a shy wee boy from Ayrshire might feel at home and so it proved. My first thought on arrival was, 'How do I get home from here?' I spent the rest of the time crying my eyes out. I could not have stayed away from Scotland, especially at such a glitzy club as Chelsea. That was a reflection on the good home that my parents had provided for me back in Saltcoats.

Ted Drake was the Chelsea manager and while I was there, in September 1959, Matt Busby's Manchester United came down to Stamford Bridge and I saw them thrash the home side 6–3. On the following Saturday, I saw Jimmy Greaves, whom I loved as a player, score for Chelsea against Burnley. Those were good games for Chelsea to take me to – there was a lot of glamour attached to Manchester United and the big crowds made the atmosphere at the matches great, but in the late 1950s Rugby Park was also packed for every game, so I didn't perceive any real difference between attending top-flight football in England and Scotland. I didn't come away thinking that English football was a cut above what we had in Scotland. Joe Kirk, the Chelsea scout who had recommended me, was an Ayrshire man. He had provided Chelsea with a lot of Scottish players and he accompanied me down to London. I played one game, on the Saturday morning, and did OK but I didn't do myself full justice, chiefly because of my unsettled state of mind.

Once I'd been down to those two English clubs I decided that English football wasn't for me. Even though I had been impressed by much of what I had seen, England was too far away from my mum and dad. Maybe I just had too soft a life back home. Neither Blackpool nor Chelsea reached the stage of asking me to sign but I definitely would not have done so, and Joe Kirk, for one, would have been well aware of that. My father, characteristically, did not try to exert pressure on me to commit myself to one of those two clubs.

Of the Scottish clubs, Motherwell were keen to sign me; Falkirk and Morton even more so. Falkirk showed a lot of interest and kept asking me to join them, but Falkirk seemed like a million miles from Saltcoats. Getting there involved three or four buses or trains and took a long, long time. I trained at Kilmarnock, who had a lot of local boys training with them, and it was while I was there that Blackpool had asked me down for a trial. Before I travelled south, Willie Waddell, the Kilmarnock manager, offered me the advice, 'If they want to sign you, refuse to do so and come back and we'll sign you.' That was a strange one. I wondered why, if Kilmarnock were that keen on me, they didn't sign me before I went to Blackpool. If Kilmarnock had not hedged their bets and had made a more positive commitment to signing me, I might have joined them because Rugby Park was just up the road and joining Kilmarnock would have meant that I'd have been able to remain at home.

I was also at St Mirren on trial and I played in a trial match for Motherwell against Ayr United reserves and scored a goal. I played another game for them against a Scottish amateur side, did well and scored another goal in a 5–2 win. I enjoyed my two games with Motherwell and in the second match we played in a fabulous all-white strip with the claret-and-amber band across the chest, which really made me feel the part. It seemed a happy club. Bobby Ancell, the Motherwell manager, wanted to sign me on provisional forms – which meant that you would train with them regularly and they would have first option on you if they decided at a later stage that they wanted you as a full-time professional – but I told him that provisional forms were no good for me. It was gratifying to know that all these clubs were keen on me but I was content to play Junior football until I was made an offer to sign for a club that would be right for me.

Our opponents in my debut match for Ardeer Rec had been none other than Saltcoats Vics. At half-time we were 3–1 up through a Lennox hat-trick. At full-time we were losers by 4–3. I went on to score quite regularly and if you do that, you tend to get noticed. The facilities at Ardeer Rec had made it easy for me to sign for them, along with the fact that I knew quite a few of the players. Ardeer, the only amateur team in Junior football, had the best pitch at that level in Scotland, bar none. ICI owned it and kept it manicured to perfection. Everything in training revolved around the use of the ball, so it was always interesting. We had a really young team – a team of boys – and although we could beat a lot of clubs in Stevenston, we weren't too clever away from home, at Irvine Meadow in particular. Ardeer never seemed to be able to defeat them at their own ground, but I helped to change that – away to the Meadow, I scored two goals right at the start of the game and we hung on to win 2–1. That's one result that I still prize highly, but an even greater reward for remaining in Junior football, when all those professional clubs were tailing me, was soon to come my way.

CHAPTER 2

LEARNING MY TRADE

Despair mingled with the deepest delight on the most significant and far-reaching afternoon of my early life. I was just coming off the pitch with Ardeer Recreation one Saturday afternoon after a 4–1 defeat by Shettleston in a West of Scotland Cup tie, puzzling over the way the game had gone so badly for us, when Joe Connors, Celtic's chief scout, broke through that moment of reverie with some of the most honeyed words I've ever heard in my life. 'Bobby,' he said to me as he took me aside on the touchline, 'how would you like to put your future in the hands of Glasgow Celtic?' He didn't need to repeat the question.

At that point I'd already turned down Motherwell's offer of signing provisional forms but when Celtic made the same offer I couldn't grab hold of a pen quickly enough. It must have been in the back of my mind all along that Celtic were the club for me and I wanted to sign for them, if I got the chance. That was actually slightly odd because at that time I wouldn't have shouted and bawled about being a Celtic supporter.

My dad and I went up to Glasgow one Tuesday evening in early September 1961 to meet Jimmy McGrory, the Celtic manager, who, in the 1920s and 1930s, had established himself as the greatest goalscorer in Celtic's history. It was almost as much of a thrill for Bobby the elder as for Bobby the younger to be there that night. My dad was a Celtic fan, even though he didn't go to a lot of the games, and he was rapturously happy to meet Mr McGrory. I accepted the terms offered without a quibble. Since Ardeer was an amateur club, any money due from Celtic under the deal would come straight to me, so I got the considerable sum of £90 as a fee when I signed.

There were still shades of the strange little boy in my make-up, even though I was by then 18 years old. They showed themselves when I subsequently proceeded to give Celtic Park and the East End of Glasgow a wide berth. I simply signed for Celtic, went back to Saltcoats and proceeded to live my life as though that trip to Glasgow had never happened. Consequently, I received a letter from Celtic, a few weeks after my father and I had met Mr McGrory, asking me if I would please start coming to training.

It hadn't been mentioned to me that I should report for training at Celtic Park and no date had been given to me to report there in the future. I had been told I would be an Ardeer Recreation player until the club had been eliminated from the Scottish Junior Cup and as I was still training with Ardeer, it had not occurred to me that Celtic might want me to train with them as well.

Punctuality has always been one of my strengths but even that went slightly awry on the first evening on which I did turn up for training at Celtic Park. I had left ICI early, taken the train up to Glasgow, the tramcar out to Parkhead and made sure I walked into the ground bang on six o'clock, thinking that that was the time when I was due to arrive at the stadium – only to discover that I was expected to be ready to start training by then. Sean Fallon, the first-team coach, was behind the wee window inside the entrance to Celtic Park and he said, 'Can I help you, son?'

'My name's Bobby Lennox,' I replied.

'Oh, Robert, great to see you, come in, we've been waiting on you coming.'

All the other 'provisionals' and part-time players were on their way down the tunnel to start training so I had to rush away and get ready to go out with them. A lot of the boys were pretty well acquainted, having played with and against each other in Glasgow and Lanarkshire, but I had never met any of them and felt every inch the newcomer. Still being really shy, I stood back a lot whenever I attended those training sessions, which took place on evenings twice a week. I found it difficult to get in among the other guys and mix with them, even though they tried to make it as easy for me as possible.

Nothing distracted me from football when I was a teenager and much of that can be attributed to my nature. Among my group of friends in Saltcoats, I was the last person to go to the dancing. I wasn't interested; nor was I interested in drinking. My dad was a good example in that respect. He didn't drink at all. I would never, ever go out on a Friday night but on a Saturday night, after the game, I used to socialise at the Café Melbourne in Saltcoats. The jukebox would be playing Elvis Presley, Cliff Richard and Buddy Holly – I was a rock'n'roller in spirit – and the café was always bursting at the seams. It was the place to be. I'd have a Coca-Cola with a touch of Irn Bru or Vimto in it and take as long as possible to drink it so that I could keep my seat. That's where I met a girl called Kathryn, who also frequented the café. A couple of her pals knew a couple of my pals and eventually I asked her out. At the time I'd be about 18 and she would be a couple of years younger.

It was always going to be difficult for a shy individual to keep the conversation flowing when we went out. On our first date I had arranged to meet her at the Regal picture hall and I was standing there on the appointed Saturday night, paper under my arm, nodding to acquaintances as they passed and then, as time clicked on, nodding to them as they passed again, going in the other direction. After a while, I was starting to become really embarrassed at having stood there for so long and eventually I decided that Kathryn wasn't simply late but actually wasn't coming. I had just turned to walk away when somebody shouted, 'Hey, Bobby, here's Kathyrn.' I turned round and she was walking up the road. Love blossomed from there.

My whole life would have changed if Kathryn had not appeared at that moment. I didn't know her very well, so I would probably have been too shy to ask her out again. She had been delayed because her mother had returned home late from Kilmarnock and Kathryn had been dutifully looking after Tommy, her younger brother. She was my first love – I thought she was terrific. She was also a bit more outgoing than I was. It was Kathryn who drew me to the dancing because she liked it so much, and that led to me starting to socialise in Glasgow, which was a big step. We would occasionally go to the Dennistoun Palais, in the East End, close to Celtic Park, but more often it was easier to go to the dancing locally, at places such as the Ingledean in Ardrossan.

Life seemed to be going well for me on and off the park, although I was not too keen on the ash pitch at Barrowfield, Celtic's training ground. Down in Ayrshire we played on grass all the time but that was not the case in Glasgow, where full-sized ash pitches were common. The Glasgow boys at the club told me how much they loved coming down to Ayrshire to play on our grass pitches. Mentioning the type of pitches we played on may sound like a trifling detail, a technicality, but shortly after I joined Celtic, I had a strong feeling that the ash pitch might just bring my career at the club ploughing into a headlong crash after only the briefest time.

I had finished training at Celtic Park one Thursday night late in

September 1961 when I was told I was expected to report to Barrowfield at ten o'clock on the Saturday morning for the third-team game that day. I'd never previously played in a Celtic team of any description but instead of the news being a cause for great rejoicing, it was quite the contrary. The game was due to be played on the wretched ash pitch and I was full of worry about whether I would be able to perform well and show what I was capable of doing on a playing surface that was entirely alien to me. The prospect troubled me as I travelled back to Saltcoats that evening, and on the following day, when I turned up for my shift at ICI as usual, it was still on my mind – so much so that I was expecting to spend a restless, possibly sleepless, Friday night into Saturday morning.

On the factory floor, time seemed to crawl by. I was working and worrying away when, at about three o'clock, the foreman came in and said that I was to report to Celtic Park at six o'clock that night and play in the reserve-team game against Falkirk. Relief cascaded over me. I was allowed to leave work early and Jim Kelly, one of the lads at the factory, together with another of my work-mates, agreed to run me up to the game. I completed my tasks, raced home to change into a collar and tie and, before I knew it, had been whisked up to Glasgow just in time for the match. It was similar to that moment when, as a 12-year-old, I had been asked by Mr Nolan to play for the Scouts in Saltcoats just as the match kicked off. I had no time to think, get nervous or turn over the consequences in my mind. I played quite well, I was pleased with myself, we beat Falkirk 2–0 and I never ended up playing in the third team after that. I've always thought that if I had played on that ash pitch on the Saturday morning, I might not have played as well as I was capable of doing. I might have struggled badly and remained stuck in the third team. That quick promotion to the second team was one of the strokes of luck that you need at every stage in your career. I think the coaching staff realised that I had never played on ash – it was mentioned to me a good while later that they had thought it better to see what I could do on grass.

A couple of thousand people would always turn out for the reserve matches. When we scored the two goals against Falkirk I can remember big cheers going up and thinking, 'This is great.' It was not long, however, before I got a chance to hear the roar of a crowd that made a reserve-team attendance sound like a couple of mice squeaking.

On the first Saturday in March 1962 I travelled up to Glasgow to meet the other reserve-team players for a bite to eat at Ferrari's restaurant in Glasgow, at the top of Buchanan Street, the habitual meeting place for Celtic teams. We were due to play Dundee reserves up at Dens Park that afternoon – the Celtic first team, conversely, were playing Dundee at home in a huge match. Dundee were the League leaders, one point ahead of Rangers and five ahead of Celtic. With only nine fixtures remaining, Celtic had to win that Saturday if they were to remain in contention for the League title.

I came down the stairs of Ferrari's with Bobby Murdoch, ready to board the team bus for Dundee, but when I reached the pavement and the bus pulled up, Sean Fallon told me not to get on board.

'Bobby,' he said, 'you're playing in the first team today.'

I had never met a Celtic first-team player in my life and I found it hard to believe that a raw youngster such as myself could be involved in a match with the League leaders.

'Go and get yourself a new pair of boots at Greaves,' Sean told me.

All the other reserve boys were really pleased for me but I had little time to discuss my big break with them – I had to rush down to the shops in Argyle Street, but only after locating a phone booth, at Glasgow Cross. I wanted to get the news of my debut to my parents. We did not have a phone at home so I called John Murray, a friend of my dad's back in Saltcoats, and asked him to let my dad know that I was playing at Celtic Park that afternoon. After that I ran to Greaves, and back to Ferrari's. I was exhausted by then, and I still had 90 minutes to face against Dundee. I knew I'd be on the field for the full match – substitutes were not allowed in Scottish football in 1962. Nerves for the shy boy? Not really. As had happened before, it helped that I hadn't known I was going to be playing until the match was almost upon me. Once again, I basically just had to go and do it.

It may seem surprising that I was selected so unexpectedly for the first team but that was the way things were at Celtic at the time. Team selections could be a bit haphazard and there were no tactics to speak of – players were simply picked to play in certain positions. A player was expected to know how to play in that position and to go out and get on with it. As a part-timer I had had no reason to meet the first-team players previously, but if I was good enough to be in contention for the first team, it was expected that I would be able to slot into the starting line-up immediately. I imagine most clubs were run along similar lines in the early 1960s.

Sean had told me that Pat Crerand, Jim Kennedy and Frank Haffey would be in for their lunch at Ferrari's and for me to go out to Parkhead with them. He must have got in touch with them because when they came in, they knew I'd be sitting waiting. It was so exciting just to meet them, let alone play alongside them. We took a taxi out to Celtic Park, for which one of those guys paid, thank goodness. Matters were a little less cordial when we arrived. In the dressing room, some of the other players took one look at me, this scrawny little kid, and began saying, 'What's this? What's he in here for?' That wasn't too encouraging but next thing I knew I was in the tunnel and on the way out for the match.

To cap a quite remarkable day, I scored on my debut. Well, I think I did. The referee had a different view – not for the first or last time in my career. Midway through the first half, Ian Ure, the Dundee centre-half, went to boot the ball clear and instead hit it off me; he smashed it off the centre of my chest. The ball broke past him and I put it in the net. I was absolutely delighted until I heard the referee blow his whistle and disallow the goal for handball against me. It had been nothing of the sort. We ended up beating Dundee 2–1. Billy McNeill scored with a header, something on which Celtic could always rely, and Frank Brogan scored with a cross-cum-shot that bounced in off the post. Late on in the match, I felt really tired, which I put down to the pace of first-team football but, in retrospect, I may have been drained because of the amount of nervous energy I had expended before the game. Running around Glasgow that lunchtime could not have helped, either.

I felt I had done well enough on my debut, in front of a crowd of 39,000, the biggest home attendance that season except for the Rangers game, but I did not feature again for the first team that season. I'd been brought in for the Dundee game because Stevie Chalmers had been unavailable and the following Friday I picked up the paper to read that, 'Stevie Chalmers has breezed back through the doors of Celtic Park fit and ready to come back in this Saturday's game . . .' I knew then that I would be returning to the reserves and I had no quarrel with that. Dundee went on to win the championship that season, finishing eight points ahead of Celtic, who ended up third.

When I was called up to go full-time, at the start of the 1962–63 season, it made an enormous difference to me because I could apply myself fully to football and was with the guys every day. Things became a lot easier. Sporadic first-team appearances followed during the 1962–63 season but I was still more familiar with my reserve team-mates, with whom I played most weeks, and I became really friendly with Willie O'Neill, Bobby Murdoch and Jimmy Johnstone. We weren't exactly a clique but we were very close. That helped me a lot, especially as we were all very quiet at that time, and I include Jimmy in that, hard as it is to believe. We were drawn together, in fact, through our mutual shyness. If we were training with the first-team squad or included for a match, we all kind of sat back a bit, trying to get used to being in among all these individuals whose pictures dotted the pages of the papers seven days a week. Before first-team games, we would troop into the snooker room and hardly a word was spoken as we all sat watching a couple of the guys playing. We were almost comically shy. It was actually quite a canny approach for us to adopt because if you breeze into a dressing room as a youngster, full of cheeky patter, you will soon find the flak flying in your direction and your witty remarks torn to shreds. You've just got to watch your step because the older, more experienced players will, from time to time, bury a young boy who thinks he's made the grade.

It was always good to get some encouragement so that you knew you were progressing in the right direction. I remember a reserve game one night, a year or so after I had joined the club. We came in at half-time and I was sitting thinking my own thoughts when Billy McNeill came in, wearing casual clothes. He must have been up at the ground to take in the game as a spectator. He had been a regular in the first team since the late 1950s. He planted himself down right beside me and started talking. He told me, 'You're doing well, keep it going in the second half.' There wasn't a lot said at half-time by the manager or the trainer and this intervention from Billy was the type of individual pep talk missing at the club. I remember thinking to myself that if Billy was suggesting that I might be good enough to break into the first team consistently, I couldn't have been doing too badly. It's amazing how potent a few small words such as that can be. When you're young it's important to think that the first-team boys rate you because it can be overwhelming to be in among them if you don't have any source of confidence. It was especially important to me that Billy offered that advice because I thought of him as the model centre-half and Celtic player.

My second League game, as with my debut, was not exactly a low-key occasion. I was selected for the match against Rangers at Celtic Park in September 1962 and was extremely nervous beforehand because of the big crowd and the Old Firm occasion. If you're not excited before games such as that, there's something wrong with you. It was a pleasant afternoon and when we came out on to the pitch, the place was absolutely jumping. There were at least 75,000 inside the ground. As we were warming up, a process that, in the 1960s, consisted of nothing more than a bit of shooting-in, we heard an enormous crash. A big door at the Celtic end had come tumbling down because so many people were climbing over it and trying to get into the ground. Strange the moments that stick in your memory, even after all those years.

It was a tight, nervy game and I remember thinking that even though Rangers were a highly rated, accomplished team – they had reached the semi-finals of the European Cup two years previously – there wasn't an awful lot of difference between them and us in terms of playing ability. We were awarded a penalty early in the match and before Paddy Crerand could take it, Jim Baxter, the Rangers midfielder and Paddy's great pal, messed about with the ball, delaying the kick and adding to the tension. Paddy missed the penalty and six minutes from time, Willie Henderson, the Rangers outside-right, broke away and planted the ball in the net for the only goal of the game. I enjoyed the match even though we were beaten. It stood out for the particularly good quality of football that had been seen on the day. It was the quality of football played by Celtic that had impressed me. Celtic had struggled to beat Rangers in previous seasons and I thought that we had deserved a draw at least that day, so I was not too despondent afterwards.

Nine first-team appearances, dotted throughout that 1962–63 season, helped me to feel my way into the top flight, but I failed to score. It wasn't until 18 months after my debut that I got my first goal in the League. It came on 14 September 1963 in a game against Third Lanark at Celtic Park. I can still see it today. A Third Lanark player, Joe Davis, was short in sending the ball back to Stewart Mitchell, his goalkeeper, and I ran in and nicked it over Stewart. That made the score 2–0 after ten minutes and I was thrilled with my goal although it was soon overshadowed in the minds of the public by the quirky nature of the game itself. We rapidly scored twice more to go 4–0 ahead within the opening quarter of an hour but Third Lanark, with Ally MacLeod at outside-left, came back at us with three goals before half-time and scored another one after the break to make it 4–4 at the end. During that era, a Celtic team could reach great heights and then plumb great depths within the same match or even, as against Third Lanark, within the same half.

Three days after that match we were in Basle, Switzerland, for the first leg of a European Cup-Winners' Cup tie and I notched my first goal in European football. We were 2–0 ahead when I made a run from the inside-right position, hit the ball as the goalkeeper came out and saw it smack against the near post and streak across goal before settling in the netting on the far side. We played well and won 5–1, with John 'Yogi' Hughes getting three of them. It was a nice pitch over there and we all came back with cuckoo clocks. We always bought a souvenir on trips abroad and cuckoo clocks were the automatic choice in Switzerland. Whether or not they were working a month later is another matter.

Those first-team outings were welcome excursions from the reserves, where I was gradually gaining more and more experience. I was playing in a reserve match at Rugby Park, Kilmarnock, one Friday in late November 1963 when terrible news from America was announced over the Tannoy. The answer to the perennially asked question, 'Can you remember where you were when you heard that President Kennedy had been assassinated?' is yes, I can remember it clearly. I thought it sounded like the end of the world.

To a certain extent, the lack of coaching at Celtic meant that I was a self-taught footballer. My bad games were important because I had to go over them on my own and learn from them. On another Friday evening at Kilmarnock we got beaten 4–1 and Sean Fallon came into the dressing room afterwards, raging. He was entitled to be angry. He went through everyone and told almost all of us to report to Celtic Park the following morning, for a friendly match away to Raith Rovers. I was one of those he picked on for special attention so I tried to make an excuse. I couldn't believe I was expected to play on the Friday night and the Saturday. Sean was having none of it and told me quite forcefully to be at the park the following day. On the bus to Kirkcaldy that Saturday I was really on a downer. That was a rare event for me – and it didn't last long. I scored four times that afternoon and was in the good books again. Instead of still being disappointed from the Friday night, when I went back into training on the Monday, I was on a high. It shows how important it is to work your way through setbacks.

I had joined Celtic as an inside-right. I had played in that position for all of my previous clubs and that was where Celtic had fielded me in the reserve team and in the few first-team matches that I played in my opening two seasons with the club. Then one Saturday in early December 1963, I was introduced to the outside-left position. Celtic were playing St Johnstone and, although I was in the first-team squad, I had not been selected to play, so I expected to be going along to Celtic Park purely as a spectator. As soon as I walked into the dressing room though, I encountered Yogi, who grinned at me and asked me if I had ever played outside-left. Yogi was injured and had heard the coaching staff decide that I would be the one to replace him in that position. I was shocked but realised that this was another chance to try to establish myself in the team. Although I was naturally right-footed, I was quite comfortable on my left foot and I was quite quick. I had never previously played a match at outside left. We beat St Johnstone 3–1 and I played a couple more games after that before Yogi returned to fitness. That episode proved to me that, if needed, I could do a job on the left wing, although I never contemplated playing there on a long-term basis.

The crowds at Celtic during that era, other than for major matches such as the one with Rangers, weren't always as big as people tend to imagine, which may have been a reflection on how much Celtic were struggling. During 1963–64, when Celtic spent the season trying to keep in touch with Kilmarnock and Rangers, who were tussling for the title, the team sometimes played in front of a home crowd of as few as 10,000 or 12,000 people in run-of-the-mill League matches. The dormant supporters would turn up in their tens of thousands for the bigger matches. In Europe, against Rangers or in the Scottish Cup, the ground would be heaving with excitement, but on routine afternoons you would see more terracing than spectators, and the size of Celtic Park would only emphasise the paucity of the fans. On days when the team were doing badly, you could feel the crowd, such as it was, getting restless about what they were seeing, and there's nothing worse than that for a player. You try to take extra care to do things properly but end up getting in a fankle – you take an extra touch and someone gets a tackle in on you, or you play the ball quickly and it's the wrong pass.

Mr McGrory was the nicest man I have ever met in football, a real gentleman, but he wasn't a coach as such – he didn't instruct the team tactically or take training. He would just read out the team in the dressing room before a match, pat you on the back and say, 'Good luck, lads' as we were about to step on to the pitch. Training was basic – a case of lapping the park – but I imagine it was pretty basic at most clubs. I once heard a story about a player at one club during that era suggesting to the trainer that it was tedious simply to lap the track in the same direction all the time. The trainer looked at him in surprise before agreeing to introduce some variety into their routine. 'Fine,' he said. 'You can lap the track in the other direction today.' At Celtic it was the same. We never trained with a ball when Mr McGrory was the manager – the only day on which you would really see a ball would be a Saturday – and nobody discussed with you how you had played the previous Saturday and how you might go about improving certain aspects of your game. At the time, I had nothing with which to compare Mr McGrory's methods, so I didn't think there was anything wrong with them. Footballers trained hard all week and played on a Saturday. That was the way it was.

If the training routines were basic, so too were the facilities. That barely mattered to me. When you're a boy training at Celtic, you don't care too much about those things. After a training session, we would put our kit in a drying room and collect it next day, still dirty but dry. The socks might have great cakes of mud attached to them, almost like small slabs of peat. You'd have to break them off before putting on your gear, and if you were first into the drying room before training, it meant you could select the cleanest of the grey polo-necked jerseys. Both the first team and the reserves wore these big jerseys for training sessions, although there was a slight class distinction in that the first-team players were allowed to wear another jersey underneath theirs while the reserves were not. It was like wearing a hair shirt, they were so scratchy and itchy on your bare skin. The kit would be cleaned once a week and by the end of the week's training, the shorts, socks and jerseys would be putrid.

I was still living with my parents and every morning I would get up at around seven so that I could catch the fast train to Glasgow from Kilwinning station. I'd be getting up at about the same time as most of the workforce but I would never have described what I was doing as 'going to my work'. It just didn't seem like it – this was pleasure. After training, I'd be back down in Saltcoats as soon as possible. I didn't have enough money to have my lunch in Glasgow and you wouldn't get so much as a cup of tea at Celtic Park. You went in, did your training and came away again. Once I could afford it, I bought my first car. It was an absolute dream – a wee two-door Ford Anglia that had three forward gears and one reverse gear. I puttered up and down to Glasgow in that, stopping every now and then to spit on a hankie and wipe the windscreen clean. A radio, working on batteries, resided on the back seat and I'd occasionally have to stop to tune it to get back on to a frequency.

That car changed my life completely. I wasn't getting up quite so early in the morning and I would be back in Saltcoats during the early afternoon. I could get home and read a book for a couple of hours – I was always great at relaxing and resting up for matches – and that was a bit better than making wooden boxes for ICI. Subconsciously, the fact that I had had such an awful job meant that I was deeply determined to keep the new one. So I tried to do absolutely everything I could to make progress as a footballer. I didn't have late nights and I didn't drink at all during my early twenties. Jimmy Johnstone, my good friend, didn't drink either. I went home to Saltcoats every afternoon and never socialised in Glasgow. That meant I was not aware of what the other players were doing socially. They would, I'm sure, go for a drink after a match but I don't believe there was a boozy culture at the club.

There wasn't extensive television coverage at that time so the players' faces weren't particularly well known and that meant we could go for a wander around the streets of Glasgow without being recognised. I never got much hassle for being a Celtic player, although one night Kathryn and I were in a place in Glasgow, Danny Brown's, having a meal, when a few nippy comments began flying in our direction from a table situated across from us. It was starting to get to me a wee bit when one of the guys got up from the table and advanced in our direction. 'Look,' he said, 'we were having a wee bit of fun there but it's gone over the top.' He had a bottle of bubbly with him and he presented it to us, which was really nice, even though we didn't drink champagne. Honestly, that was about the worst incident I ever encountered. I've never had anybody in my face confronting me about playing for Celtic or making sectarian remarks. Maybe I just went to the right places.

Robert Kelly, a Glasgow stockbroker, was the chairman of Celtic in the 1960s and I was very much in awe of him, especially as he was a man who didn't take the time to stand and speak to players. You never got to know him, but when our paths crossed he was always very pleasant towards me, and I remember him writing in one of the wee green books, which were available for supporters to buy annually, 'This boy will become a Celtic great.' That made me sit up, especially as I was still not a regular in the first team at the time. It gave me a great lift. He was also very pleasant towards Kathyrn. Celtic had played Real Madrid in a friendly at Celtic Park in 1962 and afterwards a lavish banquet was laid on back at the Central Hotel. Kathryn accompanied me – she would have been about 17 – and Mr and Mrs Kelly went out of their way to spend a considerable amount of time talking to her and making her feel welcome.

If we were training and Robert Kelly came walking down the tunnel, you would find that things suddenly stepped up and became a bit sharper. He had a strong hand on the tiller at the club. If any of the players did something of which he disapproved, it would get back to them that the chairman was displeased, although they would not hear directly from Mr Kelly. He was also picking the Celtic team during the first half of the 1960s – that was never stated but everyone knew it was happening. It was the worst kept secret inside Celtic Park. The board would meet on a Thursday night and we would buy the paper on a Friday morning to see whom Mr Kelly had decided would be playing that week. Again, I simply accepted it. As a youngster at my first professional club, I thought that was how things were done at every club in the country.

I was pretty sure, however, that not every aspect of the process of team selection at Celtic mirrored the system at other professional clubs. In fact, sometimes the chairman's incessant interference became at best quite comical and, frankly, a bit odd, not to say absurd. The team may well have been selected on the Thursday, but that wasn't necessarily the end of it – there could still be a couple of changes made, courtesy of Mr Kelly, before kick-off. You could read the team in the paper, find that you weren't included and turn up at Celtic Park on a Saturday, ready to watch from the stand. You could enter the ground, have a chat, go to the toilet, come back out and find that your boots had been laid out in the dressing room, which indicated that you were now in the team. You could then stroll into the snooker room to try to relax before the game and another player would say to you, 'I see you're not playing today.' You'd reply, 'I wasn't playing to begin with but I'm in the team now.' They'd tell you that you weren't, so you'd return to the dressing room and discover that your boots had been taken away again and that you'd been re-consigned to the role of spectator. That was a frequent occurrence. The team would be chopped and changed, at Mr Kelly's behest, several times between one o'clock and the back of two.

Although clubs were not allowed to use substitutes in European competition, Celtic always took a large party of players with them on trips abroad and I was part of the squad when we travelled to Budapest to play MTK in the semi-final second leg of the European Cup-Winners' Cup in April 1964. We felt pretty confident of making the final as we had won the first leg 3–0. I wasn't named in the team and spent the match sitting beside Dunky MacKay, who was an experienced player. Shortly after half-time, with the score 1–0 to MTK, he turned to me and said that we were in no danger of failing to go through. Within a minute, it was 2–0 and Dunky and I looked at each other, realising we could soon be on our way out of the tournament, and so we were. MTK went on to win 4–0. The instructions from the management – Mr Kelly – had been simply to attack and we had been caught out defensively. It was always Celtic's policy at that time to attack home or away and that was admirably naïve in Budapest.

The reason I mention that semi-final in particular is that it is indicative of the whole – amateurish is perhaps too strong a word, unsophisticated perhaps – approach of Celtic to European football at the time. Indeed, when Mr Kelly was running the show, European away games were treated as though they were a city break. All jolly nice! In fairness to Mr Kelly, European football was in its infancy and nobody knew the right or wrong way to approach it. We would arrive at our foreign destination on the Monday and on the Tuesday, at lunchtime, a chartered bus would collect us from our hotel and take us off for four or five hours of sightseeing. That used to drive the boys bonkers. There we were to play a key football match and spending hours sitting on a bus the day before the game. In Budapest we looked round Buda, then Pest and the island in the middle of the Danube, which was all very well but not the type of thing that would help players conserve their energies and focus on the match at hand.

Although, as I've mentioned, I played a couple of matches on the left wing, I was habitually an inside-right for Celtic, who employed the old 2-3-5 formation. Inside-right was the position I enjoyed and the system was one with which everyone had grown up – so much so that it was second nature and you barely thought about it as a formation. The five were the forwards – two wingers and a centre-forward, with the inside-left and inside-right positioned in between the centre and the wings. As inside-right, my job was to take the ball from midfield, often from the right-half, who, along with the left-half, would plough through the hard work in midfield. I would then spring forward and supply the centre-forward or spray the ball out to the wing or, if it was on, try to go through on goal and score myself. It wasn't a regimented system and there was some freedom within it to roam here and there, although the wingers were told strictly to stay wide on the touchlines. Their job was purely to hit the goal-line and cross the ball into the box. The system was geared to attack, with only one centre-half – for Celtic almost always Billy McNeill – positioned in between the two full-backs. If the other team were attacking, the right-half and left-half would funnel back to support the three defensive players. It's so hard to picture it now. I can't imagine looking at a pitch and seeing Billy standing there on his own in the centre of the defence, despite having played in that system until I was in my early twenties.

It had always been clear to me that it was a big, big thing to be going from Ardeer Rec to playing for Celtic in Glasgow. So I wasn't disappointed that I remained largely in the reserves for the initial three years of my Celtic career. I saw it as an apprenticeship and no bad thing. Sometimes, when I went into the first team, I felt a bit overawed and didn't do myself justice. Bobby Murdoch was the same – he also often didn't show how good he was whenever he was given a game in the first team. I would do things that weren't really natural to me. I would play a pass instead of taking someone on when I had the chance to do so, and later on decide that that had been the wrong option. Alternatively, I'd take someone on when it would have been more productive to pass the ball. I'd make bad decisions and I always had the feeling that people weren't seeing the best of me in the first team.

One example came at Ibrox in September 1964, when I opened the scoring against Morton in our League Cup semi-final around ten minutes from time – a goal that paved the way for us to reach the final. The ball came into the box, everybody missed it and I slipped in at the back post to poke it into the net. It wasn't a great goal but that didn't matter because it turned the game in our favour. Charlie Gallagher scored a second for us, with only a few seconds remaining, to seal a 2–0 win, but I knew I would not be appearing in the final with Rangers three weeks later because I hadn't played well enough. I came off the park knowing that I would get praise in the press and that most of the 60,000 present on the night would consider me a hero but that those inside the club knew differently. I hadn't done enough to justify staying in the side for the final at Hampden. I was never, ever despondent about being left out of the team at that time, though, because I didn't think I was doing as well as I ought to have been. I think I'm lucky with my nature. I always remained positive and was glad to be learning a job that I loved. That made me continue to try my hardest.

A story has done the rounds that I was on the verge of a move to Falkirk some time in early 1965, but no one from Celtic or Falkirk ever mentioned it to me. I don't know whether it was true or not but if Celtic had decided the time was right to sell me, I would have had to comply. Robert Kelly was the type of man who, when he decided it was time for you to go, made it impossible for you to do anything other than leave the club. Even so, I don't think I would have gone to Falkirk unless my arm had been twisted up my back. I wouldn't have left Celtic voluntarily because I still thought I had the chance to be a first-team regular. Unlike Billy McNeill, I was not feeling dissatisfied with the lack of direction on the managerial side at Celtic, although I can understand Billy's frustration. He was a terrific centre-half and the mainstay of the team, especially after Pat Crerand left for Manchester United in early 1963. A Scottish international, Billy was great at his job. He had been well established in the first team for a number of years and was irritated at not playing in a winning team. By early 1965, Celtic had not won a major Scottish trophy for eight years. That pushed Billy to the verge of leaving, but it was different for me. I was still trying to establish myself in the team, so I didn't have the wider concerns about the direction in which the club was going that would have been gnawing away at Billy.

The news that Jock Stein was returning to Celtic as manager was good for Billy. He had been coached by Jock in the reserves during the late 1950s and knew how much potential he offered the club. Jock Stein's imminent arrival was not, in contrast, a development that particularly pleased me. I had, at last, started to establish myself in the first team. On instructions from the management, I had begun to play farther forward and to use my speed and quickness of thought, and it had worked. Away to Morton in late January 1965, I had headed us into the lead and we had drawn 3–3. At home to Aberdeen the following week, we won 8–0 and I scored again. On the following day, 31 January 1965, it was announced officially that Jock Stein would be the new manager of Celtic as soon as he had freed himself of his duties with Hibernian. When I heard the news, I didn't take it well. I fretted that the new man, whom I did not know at all, might not fancy me as a player and that my hard-won place in the team could be in jeopardy. At this crucial juncture my future as a Celtic player seemed more uncertain than ever before.

CHAPTER 3

FORWARD THRUST

The speed of life increased rapidly for everyone at Celtic once Jock Stein stepped through the main door and settled his great bulk into the manager's seat. The amateurish attitude that had been hanging over the club simply evaporated as he exerted his influence on every aspect, every detail of life at Celtic, instilling a set of values and methods that would sustain the club for decades to come. His reach extended everywhere inside the club. For instance, prior to Jock's arrival, we had always played snooker pre-match in the recreation room but he scrapped the snooker and replaced it with table tennis. A game of snooker could take maybe 20 minutes for the two guys involved to complete, while the others would be doing nothing more than watching them play. A table-tennis match would be over much more quickly, enabling others to play and, unlike snooker, it gave you a wee bit of sharpness through the movement involved in playing the game. With hundreds of such small but significant actions, Jock revitalised the entire club.

Jock's arrival was delayed for six weeks because of his commitment to Hibernian to remain at Easter Road until the Edinburgh club had secured the services of a new manager. By early March, when he was finally due to take over at Parkhead, we were in seventh position in the League, so the Scottish Cup seemed a more realistic target for us. The match before Jock's arrival was a quarter-final against Kilmarnock. The final of a Cup competition is usually remembered as the most important match in lifting a trophy, but often an equally vital match, and one of particular significance to the players, occurs earlier in any Cup run. This game against Kilmarnock was the tie that fitted that description for us.

Celtic had been drawn at home and we were desperate to avoid a replay. The club had suffered a string of sizeable defeats by Kilmarnock at their Rugby Park home prior to that encounter. Five months previously, we had gone down 5–2 there. We'd lost 4–0 in March 1964 and 6–0 in March 1963, on the night on which Jimmy Johnstone had made his Celtic debut. We had also lost 2–0 in Ayrshire in August 1964, in a League Cup match. So when we were drawn at home to Kilmarnock we were determined to finish off the game on the day. Before the match, the boys were all geeing each other up, insisting that we had to make sure we saw Kilmarnock off over the forthcoming 90 minutes. After quarter of an hour, Bertie Auld slipped a neat cross into the penalty area, I headed us into the lead and we went on to win 3–2. On the same afternoon, Jock, in his final match in charge of Hibernian, did us the significant favour of eliminating Rangers by beating them 2–1 in their quarter-final at Easter Road.

During those six weeks of waiting for Jock, I had scored five goals in five games, but the thought that had entered my mind when his appointment was announced couldn't be dislodged. Regardless of my new-found good form, the new manager might simply prefer someone else when he arrived and I could find myself out of favour just when I had been enjoying my first settled run in the team. With a new manager, anything can happen. It never struck me that, although Jock might still be in charge at Easter Road, he could also be selecting the Celtic team and that my run in the side might owe more to him than to anyone else. That was what had been happening – my uneasiness about him coming to Celtic was unfounded. Jock had authorised my regular selection for the side and it was Jock who had instructed Sean Fallon to tell me to push farther forward. Jock's invisible guiding hand had resulted in my scoring more freely than ever before for Celtic. His instructions to Sean had been to alter my role from being an inside-right who chugged up and down the park linking midfield with attack, to playing up beside the centre-forward. That was the big step I needed in my career. Instead of being a traditional inside-forward, I was now to conserve my energy solely for attacking movements, and there was no requirement to work back past my own halfway line. I loved my new position – and in adjusting my role, Jock not only changed my career but began to change my life.

In the coming years, Jock played me most frequently at outside-left, but if someone had given me the option, I would always have chosen to play up beside the centre-forward. Even when I played wide left I had licence from Jock to make runs into the penalty area and seek out goalscoring chances. That was not optional – it was an essential part of our way of playing the game. Under the new manager, we became a more flexible, adaptable and quick-thinking team. We would cover for each other slickly and swiftly. If I made an angled run into the box from the left wing, Bertie Auld or Tommy Gemmell, the other left-sided players, would fill in for me to prevent my immediate opponent being afforded too much space in which to operate. Occasionally, I would end up on the right wing and that would sometimes mean Jimmy Johnstone would switch to the left until I got the chance to move back into position. We worked well as a team, with guys switching position for each other all the time. It helped me that I was comfortable on both feet. If the ball broke to me on right or left, I would feel at ease on either foot, although I would always take corner kicks with my right foot.

Jock tinkered with the team, making minor adjustments to almost every player's game. He brought out qualities in us all that we hadn't known were there. One man whom he couldn't really change, though, was Jimmy Johnstone. Jimmy had a unique talent and the best thing for any manager to do was simply let him loose on the opposition. On one occasion, Jock did try to give Jimmy some instructions. 'Now,' Jock said to Jimmy, 'when you don't have the ball, I want you to keep moving. Don't worry about where the ball is, just concentrate on staying on the move – if you do that, you will be doing a lot to help the team simply by distracting their defence.' Wee Jimmy just nodded his head repeatedly as Jock got his point across. As we left Jock and went out into the tunnel before taking the field, Jimmy turned round and said, 'Not get on the ball? Who the **** does he think he's kidding?' He went ahead and played his usual game – there was no point asking Jimmy to do anything other than to try to get on the ball and use it to rip into the opposition. Sometimes he would hold on to the ball for a good while and then lose it but even that wasn't such a bad thing. In doing so, he might have allowed the rest of the team to sort themselves out, get organised and get back into position before going again. He was great for us.

Jock also introduced that rarest of things – a ball in training. Dull lapping of the track became a thing of the past. He placed a strong emphasis on ballwork and it wouldn't be abstract – there would be goals involved every time. I always liked that, to knock the ball into the net, even in training. One morning, early in his time at the club, we were given an insight into how much detailed thought Jock put into management. He lined up a defensive wall in front of John Fallon, the goalkeeper, but arranged it so that there were two men, then a gap, then another two men. That was to allow the goalkeeper to look through the wall at what the opposing team were doing in their taking of the kick. No one at Celtic Park had ever previously shown such advanced thinking in their coaching of the team. In practice, that ploy didn't work and Jock decided to abandon the idea because if the ball was directed at the wall, it could veer off either of the defenders on each side of the gap. It still showed how prepared he was to think radically and differently about every aspect of the game. That was very impressive.

Shooting was something we practised endlessly with Jock and that was invaluable to us. The more you shoot at goal, the more relaxed you will be when the ball pops into your path inside the penalty area. If you don't see a ball from one Saturday to the next, you'll end up fluffing your shot when the moment comes on match day. We scored lots of goals from inside the six-yard box because we had gone over it again and again in training. Bobby Murdoch, Bertie Auld and Tommy Gemmell – indeed, everyone other than the front three – practised getting to the byline and sending low, fast crosses into the six-yard box. It meant that when it came to match day our players would automatically know to smack the ball across the face of goal, where forwards such as Stevie Chalmers and I would be waiting to despatch it into the net. The ball was in the opposition's box a lot and we were always on the move in and around there.

Inconsistency had dogged Celtic for the best part of a decade when Jock arrived on the scene and not even Jock Stein could immediately eradicate the haphazard nature of results that typified Celtic at that time. We did defeat Airdrieonians 6–0 in his first match in charge, with Bertie Auld netting five on the night, but we then lost 1–0 at home to a St Johnstone side that was sitting close to the foot of the first-division table. We drew 3–3 at Dundee after being 3–1 up, lost 4–2 at home to Hibs but beat them 4–0 at Easter Road, beat Third Lanark 1–0 at home, then went down 6–2 at Falkirk before a 2–1 home defeat to Partick Thistle. It was a crazy, zigzagging series of League results. The team was being chopped and changed by Jock throughout that time and that may have contributed to the way results had gone for us. He was possibly experimenting with his new set of players. It did not affect our morale – we had reached the Cup final and we were all buoyant about that. Just being in the team on a regular basis was enough to please me.

For some reason we remained potent in the Cup, defeating Motherwell 3–0 in front of 60,000 in a replayed semi-final after we had drawn the first game 2–2. The final was due to be played on 24 April 1965 and our opponents were one of Jock's former clubs, Dunfermline Athletic. We went down to Largs in the midweek before the match, where Jock named the team, providing us with one of the first of many surprises he would spring on us during his time at Celtic. Jimmy Johnstone, who had played in the home League match against Partick, was left out. Everyone was surprised at Jimmy's omission, but Jimmy, in common with the rest of us, was a young guy learning his trade, so although we knew what he had in terms of his ability, he was not the consistent player he later became. He was not, in those early days of his career, the saviour he would later become – not yet the established match winner. So although his omission puzzled us to some degree, it was not seen as a body blow in terms of whether or not we could win the Cup. It was still sad to see how despondent Jimmy was at that decision. He was really down about it.

Jock had initially built his reputation as a manager by turning round Dunfermline and putting them on the path that helped, among other things, lead them to the 1965 final. He had altered their fortunes by saving them from seemingly certain relegation in 1960 before winning the Scottish Cup in 1961. Subsequently, he had done well in his year at Hibernian, where his team had defeated Real Madrid in one encounter and had won the Summer Cup. Everybody in Scottish football thought Jock was a genius, so you trusted what he said. If he said you could do something or that something was possible, you believed it so a crowd of 109,000 congregated inside Hampden on the day of the 1965 final to see whether he could work some instant magic for Celtic, the underdogs, and upset Dunfermline by taking the trophy. The Fife club were rightly favourites. They had been challenging for the League title throughout the season and they were a good, strong, experienced side.

Shortly before half-time, Dunfermline scored to go 2–1 up and we came in at the interval slightly concerned, in the knowledge that we would be turning round to play into the wind. The dressing room was really quiet but Jock took over and assured us that if we continued playing as well as we had been doing, we could win the match. We went on to win 3–2. Billy McNeill scored the winner with a great header – the only thing that bugs Billy about that is that when you see the photograph of him rising into the air to score, I am always in frame, crouching down close to him as he sends the ball into the net. No matter how often he sees it, or from whichever angle the picture has been taken, he says, he can't get me out of that photo… After Billy scored the goal, the remaining nine minutes felt like a lifetime. That afternoon, my dad was working down in Saltcoats – being at the game would have been too much for him because of the emotion and excitement involved. When he heard that we had gone ahead near the end, he started bubbling. The thought of that still affects me deeply.

That victory has to be one of the best results that Celtic have ever achieved. The team might even have been split up if we had failed to win. We had to prove to Jock that we could win and we did it in a very hard game. Had we been beaten, he might have decided to make a few changes to get himself a team of winners. Afterwards, we were all in the bath having a laugh when someone came in and said, 'Kilmarnock have won the League championship – they beat Hearts 2–0 at Tynecastle.' The cry from our boys was, 'Who cares? We've won the Cup.'

It was fantastic to have won the Scottish Cup – I thought at the time that it had to be the pinnacle of our careers. We hadn't won the trophy for 11 years so there was a great outpouring of joy among Celtic supporters at this feat, especially as the victory could never have been taken for granted, pre-match. When we came out of the stadium, the car park at Hampden was heaving with people who had been waiting to acknowledge us. We put the Cup up at the front of the bus and wound our way down through the Gorbals, where the crowds were so dense they reduced our journey speed to a crawl. After the barren years, no one knew how long it would be before they would see Celtic lift another major trophy, so people wanted to make the most of the moment. That victory, I think, proved that Jock was the best thing that could have happened to the club. He was beginning to look invincible.

During the summer of 1965, Jock again showed how progressive he was by bringing in four Brazilians for a month's trial – Ayrton Inacio, Marco di Sousa, Fernando Consul and Jorge Fara. They hated the cold and big Tam Gemmell, for a laugh, would turn the freezing hose on them. They would go demented. They hated it. Brazil were the world champions and it was a radical move even to think of introducing South Americans to Scottish football, but those particular players were not quite up to the standard of the very top Brazilians and Jock allowed them to go home. They were no better than the players he already had at the club.

Prior to the Cup final, I still hadn't felt completely established in the Celtic team, despite having scored in every round up to the final and having been selected regularly by Jock Stein. It wasn't so much that I still felt like the shy outsider of my earlier years at the club – more that I continued to wonder if I was good enough to be in the Celtic team. After we won the Cup, I started to feel a bit more confident. I was in the team from the start of the 1965–66 season and things blossomed from there. As a young player, you don't look too far ahead. All you're really interested in is getting in the team. Once there, it's good if your pals are in it too. In my case, I'd be pleased if Jimmy Johnstone or Bobby Murdoch or Willie O'Neill were included, but the most important thing is that you are in the team yourself. That is the one and only priority for any footballer. It's why you are at a football club. Under Jock Stein, though, if you worried solely about your own game and how you played as an individual, it might not work for you. You might think you had played well in a match but if Jock was of the opinion that you had not done your bit for the team as a whole, you would not be in the side for the next game.

Under Jock, the old formation that the club had been using for decades started changing. We went to 4–2–4, and sometimes 4–4–2. Bobby Murdoch and Bertie Auld were in the middle, and wee Jimmy and I were pushed wide, either up alongside the two central forwards or operating from midfield. Bobby Murdoch and I had been the two inside-forwards in the reserve team but when Jock came, Bobby moved back into midfield and I went to outside-left. Bobby was magnificent with the game spread out in front of him rather than working away with his back to goal. As his deployment of Murdoch showed, Jock was excellent in terms of identifying where a player's energies could be best employed. He would never allow himself to be trammelled by the received wisdom about a player's best position, and he would often talk to you about how to use your abilities to the best effect so that you didn't expend energy pointlessly. No one had ever taken the time to explain small details such as that to us previously and it was so helpful. The players were highly receptive to him – everyone thought that what he said was the law.

Those improvements to the team meant that we were feeling good about ourselves as we confronted Rangers in the League Cup final of October 1965, in front of a 108,000 crowd. We hadn't beaten Rangers in a Cup final for almost a decade and they had also had the better of our League encounters during the early 1960s – in 13 matches in League and Cup over the previous three years, we had won once, drawn once and lost 11 times to them. We'd play well against our great rivals, but not win, so when we defeated them 2–1 that day at Hampden, thanks to two penalties from John Hughes, it was as if a hoodoo had been broken. I can remember Yogi slotting away the first quite neatly and Billy Ritchie, the Rangers goalkeeper, getting his hand to the second one but failing to keep it out. Those goals had come in the opening half hour and although Rangers scored in the final ten minutes, it felt like a much more comfortable victory than the scoreline might indicate. The win proved to be just what we needed, and it provided us with the impetus to go on from there and beat Rangers regularly. Confidence is a huge factor in any sport. Of course, the Rangers fans were not too enamoured about this shift of power in Glasgow. After the game, we were parading the Cup when 'Gers supporters started pouring over the wall and on to the pitch. I don't think they were about to congratulate us either. We had to race for the dressing room. I hadn't sprinted as fast as that all afternoon . . .

Jock would tell the press that a win over Rangers was only two points and although it was nice to win, it was really just the same as beating any other team. That wasn't quite what he said to us in the dressing room. He would stress how intense the competition had to be on the park, how we had to get our challenges in on them, run them, work them. His preparations made it clear to us that it was more than an ordinary game against Rangers because they were always going to be on our tail.

An extended European run was another of the benefits that came our way in Jock's first full season as Celtic manager. Go Ahead of Deventer, a Dutch side, were our opponents in the first round of the European Cup-Winners' Cup that 1965–66 season. We were drawn to play away first and our hotel was so close to the De Adelaarshorst stadium that we walked to the ground. When we got there, an hour and a half before kick-off, it was jam-packed and the crowd were having a great time, singing verses of traditional songs such as 'Daisy, Daisy, give me your answer do'. The atmosphere was wonderfully friendly, and so conducive to me that, in a 6–0 victory, I scored my first hat-trick for Celtic. On the previous weekend, we had beaten Aberdeen 7–1 at Celtic Park, and I had scored twice. The Deventer scout, after watching that game, had suggested that I would be Celtic's most dangerous player in Holland. I was happy to oblige. He had also approached me before the game and asked me to leave Celtic and join Go Ahead, telling me that his club would give me whatever I requested in terms of payment and accommodation. I had politely turned him down. After the match he sought me out again and told me that I had done him a favour. His reputation had been enhanced greatly in Deventer because he had correctly identified me as Celtic's major threat.

Denmark was our destination in the following round. We played Aarhus away in the first leg and, although we won 1–0, we struggled. They had an inside-right who was reputed to have the hardest shot in European football, so I was slightly concerned when they won a free-kick 25 yards from goal and I was drafted into the defensive wall. We were all linking together in the wall, but when the big lad ran at the ball and hit it, I instinctively ducked. The ball went hurtling through the space I had left and Ronnie Simpson had to pull off one of his fine saves to push it away. Once he had regained his feet, he started running about shouting, 'Who ducked? Who ducked?' By that point, I was already at the halfway line, well out of the road. I don't think I was ever in another wall after that.

After defeating Aarhus at home and Dynamo Kiev by 4–1 over the two legs of the quarter-final, we faced Liverpool, England's champions elect, in the semi-finals. We simply overwhelmed them in the first leg, at Celtic Park. We missed so many really good chances to put the game out of sight but ended up with a 1–0 win, the goal coming shortly after half-time when I prodded the ball into the Liverpool net from close range.

At Anfield, we were warming up when Ronnie Simpson landed on top of Stevie Chalmers' ankle. Blood was seeping from the wound but Stevie didn't want to say anything about it. He went ahead and played the match, and played well. It was a hard game, turning on a five-minute period an hour in, when they scored twice to go 2–0 ahead. That was the final scoreline but we should have been level with them on aggregate because I scored a goal that night that should have stood, definitely should have counted. The ball was played forward by Bobby Murdoch, and Joe McBride jumped to flick it on. Now I actually saw Joe play it, when he was ahead of me, so I raced past him and his marker to get the ball, went round the goalkeeper and placed it in the net – only for the referee, Josef Hannet of Belgium, to give offside.

We were all raging at that. A lot of bottles were thrown on to the field by the Celtic fans that night and the referee had to stop the game for a while. Although you would never excuse their actions, you could understand the fans' frustration, because it had been a perfectly good goal. The referee admitted later that he had made a blunder. It was all the more disappointing because the final was due to be played at Hampden and with the ground crammed with Celtic supporters, we would have been hugely confident of lifting the trophy. That rankles with me to this day.

I hurt my foot at Anfield and my ankle was really sore, so my disappointment at having my goal erased was compounded when I was ruled out of the Scottish Cup final with Rangers at Hampden Park the following Saturday. A 0–0 draw meant the game went to a replay. I trained on the Monday after the final and was fit and ready for the second game two days later, but Jock opted not to bring me back into the team. I thought I would have been back, especially with the first game having been goalless, but Jock did not explain why I had been left out of the team – he very rarely explained his selections. Being left out a second time was even more disappointing than not making it the first time, because I really expected to be in the side. Kai Johansen scored the only goal of the game to win the trophy for Rangers.

Rangers had also been our closest pursuers in the race for the League title and when we had a couple of hiccups early in 1966 – losing away to Hearts and at Stirling Albion – we fell behind our Old Firm rivals. After that, though, a great roll of results moved us clear of Rangers at the top of the table and in the second week of April, when Bertie Auld scored our 100th League goal of the season in a 5–0 victory over St Mirren, we went five points ahead. Rangers had a game in hand over us at that stage but we had four matches remaining and knew the title would be ours if we held our collective nerve.

A 0–0 draw away to Hibernian was followed by a trip to face Morton, who desperately needed points in their battle against relegation. Jimmy Johnstone gave us the lead right on half-time but the match remained in the balance until the final minute when a ball up the middle split the Morton defence. As I raced in behind their central defenders Erik Sorensen, the Morton goalkeeper, flew out towards me. I got there first and as it was a nice sunny day and the pitch was bone-hard, the ball took a lovely, high bounce and I nodded it over him to clinch another couple of vital points for us.

We knew we had to win the next game, against Dunfermline Athletic on the first Wednesday in May, to push ourselves to within a whisker of taking the title but after 29 minutes of this crucial match at a packed Celtic Park, Alex Ferguson, the Dunfermline striker, pounced to put them 1–0 ahead. Five minutes later, I got my head to the ball, at close range, to equalise. On the hour, Stevie Chalmers reached the byline and cut the ball back to me. I hit it from the edge of the box, the goalkeeper parried it but Jimmy was there to smack home the rebound, much to the delight of our support. After that, we remained steady to clinch victory.

A point at Motherwell in our final fixture, the following Saturday, would win the League for us, and only a hefty defeat, something like 4–0, would hand the title to Rangers. We had been going well enough throughout the season to be confident that we would go to Fir Park and win. Everyone was buoyant going into that game. We were embarking on a tour of North America the following week, which we were all excited about, and that helped to put us in fine fettle for the visit to Motherwell.

It was great to score the only goal of the game just a minute or so before the final whistle. Jim Craig did very well to get to the by-line and I came in and bundled the ball in off my shins from a couple of yards, which is as good as a 30 yarder really, especially when it has won you the title. It set off much dancing and singing and celebrating inside our dressing room at Fir Park – it was great to know that we were about to visit places such as St Louis and San Francisco as the champions of Scotland.

I could look back on numerous personal highlights over that title-winning season. For instance, at Falkirk in mid-October the score was locked at 3–3 with only a few minutes to go when a corner kick was delivered into the Falkirk box and I met it cleanly with a volley, on the penalty spot, to give us the win. I also scored our first goal that day, accelerating past John Lambie to smack a left-footed shot across the goalkeeper and into the far corner of the net. I can still see both of those goals, as clear as day. Then at Dundee in our next game, I scored the winning goal in our 2–1 victory when I rounded the goalkeeper to jab the ball into the net.

When the team is playing well and you are winning games, football is great fun, really enjoyable. With each victory, our faith in Jock grew ever stronger. When you are on a run like that you are delighted to go to the ground in the morning to get stuck into some training. It helped that we had got off to a terrific start to the season – and that would become a hallmark of the Jock Stein years at Celtic.

It was such a big thrill to get that championship-winning goal at Fir Park, my 25th of the season in League and Cup. We had beaten Rangers 5–1 at New Year but they had still proved difficult to shake off, finishing the season only two points adrift of us. Fir Park was packed with Celtic supporters, so much so that some opted to ease away from the uncomfortably busy terraces and find a more exclusive vantage point on the roof. We too felt as though we had scaled considerable heights. We had clinched Celtic's first championship for 12 long years and I wondered whether anything in football could top the feeling we had that day.

CHAPTER 4

EUROPEAN ENGAGEMENTS

It was very much a case of us and them when we dipped into the European Cup for the first time during the autumn of 1966. It appeared clearly to be a two-tier tournament, with the great majority of clubs, including us, there for a bit of an adventure, while a thin sliver of élite Latin clubs seemed likely to smooth their way to the final. The tournament had, until that year, always been won by one of the major footballing institutions from southern Europe, where the game seemed to be played in a manner sufficiently sophisticated and elegant to overwhelm anything that anyone else could offer. That meant that Internazionale of Milan, Real Madrid, Sporting of Lisbon and Atletico Madrid were the natural favourites for that season's Cup. Only rarely had clubs from northern Europe even reached the final. Milan, Inter, Benfica and Real Madrid had repeatedly won the tournament in style, then competed for the World Club Championship. We had also been thoroughly outplayed and outclassed by Real when they had beaten us 3–1 in Glasgow in a friendly match in September 1962, so we entertained no illusions that we might add our name to the select band of clubs who had taken the great trophy.

The opening round of the tournament placed us in a tie with

Zurich, the Swiss champions, and at that stage, all that the European Cup meant for us was a match at home in front of a bigger-than-average crowd and a trip to somewhere interesting that we had never been before. We wondered what sort of stadium our opponents would have and what their team would be like. We were determined to make the most of the match and didn't even think about what other clubs were in the tournament that year. We didn't think any further than the tie in hand. If we won it, that would be great.

Despite all the anticipation, the European Cup began with a bit of an unpleasant taste for me. I recall sitting in the North British Hotel on George Square before heading off to Celtic Park for the first leg with Zurich and the papers were all asking, 'Who will partner Lennox in Celtic's attack?' They were speculating whether it would be Stevie Chalmers or Joe McBride. When we got to the park, the team was read out and I had been dropped. The press speculation beforehand made it slightly more disappointing not to have been selected. Jock gave me no idea why I had been left out. The boss went with Stevie and Joe as his front two, the team played very well and we won 2–0. That set up Celtic nicely for the second leg.

The whole trip was organised in a much more professional manner than had previously been the case with Celtic when abroad during the pre-Stein era. It was clear that we were in Switzerland for that game and that game only. We trained at the right times and had banter with the boys at the right times. There was still some light relief when a cake with candles was presented to Jock on the day before the match in celebration of his 44th birthday.

Even though we had beaten Zurich 2–0 in Glasgow, we had felt, as we travelled to Switzerland, far from certain of our passage into the next round. A number of us were concerned that Zurich, now that they were at home, would drive hard at us in the way Celtic had attacked them in Glasgow. It meant that when Jock sat us down in a room in Zurich's splendiforous Dolder Grand Hotel before the match, it was imperative that he gave us a reassuringly good team-talk. It wasn't a big room, only about the same size as a bedroom, with people crammed in and sitting on plush, ornate armchairs. Jock surprised us all when he told us to expect Zurich to play in exactly the same cautious fashion as they had done in Glasgow. 'They're not good enough to change,' he said. 'We'll beat them here. We'll get at them.' One or two of the lads still weren't sure, so they questioned him. I think Billy McNeill suggested to him that Zurich would come out aggressively and try to defeat us. Jock was emphatic on the point. 'They've not got the players to come out and beat us,' he said. 'They're not good enough. We will beat them here tonight.'

The Letzigrund was a nice wee stadium, holding around 25,000, and so homely that when we had gone to visit it on the evening before the match, we had come across some locals jogging round the running track that hugged the perimeter of the pitch. Others had been practising the high jump and some honing their abilities for a walking race. The competitors looked like a pack of flustered Charlie Chaplins as they wiggled every muscle while continually straining to prevent themselves breaking into a run. Watching that raised a wee bit of a titter among the boys. The whole place had the atmosphere of a municipal facility. On the following evening, when I made my European Cup debut, we won very easily, by 3–0, and nobody ever doubted Jock's word after that. That meeting in the Dolder Grand was the only occasion on which I ever recall any real rumblings from the players in terms of questioning an assessment or a decision made by Jock. He had good reason for his confidence – he knew he had good judgement and I think he also had a lot of belief in his own players. Ninety-nine times out of a hundred, Jock would, tactically, get it absolutely right.

On beating Zurich, we wondered where we would go next on our big adventure. We always really looked forward to the draw for the next round of European competition. It was like taking part in a lucky dip. You could find yourself despatched to a forbidding region of communist eastern Europe or to the resplendent San Siro in Milan, the Bernabeu in Madrid or to a modest club about whom you might not know very much. It was exciting and added an extra dimension to the normal routine on the day when the draw was made, usually a Friday. We'd come in from training at lunchtime and would often be relaxing in a big soapy bath when told whom we were next to face. You would then see, written all over the players' faces, the anticipation and intrigue regarding our forthcoming test.

This time our destination was to be the Stade Marcel Saupin, home of Nantes, the French champions. We were quite pleased with the draw – it was good that we were not going to eastern Europe, a part of the world to which Celtic had often travelled in European competitions during the mid-1960s. Unlike the Soviet Union, Yugoslavia or Hungary, a visit to France would not involve a long flight plus dodgy food and accommodation once in the host country. Still, no matter whom you were drawn against, you got on with it. You were always pleased with the draw, in a way, because you were pleased still to be involved in the competition.

This time, the first leg was away from home and on a wet night we played on a heavy pitch. There was a bit of a glitch before the match – as our coach approached the stadium, Joe McBride realised that he had forgotten to bring his boots. Jock lost the place with him and Joe and Neilly Mochan, our kit man and trainer, had to take a taxi back to the hotel and then return to the ground, where they had to wade through the crowd to get to the dressing room with minutes to spare before the game began. This was one of the few occasions on which anyone was allowed to make such a *faux pas* and still play but Joe was our top scorer that season and Jock was always practical in his decision-making. Nantes scored early in the match but Joe equalised quickly. Shortly after the interval, I ran on to a ball through the middle and speared it into the net to make it 2–1. Stevie Chalmers added a third before the end and, having won 3–1, we were quite confident of the outcome as we looked forward to the home leg of the tie.

Over in Nantes, an amusing episode had occurred during the build-up to the match. During a conversation with the travelling pressmen, Jock had put it to them that it was ridiculous that they should habitually hand out so much stick to footballers and football people when they could barely boot a ball in a straight line themselves. They must have defended their abilities as footballers because the discussion escalated to such a point that Jock laid down a challenge to them to show what they could do and took the press boys out on to our muddy training pitch in France where he told them to try to hit the target from the penalty spot. Balls were soon flying off at all angles wide of goal as the hapless hacks, still in their shoes, tried to steer their shots on target.

The return match with Nantes was almost a mirror image of the first leg. On a really miserable, wet night at Parkhead we once again beat them 3–1. This time, I notched our third – Jimmy Johnstone cut the ball across the face of goal and I came sliding in, on the edge of the six-yard box, to stretch out a leg and nick the ball into the net. A 6–2 aggregate victory over the French champions was pretty pleasing.

There had been no surprises in the second leg as we went about our work of removing Nantes from that year's tournament, but minutes after the final whistle there was a bit of a shock when we were told that Ajax Amsterdam, a team of whom we had never really heard, had thrashed Liverpool 5–1. After the match, we were all in the bath when somebody came in to give us the result. How could a virtually unknown Dutch team give Liverpool such a doing? Mind you, our next reaction was to be grateful that Liverpool were out. At that stage, we were beginning to take a bit more interest in which clubs would be with us in the last eight but still, much more than that, we were predominantly concerned with where we would be heading next, rather than trying to assess our chances of winning the tournament. That still seemed a very unlikely prospect. Although Zurich and Nantes had been decent opposition, against whom we had had to work hard to win, we were well aware that the great white sharks of the tournament were still lying in wait. Real Madrid and Inter Milan still lurked in the competition's depths. Atletico Madrid, though, were no longer alive, having been eliminated by Vojvodina Novi Sad of Yugoslavia, who turned out to be our opponents in the quarter-final.

Those European midweek ties were fantastic. If we were at home, we would almost always achieve a great result and would then come into Celtic Park at around 11 the next morning for some rest and relaxation. We'd all be in the big bath, full of soap suds, and Jimmy Steele, the masseur, would be singing away while giving people a rub-down on the massage table, which was in the same room. Jock would sometimes jump into the bath along with us. We'd be lying in the bath for ages, talking about all the results across Europe, and Jock would be chatting away about this and that, on our level. As soon as he got out and got dressed, though, he was the manager again. You'd had your bit of fun. He was terrific but you always knew when it was time to get back to business.

When we went away with Celtic and stayed in a hotel on the Continent, the camaraderie among the boys was so great that Jock could mix things up every time so that players had different room-mates on each trip. The exceptions to that rule were Jimmy Johnstone and me – we were always in the same room. Jimmy and I were the two most impish and cheeky members of the Celtic team at that time. There would be big card schools in operation when we went away with the club for a night or two, but Jinky and I were too daft to be invited to play cards for money. After a while, the guys involved wouldn't even tell us the number of the room in which the card school was being held, because we would come in and throw cards about or look over someone's shoulder and say something such as, 'King of diamonds – is that a good card?' Neither Jimmy nor I played golf at that time, so, if we were down at Seamill preparing for a big home game, and some of the other boys were out golfing, we would wait until they had hit their drives, then spring out from the bushes and shift the balls around so that they were sitting in the most awkward spots when the golfers walked up to them. They'd think they had hit a cracker straight up the middle only to find their ball sitting in a bunker or in a burn. We'd do lots of small, stupid things, too. At dinner-time, for instance, we would unscrew the top of the salt and pepper canisters before our team-mates came into the dining room. There was always someone wanting to throttle Jimmy and me.

Most of us were happy to have been drawn against Vojvodina. We had never heard of them, they weren't one of the bigger names in European football and they had won the Yugoslavian championship for the first time in their history. We understood that if they were in the last eight of the European Cup they couldn't be a bad team, but we were not overawed at facing them in the same way that we might have been if we had been drawn against Real Madrid, the holders. Big names and a big reputation can carry a decisive amount of weight into a finely balanced match.

Novi Sad wasn't the nicest of places. The weather was dull and depressing and the town was grey. Such surroundings mattered little to us, though. On away trips in Europe, we would get to our hotel on the Monday, have a cup of tea, go for a walk and get to bed early. On the following day we would train in the morning, then have a wander round the local shops during the afternoon and buy a couple of souvenirs before visiting the stadium in the evening. On the day of the match, we'd have a short walk in the morning and take to our beds in the afternoon in preparation for the match. We were pretty much self-contained and focused on the job in hand.

Two absolutely enormous floodlights, one at each end of the ground, towered over the Gradski Stadium, and the Novi Sad fans were noisy, but as we trotted on to the park to warm up they were playing 'Mellow Yellow' by Donovan, the Glasgow-born folk-rocker – hippy-dippy music of the sort you did not expect to hear in communist eastern Europe. Some of the boys took that reminder of home as a good omen.

If the city of Novi Sad embodied grey mediocrity, the city's footballing representatives most certainly did not. It was clear from kick-off that we were up against a top-class side, one that was several notches higher than Nantes and Zurich. Vojvodina had highly skilled players who shuttled the ball around quickly, were well organised and kept things tight at the back. We were, nevertheless, looking good for a 0–0 draw when, with 20 minutes remaining, Tommy Gemmell was short with a pass in the vicinity of our penalty area and that gave Vojvodina the opportunity to score the only goal of the game. One or two of the boys were raging after that. We were all great pals but we were also fiery competitors and if, on the pitch, someone wasn't doing their job, the others would soon let him know. I remember a lot of bickering going on among our players as we walked off the pitch, with recriminations flying around about the manner in which we had lost the goal. Jock intervened once we had all reached the dressing room, telling us to calm down. He was unhappy at the way we had conceded a goal but I think he would have interpreted the guys having a go at each other as a good sign. It meant that the competitive spirit among us was strong without him having to work too hard at it.

The quality of Vojvodina was again evident when they came to Celtic Park and kept the second leg goalless for almost an hour before Stevie Chalmers popped up in the penalty box to put us ahead on the night and level on aggregate. It was so good to see the ball slip past Ilija Pantelic, the Vojvodina goalkeeper, who was a big, arrogant man. At one point in the game in Yugoslavia, I had gone sliding in for the ball and had failed to reach it but had fallen on the ground. As I lay there, Pantelic had pulled me up by the hair and milked the moment for the benefit of the crowd, who had gone wild at the sight of his belittlement of me. When we equalised in Glasgow, all the boys ran to Stevie to congratulate him but I ran to Pantelic, just to get my face in his face, to emphasise to him that we had scored and planned to take the tie. That was the only occasion in my career on which I ever did something like that.

Even with our tails up, the aggregate at 1–1 and 75,000 Celtic supporters urging us on, the Yugoslavs, who were as sublimely skilful and controlled in their football as they had been at home, retained their cool. As full-time approached, there had been no further scoring. During a lull in the play – I think someone was down injured – I remember thinking to myself that we were still in the tie but that we would now be travelling to Rotterdam for a play-off. In 1967, any European Cup tie drawn over two legs was settled at a neutral venue. Then, with seconds to go, Charlie Gallagher sent the ball sailing into the box from a corner kick and Billy McNeill powered forward and climbed to reach the ball, guiding home yet another winning header for us. The whole place erupted. Vojvodina had just enough time to centre the ball before the referee blew for the end of the match. It was incredible. Jock came shooting out of the dugout and on to the park to congratulate us. I shook Pantelic's hand at time up – once the game is over, any animosity produced by a match situation should be put aside.

Even though we were now in the semi-finals and had beaten a first-class side, in the shape of Vojvodina, our thoughts still did not turn towards winning the tournament. We had in prospect a two-leg tie against Dukla Prague, the Czechoslovakian champions, led by Josef Masopust, European footballer of the year five seasons previously, and that ensured that we could not allow ourselves the luxury of looking ahead to the final. We had been happy to avoid Inter, who had eliminated Real Madrid in the quarter-finals, but we knew that Dukla were deserving of huge respect. They had knocked out Ajax, Liverpool's conquerors, in the quarter-finals, had won their own domestic title in five seasons out of six and had frequently reached the latter stages of the European Cup during the 1960s.

The first leg of the tie against Dukla provided me with one of the strangest experiences of my career. We were at home first, so on the Monday before the match we all went down to Seamill to prepare. That afternoon, John Clark and I took a walk from the hotel up to the town to buy some newspapers. John read every paper he could because he liked to be right on top of the latest football news. He always studied the game as a whole very closely. As we were strolling along, John said to me, 'I think you will be playing for Scotland on Saturday, against England at Wembley.' It seemed a strange suggestion to me.

'John,' I replied, 'I might not even be playing at Parkhead on Wednesday night.' I was aware that Jock might opt to play Yogi instead of me. John was adamant on his point.

'You'll be playing for Scotland,' he insisted. 'The way Scotland have been playing and with the team they're likely to put out on Saturday, you'll be playing. You'll be the wide player.' Just at that moment, by bizarre coincidence, Jock pulled up alongside us in his car.

'Wee man,' he said to me, 'congratulations. You've been picked to play for Scotland against England at Wembley on Saturday.' He drove away, leaving John to give me the 'I told you so' routine.

Later that day, Jock had a less welcome piece of news for me when he announced the Celtic team to play Dukla and I wasn't included. The disappointment was enormous but it's not in my nature to mope about something like that. If there's nothing you can do to improve a certain situation, there is no point in worrying about it. It was of some compensation to know that I was playing for Scotland on the Saturday but, given the choice between the two, I would rather have been playing for Celtic against Dukla Prague.

You have to believe, if you are omitted from a football team, that you can get back in the side. Also, with Jock, you never knew just how he would shake up his selection for each match. Yogi had been given the nod at outside-left for the first leg against Dukla but Jock could decide he wanted a different team for the next game. He also played me in every away game in Europe that season – possibly because, with Celtic playing a bit deeper away from home, my pace could be invaluable in getting in behind opposing defenders if they had pushed up as part of an attacking team. As it turned out, I played well in a very good Scotland team at Wembley, was restored to the Celtic team for the next match and retained my place in the side until the end of that momentous 1966–67 season.

The team had put on a good performance to beat Dukla 3–1 in the first leg and we were hoping that would be enough of a lead to see us safely through the second leg at the Juliska Stadium. Prague was another chip off the eastern bloc, a bleak place, although we did stay in the quite magnificent International Hotel, close enough to the ground for us to walk there on the day. Dukla's stadium was, that spring of 1967, under reconstruction. The largest side of the ground was a wooded area that was being transformed into terracing and when we went there, that steep hillside was dotted densely with freshly hewn tree stumps. This was where the bulk of the fans would be situated once the rebuilding work was complete but it was depopulated for our semi-final. There were spectators behind both goals and also in a modest stand on one side of the pitch but there were not enough of them to create any sort of special atmosphere. The ground had no floodlights, so we played the match during the afternoon. All in all, the setting wasn't quite as intimidating as a lot of grounds that we had visited.

The match still proved to be an exacting experience. Dukla needed to go all out for the win and they pushed us back so far that I spent much of my time alongside Tommy Gemmell, on the left side of our defence, while Jimmy Johnstone was doubling up in defence alongside Jim Craig, on the right. Stevie Chalmers was on his own up front and, with the tirelessness of a young sheepdog, he chased every ball into the corners and along the Dukla back line. At one point, his enthusiasm for the cause led him into a bit of pushing and shoving with three or four Dukla defenders and there was no help at hand for him because the nearest Celtic player was about 70 yards away.

With so many of us having been pressed back by Dukla, it meant that when we did get the ball, there was a lot of ground for us to cover if we wanted to break into attack. That prevented us building up many cohesive forward movements and with Dukla having a lot of possession, we were under pressure almost completely from start to finish. It was one of the toughest games I ever experienced and certainly the one in which I had to do most defending. The longer it went without them scoring, the more comfortable I felt, although you are always aware that a team needs only one small break to score a goal and that if Dukla did so, it would lift them enormously and they would really force things hard to seek a second. At the final whistle, Dukla, for all their intelligent football and pressurising of our defence, had failed to score and the 0–0 draw put us in the final. It was an experience that pinched the nerves and I had no wish to go through something such as that ever again. The game had been foreign to our style of play. The relief at getting into the final was, though, heightened by a sense of achievement at the professional manner in which we had gone about our business.

During the month that elapsed between that victory in Prague on 25 April and the final in Lisbon, with Internazionale, on 25 May 1967, we were far from idle. On the Saturday after the European Cup semi, we faced Aberdeen in the final of the Scottish Cup and it was a re-run of the Dukla match, except that this time it was Aberdeen who were barely able to get out of their own half. Shortly before half-time, Bertie Auld and I worked a short corner and I cut it back from the goal-line for Willie Wallace to deliver it, cutely, into the net. There was no way back for Aberdeen after that. We won 2–0, in front of 127,000, with Willie also getting the second, but our pressure was such that it should have been a lot more. I think the Aberdeen players were quite disappointed in themselves that day. They had failed to put on a show but they were a good side, just one of a number of accomplished teams in Scotland, among them Rangers, who reached the final of the European Cup-Winners' Cup that season, and Kilmarnock, who got to the semis of the Fairs Cup in the spring of 1967. Competing in a League with accomplished opponents such as those prepared us well for the rigours of European football although the European Cup itself always felt like a step up – you knew that whatever club you were facing were the champions of their country.

The Scottish Cup was, incredibly, the third domestic trophy we had won that season. One side effect of European football, which was growing rapidly in importance, was that over the years it would eventually overwhelm the Glasgow Cup and relegate it to a second-string tournament. For a time, though, the city's cup, for which Celtic had been competing since the club's earliest days, continued to thrive in tandem with European competition. Early on in the 1966–67 season, that had worked out quite nicely for me when we had travelled to Ibrox for a Glasgow Cup tie and, in front of a 75,000 crowd, Billy McNeill scored early – unusually, with his boot – and I hit a hat-trick for the club in a 4–0 victory. That made me the first Celtic player to score three times against Rangers at Ibrox. The first of my goals was the one I really liked – a left-footed shot that kissed the underside of the bar on its way into the net. That was a major victory for us and at full-time Mr McGrory came in and congratulated me on my goalscoring achievement. We almost hadn't made it to the game at all. Prior to the match, a particularly officious policeman had prevented us entering Edmiston Drive in our coach, telling us the road was closed. It didn't seem to strike him that the road was closed because there was a match on and that if he didn't let the coach carrying the Celtic Football Club access, there might not be. After a lot of fiddling about, a senior policeman finally came on the scene to sort the matter out.

We eased to a 4–0 victory over Partick Thistle in the final of the Glasgow Cup in early November, nine days after we had defeated Rangers in the final of the League Cup. The sole goal in the latter match was another particularly pleasing one. Bertie Auld curved the ball, from deep on the left, into the penalty area, where Joe McBride reverse-headed it in my direction. Ronnie McKinnon, the Rangers centre-back, had been drawn towards Joe so when the ball landed in front of me, 10 yards from goal, I was free to volley it home. Jock had devised the move and we had practised it on the training ground. Only 20 minutes had passed when I scored and although we didn't play particularly well after that, we held on to win 1–0 when, a season or two earlier, Rangers might have come back to beat us. It was enormously thrilling to score the goal that won a Cup final against Rangers. The split-second the ball hits the net you feel sheer euphoria – and that feeling lasts for the rest of your life. When you're a wee boy you dream about doing that and the reality of it does not disappoint one bit.

We had also topped the Scottish League from the start of that 1966–67 season, scoring 33 goals and conceding nine in our opening eight consecutive victories but Rangers had pursued us closely throughout the season and we travelled to Ibrox on 6 May 1967 needing a point from the Glasgow derby, postponed from New Year, to secure the title. Our first goal came when I hit the post with a shot and Jimmy Johnstone squeezed the ball over the line from close range. That equalised a very good opening goal from Rangers' Sandy Jardine and it remained 1–1 at half-time. On that rain-sodden afternoon (well, it was Glasgow in May . . .) the pitch got heavier and heavier as the game progressed and with quarter of an hour remaining and the rain still slewing across the field, Jimmy collected the ball close to the touchline. He looked a bedraggled figure, with the sleeves of his shirt weighed down by water and his socks flapping around as he cut inside and veered across the muddy, strength-sapping pitch, 20 yards from goal. It was quickly clear that he was lining up a shot and I was saying to myself, 'Don't hit it, wee man! Don't hit it!' Jimmy, master of the unorthodox, did just that to send the ball sweetly into the roof of the Rangers net. He scored a lot of goals in his time but they would usually be converted from much closer to the target. It was fittingly special that he should conjure up such an unusual effort to clinch, effectively, the League title for us. Roger Hynd did score close to the end for Rangers but it didn't perturb our team. The 2–2 draw was all that we required. We had the upper hand on Rangers then. We were the better team, with better players. Every time we played them, I felt hugely confident that we would get the result we wanted.

Four days later, the line-up of the Scotland team for a friendly match at Hampden Park reflected the impact that Celtic had made that season but it was a tribute that we could have done without. Scotland had a friendly arranged against the Soviet Union for 10 May 1967 – the first international after the victory at Wembley – but no Rangers players were available because they were busy with a European Cup-Winners' Cup semi-final against Slavia Sofia of Bulgaria. Instead, six Celtic players began the game – Ronnie Simpson, Tommy Gemmell, John Clark, Billy McNeill, Jimmy Johnstone and me – and by the end seven of us were on the field, with Willie Wallace having replaced Denis Law. This was just a fortnight before we were due to play Internazionale in the European Cup final. They should maybe have left out a group of Celtic players rather than bringing in so many.

I think it was wrong for so many Celtic players to be drafted into the team for that match and it's fair to say that a number of us weren't too keen on playing. The possibility of injury loomed over each of us when we were so close to the biggest match of our lives. I'm not saying we didn't give all we could to the game with the Soviets, and once you start playing, you try to do your best, but the team did not play particularly well and lost. Tam Gemmell scored a great goal that night – he lobbed Ronnie from the halfway line. Tam had turned and lofted the ball back towards Ronnie only to find that Ronnie was standing on the 18-yard line and the ball floated high over him and into the net, ushering the Soviet Union side towards their 2–0 victory. Lev Yashin was in goal for the Soviet Union that night and he, at the time, was the most widely admired goalkeeper in the world. At one point, I hit a shot from the edge of the penalty area and he treated it with contempt, bending down to take the ball as easily as if he was plucking a flower out of the ground.

Celtic's final League match that spring, against Kilmarnock at home on 15 May, afforded us the opportunity to display the four domestic trophies we had won that season. Afterwards we retreated to Seamill for a week of sharp, hard training combined with relaxation. We went for long walks, played cards and snooker, read books and had good chats over cups of tea. It was never too organised at Seamill. We'd be left to enjoy ourselves when we weren't training and I think everyone enjoyed the informality of our favourite hideaway. Jock was in a light-hearted mood that week, with a big smile on his face – this was the time to keep everyone feeling good about themselves and feeling as though there was no pressure on them. It helped that we had a bunch of guys who all liked to be in each other's company, although when we trained hard and guys went clattering into each other, sometimes fists were raised. Once we returned to the dressing room, though, such incidents became history. Tempers might be lost occasionally but no lingering grudges were held.

After a long weekend at home with our families, we flew out to Lisbon on Tuesday, 23 May, and took up residence at the Hotel Palacio in Estoril on the Portuguese Riviera. In that magnificent establishment the ornate surroundings emphasised the special nature of the business to which we were attending. We had heard that Helenio Herrera, the coach of Internazionale, had been at the game against Rangers on 6 May but that wasn't on anybody's mind. We were quite happy to let him worry about us. The final would be a one-off game and we were content to be facing Inter. If we had had the choice of Inter or CSKA

Sofia, their semi-final opponents, we would probably have chosen CSKA. On the other hand, Inter were the richest club in Europe, twice European champions in the previous three years and a team featuring some of the most famous footballers in the world, including Sandro Mazzola and Giacinto Facchetti. Their presence in the final made it the most prestigious occasion possible. There was no mistaking that this was going to be the game of our lives.

CHAPTER 5

MASTERING THE MASTERS

A magnificently freewheeling approach to football characterised Jimmy Johnstone on the field of play but away from the action he was a bit of a worrier about the game. As we sat in our hotel room inside the Hotel Palacio prior to the European Cup final, Jimmy was fretting about the quality of the opposition we were about to face and began reeling off the names of the great stars in the Internazionale team. My response was to be positive and to stress to Jimmy the qualities of Billy McNeill, Bobby Murdoch, Bertie Auld and Tommy Gemmell. I told Jimmy that once he got on the ball he was going to be great. There was no doubt in my mind that we had the players capable of winning the trophy.

We were a bit late in arriving at the National Stadium, the venue for the final, which is situated in parkland outside the suburbs of Lisbon. Our coach driver had initially made the mistake of going in the opposite direction to the ground so by the time we got there, there were only about 50 minutes remaining before kick-off. Habitually, we would get to a ground a good bit earlier than that but our latecoming did us good. By the time we had had a walk on the pitch – which was in excellent condition – and got changed, it was time for the match to begin. There was no sitting around and no time for a build-up of nerves.

We received another boost when we heard that Luis Suarez, the superb Spanish midfield player who had cost Inter a world record transfer fee, was injured, had not travelled and would not play. Jock quickly tried to set us right on that one. 'Treat that with contempt,' he said. 'He will be here and he will play.' The manager was convinced that even though Suarez had been absent from Inter's training sessions, this was just a ruse and he would have flown in from Italy in time for the match. Once the official team lines were issued, it was clear that Suarez really was injured and when Jock relayed this message to us, it gave us another little jolt of confidence just at the right time.

One of the oddest aspects of the final was the dressing room, which was I-shaped and divided in two by a shower in the middle. Half of the team – the defensive players – were changing in one section and the other half – the attacking players – in the other section, so the two groups were separated. We crossed a courtyard to get to the players' tunnel, which descended underground before climbing upwards into the light. We lined up alongside the Italians inside the tunnel and at that point all we wanted to do was get out on the pitch and get started. For any big, important game, once you reach the tunnel your main thought is simply to get on with it, just as it is in any other game. The athlete in you is more interested in the action than in the ceremony or significance of the event. A wave of heat washed over us as we ascended the stairs from the cool, dark tunnel. When we had inspected the pitch earlier, a great number of our fans had already arrived inside the ground, and they had given us a great reception. Now another huge roar greeted us and, after a few formalities, the game was under way.

We started well but after seven minutes Jim Craig gave away a penalty when he sent Renato Cappellini tumbling inside the penalty area. Sandro Mazzola stepped up to sweep the spot-kick past Ronnie Simpson and into the net. At the time, I was convinced it wasn't a penalty – during a game, you don't ever see matters objectively or neutrally and we all felt we had been dealt with harshly. On reflection, we knew that the decision was correct and we would have been annoyed if we had not been given a penalty in similar circumstances.

Losing that goal wasn't as much of a blow as it might have been because we were playing well, creating a lot of chances and felt sure that a goal would eventually come our way. It was still 1–0 to Inter at half-time but Jock Stein reassured us that he was happy with our display and that we should continue in the same vein after the interval. There was no ranting and raving from him at the break even though we were behind. He told us the chances would continue to come if we kept moving Inter about in the way in which we had been doing. There was nothing for Jock to change at half-time. We weren't under pressure and we were doing everything well in attack.

I felt that it was only a matter of time before we scored the equaliser – Bertie Auld had hit the bar and Giuliano Sarti, the Inter goalkeeper, had made a couple of good saves, once to stretch and tip a header from Jimmy over the bar and on another occasion to get to a volley from Tam Gemmell. When you see chances such as those coming the way of your team, you always think that you are going to get the breakthrough.

The pattern of the match was shifting our way because the Italians sat back after they had gone ahead. Once they had scored, it seemed as though they thought that, because they were up against a team from Scotland, wherever that might be, it shouldn't be too much trouble to cruise through the remainder of the match. They hadn't reckoned on the exceptional use that passers such as Bobby Murdoch and Bertie Auld could make of a football, or of the sterling qualities that John

Clark, our sweeper, showed in coming forward and using the ball well. In a 50-50 situation, few players ever got the better of John Clark. The Italians were also overwhelmed by the manner in which Jim Craig and Tam, our full-backs, got forward. They talk about athletes in the modern game – we had athletes then, especially in the shape of those two full-backs. I don't think Inter had anticipated that we would have so many players auxiliary to the forwards who would have the ability to open up the famed Italian defence – and we did. The Italians were also so determined to defend in depth that if we had mirrored their approach and left the ball in the centre circle, I believe it would have stayed there.

It was an unusual game because the forwards didn't get on the ball an awful lot. The Italians were so intent on defence that they marked us attacking players with cloying tightness. Jimmy and I were man-marked by Giacinto Facchetti and Tarcisio Burgnich, the Italian full-backs. Burgnich began by marking me but he and Facchetti later switched flanks. That close marking might have worked for them on another day – perhaps against a team that relied too much on their attacking players to unlock a defence – but we were able to penetrate from other parts of the park. The task for Jimmy and me on the day was not so much to get on the ball but to move around a lot so that we could move our markers out of position and create the space in which the supporting players in our team could do their stuff.

Movement creates room and that's how footballers play. That was one of Jock's principal tenets and it never worked more beautifully than on that hot late afternoon in Lisbon. He later told Jimmy and me how pleased he'd been with the way we went about our task.

Sarti, whom we had been told was Inter's weak link, turned out to be their best player. He still needed a bit of luck when, early in the second half, he grabbed Willie Wallace's legs inside the penalty area. It looked a certain penalty but Kurt Tschenscher, the West German referee, for whatever reason, failed to give it. We should also, I thought, have had another penalty in the second half, but were awarded an indirect free-kick inside the box instead. It's very rare to be given an indirect free-kick inside the penalty area. I felt it should either have been a penalty kick for us or the referee should have waved play on – an indirect free-kick seemed an unsatisfactory compromise.

Inter, I'd suggest, were disappointing to their own people that day. It wasn't that they played particularly badly – simply that they didn't shine and that was, in large part, due to us. It was hard for Mazzola, at centre-forward, to excel because he was an isolated figure for them up front. Facchetti, their great attacking defender, was kept busy by Jimmy and me and by our overlapping full-backs. Facchetti barely got an opportunity to motor forward on the overlap, a tactic at which he could be marvellously effective. Mario Corso, their star wide player, was another Italian known throughout Europe. 'Corso plays in the shade of the San Siro' was how he was tagged because he was so special he was said to have dispensation from the Inter management to switch wings in each half of a home game to be sure he played in the cool shade. We managed to keep him in the shade for the entire match.

Thrown into the mix, one pleasingly eccentric moment stands out when Ronnie Simpson ran from his goal to midway inside our own half as Cappellini chased the ball through on his own. Ronnie, instead of whacking the ball forward as would have been conventional when facing a fast and skilled forward, instead coolly backheeled it away, for it to be collected by John Clark. There was a good reason for Ronnie taking the action he did, apparently. He said that if he had hit the ball in the direction in which he was facing, it could easily have rebounded off the Italian and left him with a clear run on goal. Ronnie also claimed that he knew John was behind him, waiting for the ball, but whether that was true I don't know. I'd never previously seen him as far out of his goal as that and the fact that he was able to do so shows how far the Italians had been pushed back. Ronnie was great for us – older and more experienced than the rest of us. A cool, witty, laconic guy, he was great to have around, a calming presence. Later, he said that he really ought to have taken the ball forward at that moment in the match and had a shot at goal.

Even the best of managers – and Jock Stein clearly came into that category – can only lay out a plan for the players to follow. Once the game starts, the players have to use their initiative. Any player who can't work out situations for himself, and judge the right thing to do at any given time, is not a player at all. That was what Tommy Gemmell was doing when, after 63 minutes of the final, he streaked upfield to latch on to a pass from Jim Craig. It was taboo, under Jock's instructions, for both full-backs to be attacking in the opposing team's half but Tommy, as a good, thinking footballer, had judged that the Italians were not enough of a goalscoring threat for it to be a problem for him to join the attack. It had always looked to me, throughout the match, as though Bobby or Bertie or Tam would score from the edge of the box and that was exactly what happened, with Tommy smacking a fine 20-yard shot past Sarti's right shoulder for our equaliser.

Our second goal, which came five minutes from time, was scored by Stevie Chalmers and I was so pleased for him. He was a modest, hard-working guy whose efforts were occasionally overshadowed by the more extrovert individuals in the team but he was a magnificent goalscorer for Celtic. His goal on the lush turf in Lisbon was the result of hours of practice on winter mornings on the muddy, churned-up surface at our Barrowfield training ground. A lot of people think Stevie's was a lucky goal but three mornings a week in the preceding years we had trained incessantly to be able to do just that if such a situation arose. Stevie and I, or Wispy Wallace and I, or Yogi and Stevie would be told to hover in the heart of the penalty area and Neilly Mochan and Jock, one on each wing, would play the ball to other players to hit crosses for us to nick into the net from a few yards out. If the goalkeeper – Ronnie Simpson or John Fallon – blocked it or parried it, you had to follow up to jab the ball into the goal. If Jock saw the striker make a mess of it, he would go off his head. His idea was that if you weren't doing your work properly on the training ground, you wouldn't be able to do so on the park when the game came around. He abhorred slackness or sloppiness – everything had to be carried out with meticulous attention to detail. That all paid off when Tommy advanced up the left wing at the National Stadium and cut it back to Bobby Murdoch, who played it into the centre, where Stevie got just enough on the ball to nick it into the net.

When we scored that second goal to go 2–1 up, Facchetti came up alongside the Inter forwards as we all lined up for the restart and I remember looking at him and thinking how tired he looked. All of the Italians looked extremely drawn at that point. They didn't hurry to get the ball back on the centre spot. They looked dejected and demoralised. Their heads were down. They were gone, knackered. They had nothing left to offer. On the day, we got on top of them and never gave them a minute. I think they would have liked to play the game slowly but we never gave them the chance to do that.

We played out time after we had taken the lead and as soon as the final whistle went, I turned and ran right into John Clark. The two of us jumped up and down and rolled around on the ground but before we knew it, hundreds of people had swarmed on to the park from the terraces and we had to make a beeline for the tunnel. I met Burgnich there and swapped strips with him. At half-time I had stashed the strip

I had worn during the opening 45 minutes in my bag, so I had two priceless souvenirs of the match.

Everybody in that Celtic team could perform with excellence in his own position. Individually, we probably weren't the best players in the world but as a unit we were very, very good, if not great. We all had different roles. Stevie Chalmers and I would, in some games, not be on the ball as much as Bobby Murdoch, Bertie Auld and Jimmy Johnstone and supporters might go away from a game thinking we hadn't done a lot. But as I've said, sometimes our task was to work in behind people and create space for other players and generally open up the game. We would win corners or throw-ins and that would bring the team up the park and into attack. Other times, when playing wide left, I'd be on the ball a lot. It was a great compliment to me when Jock came and told me that Don Revie, the Leeds United manager, had said that he thought I was the best blind-side runner in Europe. You can't have a team where everybody is on the ball all the time. We knew our jobs, knew what we were good at doing, and the manager never asked us to do any more than that. Willie Wallace was another player who worked away quietly and instructively without an enormous fuss but he was hugely appreciated by his fellow players. He was a smashing all-round player, a terrific goalscorer and talented enough to play in Midfield if Bobby Murdoch or Bertie Auld were unavailable. He was also a lot of fun; great company off the park. Jimmy Johnstone was the most eye-catching member of the side – rightly so – and his abilities tended to distract attention from the work that the other players were contributing to the team effort but Jock Stein was a great believer in the value of work done off the ball being just as important as that done by the players who had the ball at any given time.

A lot of people were milling in and around the dressing room at the National Stadium when we eventually found our way back through

As a boy.

As a teenager in my Ayrshire Amateurs blazer.

HERALD & TIMES

Early Celtic days.

HERALD & TIMES

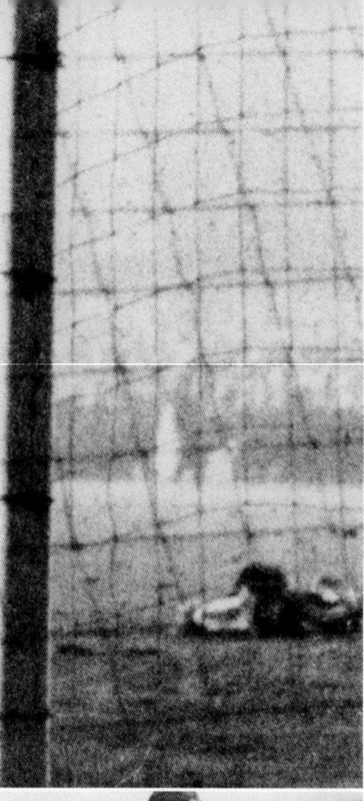

SCOTTISH DAILY EXPRESS

Above: Scoring a vital 90th minute equaliser in the League Cup semi-final against Hibs, October 1965.

Right: Returning with tulips from Amsterdam after scoring my first hat-trick for Celtic in the 6-0 Cup-Winners' Cup victory over Go Ahead Deventer, September 1965.

Below: With Jock Stein, backroom staff and the winning Celtic players after our landmark victory over Rangers in the 1965 League Cup final. I am on the extreme right, beside Jock.

SCOTTISH DAILY EXPRESS

SCOTTISH DAILY RECORD AND SUNDAY MAIL

Above: One...

Right: Two...

Below: Three against Rangers at Ibrox in the Glasgow Cup tie, August 1966.

SCOTTISH DAILY EXPRESS

Above: Celebrating Celtic's defeat of Aberdeen by 2–0 in the 1967 Scottish Cup final with Billy McNeill and Jimmy Johnstone.

Right: Sean Connery shows us his skills before the Scottish Cup quarter-final against Queen's Park, 11 March 1967. I am third from left.

EMPICS

EMPICS

Left: I am looking back at Jock Stein as he is chaired onto the pitch by the players before the final match of the 1967 season after the League Championship had been wrapped up in the penultimate game against Rangers.

Left: On the road to Lisbon. Scoring against FC Nantes at Celtic Park in the second round of the European Cup campaign.

EMPICS

SCOTTISH DAILY RECORD AND SUNDAY MAIL

Right: Enjoying an ice-cream with Jimmy Johnstone and Willie O'Neill in the hours running up to the European Cup final in Lisbon, 25 May 1967.

Below: The Celtic team line up before the kick-off of the European Cup final, 25 May 1967: (back row, l–r) Jim Craig, Tommy Gemmell, Ronnie Simpson, Billy McNeill, Bobby Murdoch, John Clark (front row, l–r) Steve Chalmers, Willie Wallace, Jimmy Johnstone, Me, Bertie Auld.

EMPICS

Above: Celebrating Stevie Chalmers' match-winning goal in Lisbon. I'm on the far left, with Jimmy Johnstone, Willie Wallace, Stevie, Billy McNeill, Bertie Auld and Tommy Gemmell and the other happy Celts. Mauro Bicicli and Aristide Guarneri are the dejected Inter players.

Left: Jimmy Steele, Willie O'Neill, Jimmy Johnstone and myself celebrating with the European Cup.

SCOTTISH DAILY RECORD AND SUNDAY MAIL

Below: Kathryn and I making our way across the pitch at an empty Celtic Park, before slipping out the back door, hours after the stadium had been packed to the rafters with fans celebrating Celtic's European Cup final victory.

EMPICS

Police helping Kathryn and me through smiling crowds on our wedding day, 14 June 1967.

IAN HOSSACK, DAILY MAIL

Celebrating scoring the third goal in Celtic's victory over Rangers in a League Cup tie at Celtic Park – watched by over 75,000, August 1967.

EMPICS

Hurdling Racing Club goalkeeper Cejas during the first leg of the World Club Championship, Hampden Park, October 1967...

... and being escorted from the pitch by an armed soldier after being sent off in the play-off in neutral Montevideo, Uruguay, November 1967.

the crowds. After a while we began to ask each other, 'Where's the Cup?' and 'Where's Billy?' It was only once he arrived back with the trophy that we found out he had been forced to collect the European cup without us. So many people had thronged the pitch that, automatically, we had sought refuge in the dressing room and that had precluded any chance of us all going up to receive our medals and lift the trophy. Billy had struggled through the supporters to receive it and eventually brought it back to the dressing room.

The strange design of the poky little dressing room meant that the ensuing celebrations were slightly odd because the team was split in two to a certain extent. In one photograph taken soon after the game the only people pictured are Bertie, Jimmy, Stevie and me because the two halves of the team were compartmentalised. The enormity of conquering Europe certainly had not yet sunk in during those moments – winning games, even the biggest games, such as that one, often produces a more subdued feeling than you might expect. The feeling of elation in victory is nothing like the feeling of despair when you get beaten.

Exiting the dressing room, we again had to wade through a mass of people to reach our coach, which took us into Lisbon and up to a lovely restaurant where the two teams were to eat together. Once there, Billy produced a shoebox and distributed the winners' medals, one to each of us. We had to wait for about an hour and a half for the Italians because they had spent so long in their dressing room being harangued by Helenio Herrera. We still managed to enjoy ourselves before heading off to another restaurant where the wives and girlfriends were having a meal.

The girls were heading off to the airport after that, so we joined them in what we thought would be a simple trip out and back. That was a bad mistake – thousands of people were at the airport and the girls got squashed before we could find them a lounge in which to wait. Their flight was delayed and we waited there with them for several hours before their departure was announced. By the time we got back to the Hotel Palacio it was two o'clock in the morning and the bar had closed, so we didn't enjoy much of a celebration at all. I went to bed but was soon awoken by Jock rapping on the door to say that the girls' flight had been delayed again and they had come back to the Palacio. We stayed up until 6.30 a.m. keeping them company before they finally left. It was a strange conclusion to a momentous 24 hours.

We arrived back at Abbotsinch Airport in the middle of the afternoon of 26 May. People cheered us on every corner of our route from there to Celtic Park and the ground was mobbed. We proceeded to climb on to the back of a lorry, which, escorted by a marching band, took us round the running track at the edge of the pitch. From the back of that lorry we displayed the European Cup to the supporters, who filled every corner of the stadium. After that, we hooked up with the wives and girlfriends in the boardroom but we couldn't get out of the front door because there were so many people outside. Brothers, aunties and uncles were dispatched to drive the players' cars round from the car park to Janefield Street and we walked across the pitch, through a rear exit and drove home from there. Kathryn and I motored home to Saltcoats, went to my parents' house, had a cup of tea and life resumed as normal.

C H A P T E R 6

INTO THE BLUE

Anyone expecting five-star luxury when selected for Scotland in the 1960s and 1970s would quickly have been disabused of that notion. The Queen's Hotel in Largs was the base for Scotland during my time with the national side and there were only two baths in the entire establishment. After training at nearby Inverclyde, where it was always muddy, we would return to the hotel to clean up – maybe 18 guys had to wait to take their turn in one of these two baths. You would troop in from training and stand around wet, with mud dripping off you, for maybe 20 minutes, and chap the door of the bathroom to ask the player in front of you if he was finished. After several players had taken their turn, the baths would be filthy and if you were last in line it was dreadful. There would be so much residue that it was like slipping into sludge. That only helped to reinforce the feeling that, when going away with Scotland, you weren't exactly taking a step upwards.

If the washing facilities were limited at the Queen's, the same could not be said of the food, which was magnificent. The staff were exceptionally friendly and looked after you tremendously well, and the hotel offered a lovely homely atmosphere. Unfortunately, you need rather more than that if you are preparing for an international. We'd maybe be playing England or West Germany the next day and know that they would be luxuriating down the coast at the top-notch Marine Hotel in Troon. We'd be taking off our training gear, giving it a quick rinse, then putting it over the pipes to dry so that we could use it again the next day – hardly top notch.

My first involvement with the Scottish international squad was of a slightly haphazard nature. Scotland were due to travel to Italy for a vital World Cup qualifying match in December 1965 – one that would decide whether Scotland or Italy reached the 1966 World Cup finals – and I was brought into the squad at, literally, the eleventh hour. A few days before the match was due to take place, Kathryn and I went to the pictures in Saltcoats and at about ten o'clock headed back to her mum and dad's house for a cup of tea. We had been there for a while when a knock came at the door and standing there was Walter McCrae, the Scotland trainer, who was, effectively, assistant to the Scotland manager. Walter had zipped along the road from Largs, where the Scotland squad were billeted, and was at the door to ask me if I would like to report to the team hotel the following morning because they had suffered a number of withdrawals and now had only 15 players available to travel. I was given the Scotland blazer that had been earmarked for Billy Stevenson, the Liverpool player, and it fitted me perfectly; I don't quite know how because he was a much bigger guy than me.

Travelling to Italy with the squad proved to be a sickening experience. The bus that took us from the airport in Naples to our hotel in Sorrento went along so many winding coastal roads that they had to stop it three times for me to throw up. I was subsequently laid up for a day and I didn't even join in with the training when I did make it out of my sickbed. On the day of the match, for which Jock Stein was

Scotland's caretaker-manager, the only two players who didn't get stripped for action were Willie Johnston and me. We watched from the stand as Scotland were beaten 3–0. It was still pretty exciting just to be there.

Almost a year later, in November 1966, I made my debut for Scotland, in a Home International against Northern Ireland at Hampden Park in front of a crowd of 46,000. There were five fellow Celtic players in the team that night – John Clark, Tommy Gemmell, Bobby Murdoch, Stevie Chalmers and Joe McBride. John Greig, Ron McKinnon and Willie Henderson made it nine Old Firm players in the team, with the balance consisting of Billy Bremner, the Leeds United midfield player, and Bobby Ferguson, the Kilmarnock goalkeeper. Having so many fellow Celts in the side made the transition from club to country a particularly easy one and I felt right at home immediately. I was less overawed than I might have been on winning my first cap.

It was a cool, crisp evening when we played the Irish and I remember how they looked the part in the lustrous green of their shirts as we lined up before kick-off. We won 2–1 and I scored the winner. The ball came over from a corner kick on the right, at the Celtic end of Hampden, Joe McBride headed it down and from four yards out I flicked the ball over the top of my head, past Pat Jennings, the Irish goalkeeper, and into the roof of the net. I was delighted with it and jumped into Billy Bremner's arms. Scoring that goal was especially pleasing as Pat had made a terrific save from me earlier in the match. I had been clean through on goal and he had raced out to snatch the ball from my feet. It was a good performance all-round from Scotland and there was a greater margin of quality between the two sides than reflected in the narrow scoreline.

Small details always pleased me. As a player at Ardeer Recreation, I had often admired a board inside the club that was inscribed with the names of all those from Ardeer Rec who had represented their country, whether it was for cricket, hockey, darts or something else. I had always wanted to have my name up on that board. Within weeks of playing against Northern Ireland, my name had been etched on to it and, although I had long left Ardeer and Junior football, knowing I was on that board mattered to me. I'm glad to be Scottish, without shouting about it from the rooftops, and I was proud to have represented my country.

My debut performance had gone well and, all of five months later, I was chosen for the next Scotland fixture, a game that would prove to be one of the most momentous in which Scotland have ever participated – the third Home International of that season, against England at Wembley Stadium on 15 April 1967. The English had not lost for 19 matches, a run that included the World Cup of 1966, which they had won nine months before we ventured south to face them. We were wasting our time even bothering to travel, according to the more arrogant and ignorant sections of the English media, who believed that England were close to invincible. It has to be said, though, that England had some exceptional players. Jimmy Greaves, Bobby Charlton and the classy Bobby Moore were on the pitch against us. People used to say Moore was slow, but I never saw anybody sprint away from him.

At training, in Hendon, north London, I remember being hugely impressed by Denis Law, who was to play in the Scotland side alongside me for the first time. He would have a bit of fun in training but, other than that, everything he did was carried out with precision and professionalism. It was great to have Denis around – he had so much charisma that it rubbed off on everyone and lifted the spirits. He was also a character of some depth. John Lunn, a young and exceptionally promising left-back with Dunfermline Athletic, had been diagnosed with leukaemia in January 1967 and a benefit match had been held for him, with Dunfermline playing against a side featuring five Celtic and five Rangers players – plus Denis Law. I thought it had been a fine gesture by Denis, then at the height of his fame with Manchester United, to travel up to Fife for that occasion.

On one of the evenings before the England match, we went to the cinema in London and the English team came in and sat watching the same film. On the way out, we mingled with them. Billy Bremner, Denis and some of our other England-based players knew a few of the English guys so the banter was good. That close relationship with the English players helped us – Denis, Billy and Jimmy Baxter were playing against them every week and told us that we had nothing to fear. Their belief in the ability of our team was infectious and their practical knowledge of our opponents was invaluable. At training, Billy told us that, at corner kicks, Jack Charlton would stand on the goal-line, in front of the goalkeeper, and that when the ball came across he would use his height and weight to prevent the goalie getting to the ball. Billy, a team-mate of Jackie's at club level, said that Leeds had scored a number of goals in that way. As a means of stopping this tactic working, Billy suggested that we should post a player either side of Jackie Charlton but Ronnie Simpson, our goalkeeper, quashed that idea immediately. He said that, now that he knew about Charlton's ploy, he would not stand close to Charlton but would instead time his run and jump so that he could get into the air just as the corner was coming over and use his momentum to catch the ball or punch it clear. If there were players standing around Charlton, Ronnie said, it would hamper his efforts and he would be scrambling to get past people to clear the ball. There was a lot of debate about that but eventually we decided that, as Ronnie was the goalkeeper, we should go with his advice.

One or two other little tips such as that one helped us to get the measure of our English opponents. Tactics were worked out by the players and not by Bobby Brown, who was taking charge of the Scotland team as manager for the first time. It's difficult, sometimes, for Scotland managers. They get the players for two or three days only, so their influence can be a bit limited.

It was good to go to Wembley on the day before the game to get a look at the pitch. We found that preparations for the game were well under way at the ground and the scoreboard had been readied with the starting scoreline of 'England 0 Scotland 0'. Eddie McCreadie, our left-back, who was with Chelsea, looked at it and said, 'If that scoreline has stayed that way by quarter to five tomorrow afternoon, I'll be walking into Stamford Bridge wearing my Scotland strip on Monday.' We were playing the world champions on their own turf so if someone had offered us a draw, we'd probably have taken it.

A stroll around Golders Green kept us fresh on the Saturday morning and yet again the English press helped us with their pre-match previews – we were given no chance at all. It was clear that they regarded us as inferior talents who would be crushed by the mighty world champions. That motivated us enormously. We came back to the hotel, had lunch and were soon driving up Wembley Way, through thousands of Scottish supporters, who were mobbing our bus. As the vehicle came close to the stadium, the driver had to take a sharp left to go through a big wooden gate into the part of the ground nearest the dressing rooms. Just as the bus was turning, my eyes were drawn in one direction only and among all those supporters, I was looking directly at the figure of my father, sitting on the steps outside Wembly in his three-piece suit. It was quite uncanny how I had been guided subconsciously to look in exactly his direction and see him amidst all those thousands of people. That was a big thrill for me. My uncle had come to pick up the tickets from me earlier. My dad was too shy to do so.

We got into the dressing room and began our preparations, which were quite detailed. The Scottish Football Association provided a wee booklet of regulations that guided you on how you ought to conduct yourself when with the Scotland squad. One of their special rules was that every player had to turn down the red tops of their navy socks a specified number of inches, and have their shirt tucked inside their shorts at all times. There wasn't a great deal of tactical discussion with Scotland but you had to dress correctly. Those were our closest and most coherent instructions. The booklet also provided us with other pieces of key information, such as to be in the tunnel precisely six minutes before kick-off and how to address the various dignitaries who would be presented to the teams prior to the match – invaluable when taking on the world champions.

As the minutes before the game ticked down in the dressing room, Ronnie Simpson, who was making his Scotland debut at the age of 36, said, 'I could have done with a wee sip . . .' At Celtic Park, a cup of whisky was kept in the dressing room before matches for anyone who needed something to settle their nerves. Stevie Chalmers, who was the Scotland substitute at Wembley, piped up, 'I bought a half-bottle in Golders Green this morning.' Next thing, Ronnie, Jimmy Baxter and one or two others had disappeared into the toilet to have a quick gargle of Stevie's whisky. That would almost certainly not have had the approval of those who compiled the SFA's booklet of pre-match advice. Stevie was a non-drinker but, in his typically considerate way, he had known that one or two of the boys might like a wee nip before the match, so had come prepared. It got the boys up for it. Soon,

Jimmy Baxter was strolling around, saying, 'Ach, just give the ball to me and we'll take it from there . . .' The Scottish dressing room was really buoyant and bubbly before that game. No one was sitting there worrying what the English might be able to do to us. Instead, the boys were saying, 'We're going to do them . . .'

Bobby Brown did his bit by coming round and talking to us. With it being his first game, it must have been hard for him. He'd been St Johnstone manager prior to his appointment with Scotland, and to come in among guys such as Billy Bremner and Denis Law, who were at their peaks with leading clubs, can't have been easy. Bobby helped calm the boys down before the game but I don't remember him sitting down and discussing tactical matters with us. It was really up to the boys simply to go out and play as well as they could.

As I remember it, Denis blanked Nobby Stiles, his Manchester United team-mate, in the tunnel before we went out and a lot of verbals were exchanged between the Scottish and English lads. The tunnel from the Wembley dressing rooms to the field sloped upwards gently so that gradually you got to see more and more of the terracings as you walked along. When we came within sight of the crowd, we were greeted by a sea of lions rampant and an enormous roar from the Scottish supporters. There were so many of them that it seemed almost like a home match. The pitch was as good as you could have wished for and it was a nice, warm day – perfect conditions for a match that would measure which was the better football-playing team. Although it was often said that the England–Scotland match was more important to the Scots, that wasn't true of players on the English side that day. Alan Ball and Bobby Moore, to name just two, were desperate not to concede their unbeaten record to 'the Jocks' of all people. We were equally desperate to win because we had been written off so comprehensively by the so-called experts.

There was a gritty determination about us as we swung into action, passing the ball well from kick-off. The pitch suited us perfectly and after 10 to 15 minutes of us pinging the ball about, I think everybody realised that London could belong to us that fine spring day.

Early on in the match, Jack Charlton administered a hefty tackle. He came flying at me with a lunge and caught me on the knee. He came out of it worse. The story is that he had a flaw in his stud and that when he made contact with my knee, this stud broke, went up through the sole of his boot and broke his toe. I thought that was fair enough. If his stud hadn't broken, he might have broken my kneecap – six weeks before Celtic were due to appear in the European Cup final. There was a lot of blood spilled as a result of that challenge and I discovered that I had a deep gash in my knee. Both of us were down on the turf for quite a while and I reckoned that he was pretending to be hurt in the hope that the referee would look on him more leniently in the light of his over-the-top challenge. At half-time, my knee was cleaned up and was fine. The wound wasn't stiffening, but it was still a nasty one, nonetheless.

A slice of sharpness from Denis Law had put us 1–0 ahead early in the match. Gordon Banks, the England goalkeeper, parried a shot from Willie Wallace and Denis whipped the rebound into the net. From there we proceeded to prove ourselves the better side, but by midway through the second half we had still to accumulate hard evidence, in the shape of additional goals, to substantiate our dominance. With around 15 minutes remaining, Tam Gemmell headed the ball towards the English penalty area and after it had bounced on the edge of the box, I caught it crisply on the turn. I knew as soon as I hit it that the ball was sweeping away from Banks. There was such a feeling of delight to see it hurtle low into the corner of the English net. I was quickly engulfed by all nine of my outfield team-mates, which says a great deal about the togetherness of that team on the day. It was a major moment in my life. I also became the first Celtic player to score for Scotland at Wembley. As soon as the ball went in I thought about how delighted my dad would be. I didn't know that if I had kept on running after scoring the goal, I would have ended up beside him. I wish I had done exactly that.

At one stage, when we were ahead and looking comfortable, Jimmy Baxter indulged in a bit of keepy-uppy, as if to emphasise how easy the game was for us. Billy Bremner, Tam and Jimmy knocked the ball around numerous times between them with exaggerated ease, again to show the English how much we were on top. Denis Law was screaming at them to get up the park. If there had been a bit less of that, it is quite possible that we could have scored a few more goals that day. As it was, our failure to bury the game left England with an eyelet of hope and with five minutes to go, Jack Charlton squeezed the ball over our line to reduce our lead to one. Jim McCalliog quickly restored our two-goal advantage but the flurry of last-gasp goals didn't stop there, Geoff Hurst notching a second for England during the dying seconds.

On the day, we were quite happy to have won 3–2 so it didn't matter enormously that we hadn't emphasised the margin of difference between the two sides. The scoreline, as it stands, makes it look as though the English were in the game but they weren't really – not at all. When I scored to make it 2–0, I thought that was the way the game would finish – either that, or we would score another one.

I was pleased with my performance. I had taken players on, cut up the wing several times and got on the scoresheet. I had done my bit and I was proud of the result. After the game, they played 'God Save the Queen' for the second time and as the players of both sides stood alongside one another on the pitch with the stately national anthem wafting over us, a Scotland supporter came tearing on to the field and stuffed a bundle of notes and coins into Denis Law's hand, exclaiming, 'Get the boys a drink! Denis, get the boys a drink!' It was quite hilarious.

After the final whistle, I approached Jimmy Greaves, the England striker, of whom I was a great admirer, and asked him if I could swap shirts with him. He said that would be fine but we would have to do so inside, not out on the pitch. So, after a few celebrations with our players, I headed for the English dressing room and was greeted by absolute silence. Their players were sitting stunned, heads bowed down with disappointment. People can say what they like about the game mattering more to one side than another but when Scotland and England collide, the ground rumbles. It is not a wee kiddie-on affair and that was clear in the desolation shown in defeat by those England players. Jimmy was as good as his word and courteous to a tee as he handed over his jersey.

Billy Bremner later told me that a great photo had been framed and displayed at Elland Road, Leeds United's home ground. It was of Jack Charlton with his studs on my knee, ready to provide me with a souvenir of my Wembley visit. Following the game, that knee was wrapped in a swathe of bandages but blood still seeped through and on to my nice grey suit, ruining it. It didn't seem to matter much as we celebrated at the joint reception with the English team at the Café Royal in the West End of London. As for us being unofficial world champions after that game, the thought never occurred to me until someone else mentioned it. If that's what they want to call that team, it suits me. On the following day, we flew back to Glasgow and I took the train home to Saltcoats from St Enoch station and wandered up the road to my mum and dad's house with my bag over my shoulder and my boots under my arm. Unofficial world champions or not, normal life had to continue.

I never did discover whether Eddie McCreadie wore his Scotland strip into training at Chelsea on the Monday morning. I do know that the next time Chelsea played Leeds, Jackie Charlton was blocked off by McCreadie at a corner, thanks to Eddie having found himself privy to Leeds' tactics via Billy Bremner when on Scotland duty. There was also a repercussion for me from that game at Wembley. As mentioned previously, I think it got me back into the Celtic team after I had been omitted from the European Cup semi-final first leg with Dukla Prague during the previous midweek. The way I played against England wouldn't have done me any harm in the approach to the European Cup final.

Despite Celtic's sizeable representation in the teams for both the game with England and my international debut against Northern Ireland, few Celtic players could be considered regulars for the Scotland team. Tommy Gemmell was one but Scotland line-ups fluctuated frequently. Billy McNeill and Ron McKinnon, of Rangers, alternated at centre-half, for instance, and Jimmy Johnstone and Willie Henderson, the Rangers winger, took turns at outside-right. Aside from Tam possibly, no Celtic player could look ahead and be confident that he would be playing in the next three or four international matches. I have no reason to think that there was a particular bias against Celtic players – it was more that Scotland at that time could draw upon a variety of tremendously talented players in both the English and Scottish Leagues. I do still think that some Celtic players should have been given a lot more caps. Bertie Auld, for instance, was a great player but he got just three caps. None of them came after he had rejoined Celtic and had started to perform magnificently in Jock Stein's teams.

However, it has to be noted that, often, Jock Stein would withdraw Celtic players from Scotland squads if they had the slightest injury or if he felt they needed a rest. There were two or three games when Jock told me to take a week off rather than joining up with Scotland. 'You're not quite as sharp as you could be just now, so you're not going away with Scotland,' is how he would put it. That happened to everyone, not just to me. If Celtic had a big game coming up, you wouldn't be risked playing for Scotland. Also, there were times when Celtic would be playing so well that we would think four or five players would be chosen for Scotland but, instead, discover that only a couple had been picked. Possibly, on such occasions, Jock would think to himself that the next time Scotland wanted a bunch of his players, he would just keep them back. That's only speculation on my part, though. I don't know that for sure.

My third cap was against the Soviet Union in the game that preceded the European Cup final by a couple of weeks, and following that I was in the squad for the next match, away to Northern Ireland. On the Wednesday before the game, I suffered a perforated eardrum while playing for Celtic against Racing Club of Buenos Aires. Jock Stein told me there and then that I wasn't travelling to Belfast. Walter McCrae and Bobby Brown appeared in the Celtic dressing room after the match and were peremptorily informed by Jock that I was being withdrawn from their Scotland squad. They could have no argument with that. The final decision about whether a player would join the Scotland squad was entirely down to his club manager.

Most of us Celtic players were regular attendees at Hampden Park for Scotland international matches if we were not included in the squad. We had a keen interest in the national team and this was also one of the few ways, in the 1960s, of seeing international football. Jock always arranged for us to get tickets and we would meet at Hampden's front door before taking our seats in the stand. The Scottish team, for all the talent at our disposal, or perhaps because of it, was remarkably inconsistent in the 1960s. With so many top players available, we never had a settled side, and I think that important element would have helped in gaining better results. Only Billy Bremner, John Greig and Denis Law could count on featuring in almost every match during the mid to late 1960s. Scotland would play just a handful of matches every year so a player could be doing well in a game or two in the national team only for club form, several months later, to determine that someone else should replace him in the side. The team that had beaten England had shown six changes from the one that had faced the Northern Irish, on my debut, and, despite its success, that Wembley team never played together again.

Scotland had missed out on the 1966 World Cup – a defeat by Poland at Hampden in autumn 1965 had done much to torpedo our hopes prior to the match with Italy in Naples. I was at the Poland match, but with Scotland leading 1–0 through a Billy McNeill goal, as the end of the match drew near, I left my seat in the stand to get to my car and nip off early to Saltcoats. By the time I switched on my car radio, Poland were 2–1 ahead, having scored twice in the final six minutes.

The match against England at Wembley had been one of the Home Internationals – the four-nation tournament between Scotland, Wales, England and Northern Ireland that had been contested annually since the earliest days of international football but encounters in the Home Internationals in the two seasons that spanned 1966 and 1968 had extra spice because they doubled up as qualifiers for the final stages of the 1968 European Championship, a new international tournament in which Scotland were competing for the first time. Beating England had put us a point ahead of them in the qualification table at the halfway stage but a Scotland team showing several changes from the Wembley side proceeded to lose 1–0 to the Northern Irish in Belfast.

For us, everything about playing against England at Wembley had you tingling with anticipation, from the moment you joined up with the squad. Other matches maybe didn't quite raise similar levels of determination and derring-do. That was Scotland at the time, veering from glory to disaster. England's simultaneous 3–0 victory over Wales put them back at the top of the table.

We managed to beat Wales 3–2 in our next match, at Hampden, in which I supplied Alan Gilzean with a couple of crosses that he headed home – one at the near post and one at the back post. That set up a decider with England at Hampden Park in February 1968. A draw or a win would ensure that England qualified for the last eight of the European Championship. A victory for Scotland would mean that we achieved the same feat.

Both Willie Johnston, the Rangers winger, and I had been playing well and I thought that I would be utilised through the middle with Willie out wide. Instead, when the team was chosen, it was the other way round – Willie through the middle with me on the wing. That put a slight dampener on things for me, even though I was delighted to be picked. Prior to the match, at about half past two, Willie and I were warming up on the pitch and having a wee blether. Both of us were wearing rubber studs and we agreed that, although the park was rather firm, the surface was fine. As both of us were pretty quick, we anticipated being able to glide across the turf. We came out for the preliminaries at ten to three to find that the sun was on the point of retreating behind a great bank of cloud, not to be seen again that day. Soon the surface was a treacherous one and both of us were slipping and sliding around all over the place during the first half. Martin Peters scored for England after 20 minutes and although John Hughes equalised shortly before half-time, it remained 1–1 at the end. We were actually glad to come away with the draw. England had played really well on the afternoon to earn themselves a place in the final stages of the European Championship. It was always better for us, I felt, to play England at Wembley because of the bigger and better build-up.

One of my best moments in a Scotland shirt came in my next appearance – a friendly match in Denmark. I took possession of the ball close to the edge of the area and Eddie McCreadie went powering past me on the left, screaming at me to give him the ball. I shaped to pass it to him but instead hit it into the roof of the net. It proved to be the only goal of the game and few feelings are better than to have scored the winning goal for your country.

I appeared for the Scottish League team on a trio of occasions in the late 1960s. One game, at Middlesbrough, was as good a match as I ever played in, even though we lost 2–0 to England. The English team was virtually the same as the one that had won the World Cup, except that Keith Newton was at right-back and Jimmy Greaves was in the attack. Keith scored a fabulous goal that night, from 30 yards. I was right behind him when he hit it and he put a fantastic amount of swerve on the ball, something that you rarely saw in the 1960s.

My debut for the Scottish League had actually been at Celtic Park, in September 1966, against the League of Ireland. I was nearly barred from playing, mind you, in the most comical fashion, and was lucky even to get into the ground. Bill Peacock was the doorman at Celtic Park and the most zealous observer of regulations, especially with regard to people not being allowed through the front door without the correct ticket. When playing for Celtic, we had *carte blanche* to wander in and out but, on attempting to do the same on the night of the

Scottish League match, Bill told the Celtic contingent that we couldn't enter without tickets and he would not be swayed from that even though he obviously knew us. A scramble ensued to obtain the necessary accreditation. It was a bit of a hoot but we duly got in and proceeded to give the Irish team a good beating.

After the disappointment of losing out on the European Championship, another World Cup was soon on the horizon – the 1970 finals in Mexico. Austria were our opponents at Hampden Park in November 1968 for our opening qualifier for that tournament. I remember it as being a dour, hard game in which we really had to slug it out against a side that was our equal. It wasn't a kicking match or anything – just a bit of a grind to eke out the necessary victory. We won 2–1. Tam Gemmell and I were afterwards standing in the foyer inside the stadium when the press approached us and asked us what we thought of our bookings. That was news to me. I could not even remember the referee having spoken to me but he had still managed to jot down a booking in my name.

A 5–0 victory over Cyprus, the group's whipping boys, in which I came on as a substitute for Colin Stein, preceded our vital encounter with West Germany at Hampden in April 1969. During the match in Nicosia, a bunch of squaddies, stationed over in Cyprus, kept shouting to the management throughout the match that they had to get me into the game but I don't know whether that was the reason for me being thrown into the action on a horrible, big, black pitch.

At Hampden against the Germans, a crowd of 115,000 generated a more frenetic atmosphere. An exceptional, long-range shot from Bobby Murdoch, two minutes from time, enabled us to snatch a 1–1 draw with a very good German side. Franz Beckenbauer had been calmness personified as he smoothed a path through the game for his team. The Kaiser played very well on the night and returned home with the result for which they had come. Beckenbauer, as with Bobby Moore of England, really stood out in that team. Both of them organised their defences impeccably and both were able to step out from the back and set up moves as and when required.

International football was, for me, interestingly idiosyncratic. It seems strange, for example, that I don't recall an awful lot of detail about those two major World Cup qualifiers, against Austria and West Germany, even though they were massive matches, contested in front of teeming, heaving crowds at Hampden Park, and fixtures that could have led to us Scots parading our talents for a global television audience at the 1970 World Cup finals in Mexico. International football seemed somehow less all encompassing than the game at club level. I always felt much more wrapped up in playing for Celtic, which was possibly just as well because after that match against Beckenbauer and his cohorts, I did not pull on a Scotland jersey again for more than a year, when I came on as a substitute to replace Tommy McLean in a drab 0–0 draw with Wales. That Home International, played on a really miserable Wednesday night at Hampden in April 1970, looked like turning out 0–0 almost from kick-off. I failed to brighten a dull encounter when I took the field.

My greatest loyalty was always to my club and if Scotland picked me to play, that was fine. If they didn't pick me, I wouldn't get depressed or upset. I was actually happier in my own environment, with all the Celtic guys around me. With Scotland, I was a bit quieter than I would normally be. Everyone involved with Scotland was very friendly and I got on very well with the Rangers players, particularly Willie Johnston, who wasn't especially popular with the Celtic supporters but whose easy-going demeanour and ready wit made me warm to him greatly. However, I still felt generally less relaxed, going away with Scotland. I guess it was because I was trying to prove that I deserved to be there. Also, as I wasn't that familiar with the people with whom I was preparing for the match, I had to be on my best behaviour. I didn't want to do anything to let myself down, so no acting the clown as Jimmy Johnstone and I often did, to release tension, with Celtic. It must have been even more difficult for players from smaller clubs to integrate into the Scotland squad.

It remains a mystery to me how it was that, at the age of 26 and at the peak of my career, I made my final appearance for Scotland in that match with Wales in 1970. I was never involved again, although I did get close in 1973, when Scotland were about to face Czechoslovakia in a qualifying match for the following year's World Cup. I was receiving hints that I might be included for that vital game but a fortnight beforehand I injured my ankle while playing at Motherwell in a League Cup match, an injury that kept me out of action for more than a month. Scotland won 2–1 against the Czechs to qualify for the 1974 World Cup finals and my chance of selection had gone. It would have been very enjoyable to be involved in a World Cup but it would not be true to describe missing out as having been a crushing blow for me. When you are a young player, I think you are extremely keen to represent your country but once you get older, you're not sitting waiting desperately for the call from Scotland. You're more ambivalent about the whole thing. At that stage in your career, I think you've more or less come to the conclusion that playing for the national side is a nice bonus but not something that's essential. Nevertheless, I would still like to have won more than ten caps. I scored three goals in six wins, three draws and one defeat. It's not a bad record. I'd also have liked to play more through the middle for Scotland rather than out wide. It just didn't happen.

There were lots of good moments and laughs with Scotland. On one trip with the national side, Walter McCrae, the trainer, who was attached to Kilmarnock, recalled the days when I had been training, as a boy, with his club. He remembered well how the manager Willie Waddell had pondered whether to sign me or not. 'You were unlucky, Bobby,' Walter said to me. 'You were nearly at Kilmarnock. We were keen to sign you but we just thought at the time that you were a bit too small.' John Hughes and Bobby Murdoch were also in the room and all three of us looked at each other, bemused, wondering what Walter was thinking about. I looked at him and said, 'I was unlucky? I've got a European Cup-winner's medal and several championship medals . . .' He started laughing and said, 'I see what you're saying.'

At the beginning of the millennium, a Scottish television poll was carried out to choose the country's greatest sporting moment of the 20th century. Top came the Lisbon Lions and the European Cup victory of 1967 with, in second position, Scotland's 3–2 victory over England in April of that same year. At midnight that night I was surprised to hear the telephone ring. On the other end was Billy McNeill.

'Great to be at number one, isn't it?' he said to me.

'Some of us have made it to number one and number two,' I replied.

'You wee so-and-so,' said Billy. 'I wish I'd never phoned you now . . .'

CHAPTER 7

TURBULENT TIMES

There was no possibility of dwelling on the past at Celtic, even in the wake of achieving the greatest triumph in the club's history. Jock Stein made sure of that. When we went back to training at the start of the 1967–68 season, it was great to know that we were doing so as European champions but the manager quickly provided us with a glimpse of the future when he introduced Kenny Dalglish and one or two other young players to the first-team squad at the beginning of that season – a reminder that, whatever we might have achieved in the past, there were always going to be players challenging for our places. I also remember Jock telling us on our return that things were going to become harder in Europe as teams would now know all about us and our abilities, and would be steeling themselves to knock us from our perch. We would just have to ready ourselves for the challenge by attempting to improve on the standards we had already set.

There had not been too long a holiday for us in that summer of 1967. Following the European Cup final, we had been invited to provide the opposition for Real Madrid in the testimonial match for Alfredo Di Stefano, the Argentinian who, during his years with Real, had proved himself one of the greatest footballers the world has ever seen. It had been billed as a friendly match, but on our arrival in Madrid, less than a fortnight after our feats in Lisbon, we realised we were in for something quite different. In the press before the match, Real were repeatedly reported as saying how they were the true champions of Europe, a fact they would establish beyond doubt by giving us a sound thrashing when we met them at the Bernabeu. The headline in one Spanish newspaper was: 'We will prove we are the real champions.' Another headline was: 'We will prove Celtic are false.' This was, allegedly, the Real players talking. They must have been hurting at us having taken over the mantle of European champions; they had won the European Cup the previous year.

There were 135,000 crammed into every cubic centimetre of the Bernabeu stadium that early June evening in tribute to Di Stefano, the man who had spearheaded Real's record five successive European Cup triumphs. He participated in the first 15 minutes of the match and was flicking the ball this way and that. Even though he had finished playing for Real three years earlier and was now 40, the boys in our team were relieved to see him leave the pitch. He walked off and up a red carpet that had been rolled out for him before receiving a mini-replica of the European Cup in the president's box. It was a highly emotional moment for everyone present.

Those of us left in the thick of the action found ourselves in a hate game. Bertie Auld and Amancio Amarro, one of the Real forwards, were dismissed by the referee for violent conduct. Prior to the match, Jock had told Bertie that Amancio was the man who made Real tick and that Bertie had to get tight on him and work him hard to stop him playing. Bertie said afterwards, 'I solved the problem. We had a fight twenty minutes into the game. The two of us were put off – problem solved.' There were battles all over the field that night. It was a tough encounter and just as tense as any European Cup tie. Real might have had great players but they could all handle themselves. Their right-back gave me a thoroughly solid punch on the back of the head at one point – I hope he broke his hand. It was still as good a game of football as you could hope to play in, with two teams really going at each other, desperate to get the win. It turned out to be us who confirmed to the Spanish that we were deservedly now among the élite of Europe. We turned them over and I was pleased to get the winning goal. Jimmy Johnstone, who played what he considered his best-ever game for Celtic that night, jinked past four Real players before angling the ball into my path for me to send a low shot across the goalkeeper and into the net.

We had lost 3–1 to Real Madrid in Glasgow in 1962 and at that time we had thought that clubs such as Real were untouchable. Now, less than five years later, we had beaten them in the Bernabeu. It was quite amazing. I would say that, after that game, on that night in Madrid, we truly celebrated winning the European Cup. With that group of players we could have gone anywhere and got a result. We had proved we were the best and we were supremely confident in our abilities.

Confidence is the most important thing in football. If you are feeling good and playing well, you'll play the ball first time when it comes to you, certain that it will go where you want it to go. If you're not feeling confident, you'll maybe want to take two touches on the ball but find that just as you've taken your first touch, someone comes in and tackles you before you can take your second – or you take a wee look to see what's on, only for someone to take advantage and steal the ball away from you. When your confidence is up, you do everything well and you're certain that the next thing you do will also go as planned. It's infectious – if you're scoring regularly, your team-mates will come to you before matches and tell you how they're hoping you'll get an early goal to settle your team, and that won't faze you or make you feel under pressure. It will actually make you feel even surer of yourself.

A tough test was in store for us as we began our defence of the European Cup early in the 1967–68 season. We had been drawn against the powerful Dynamo Kiev, champions of the Soviet Union. The first leg was in Glasgow and I scored after an hour of the match: the ball broke to me and I just thumped it into the net. The problem was that Kiev were, by then, already two ahead.

I was not unduly worried at finishing the game a goal down because I thought we were good enough to beat them over in the Ukraine, but the return leg proved to be one of the most frustrating matches of my entire career – and our pre-match preparation wasn't helped by some state-sponsored workmen digging up the street outside our hotel in Kiev all night.

We had played Dynamo off the park in the first leg in Glasgow, after we had gone two down, and at their Central Stadium we were again on top of our game, playing as well as we knew how. Early in the match, Billy McNeill timed a run to arrive at the back post and score, only for the goal to be given offside. Billy was never offside in his life. That was only one of a string of decisions that went against us from Antonio Sbardella, the Italian referee, although he did allow us to score the opening goal. A free-kick was played into the penalty area and Billy and some other players went for the ball. It eluded them and reached me at the back post, where I slid in to put the ball in the net. As we sought a second, Yogi went through with the ball, the goalkeeper dived at his feet, Yogi dragged the ball away from him and put the ball in the net. The referee disallowed the goal and gave a free-kick for dangerous play. Bobby Murdoch was sent off for next to nothing – throwing the ball to the ground after yet another dubious free-kick had been awarded to Kiev. With the score at 1–0 to us on the day, a 2–2 aggregate was going to send us out of the European Cup because of the new rule under which away goals counted double. So we had to flood forward in the closing stages to seek a decisive goal. With seconds remaining, every Celtic player other than John Clark went up into the Kiev box. The ball was cleared and Kiev swiftly spirited the ball up the park for Anatoly Byshovets to score on the break. It put them through and made us only the second defending European Cup holders to go out in the opening round of the tournament.

We should never have lost that tie. We were the better side over both legs. It was a disaster for us to have gone out at such an early stage and for weeks afterwards I found it hard to accept that we had been removed from the tournament in such a fashion. I felt totally dejected about it. All of the luxuries we had enjoyed in the previous season were now out of our reach – our regular pre-European-Cup-tie midweek sojourns at Seamill, continental travel and a gentler training regime to take account of the demands of playing all those extra matches in European competition.

However, elimination from the European Cup did not signal an end to international competition for us that 1967–68 season. The World Club Championship, in which the champions of Europe and South America faced each other home and away, was on the horizon and was seen as being on a par with the European Cup in terms of its importance. Racing Club of Argentina were our opponents, and the first leg was to be played at Hampden Park to accommodate an expected crowd of 90,000. The match was given a massive build-up and everyone expected an evening of exquisite football, but Racing Club turned it into a kicking match, hacking away at us at every turn. Billy McNeill scored with a good header and we missed one or two chances but Racing Club's cynicism turned a keenly anticipated contest into a non-event. It really agitated us all – there was a lot of shouting going on on the park among our team whereas we normally preferred to express ourselves by playing smooth, controlled football. Following the game, Sean Connery, a committed Celtic supporter, came into the dressing room and was telling us that he was going to go on televison to publicise how dirty the Argentinians had been. There was even talk before the return leg of us not even travelling to Argentina, which shows how big an impact Racing Club's negative approach had on everyone in Scotland.

We did go to Buenos Aires, though, and we went in good spirits, having won the League Cup just a few hours before embarking on our Saturday evening flight. Dundee had been our opponents in an exciting final late that October of 1967. The score had been standing at 3–2 in our favour when, ten minutes from time, I turned on the edge of the box and used my left foot to hit the ball home from the inside-right position. Dundee scored again five minutes later before Willie Wallace made it 5–3 to us with a couple of minutes remaining.

We had trained at Ardeer Recreation before our departure for Argentina, which added a nice, sentimental tinge to the occasion for me. Overall, though, there was a feeling of foreboding among our players, a sense of apprehension about what Racing Club might have in store for us once we got on to the park at Buenos Aires' Avellaneda Stadium. Things started to go wrong even before that. Our accommodation was to have been at the Hindu Club, which we had been promised would be an exotic, well-kempt country establishment, but proved instead to be a countrified doss-house. We had never experienced worse accommodation. The paper was peeling off the walls; to enter some bedrooms you had to go through a couple of other bedrooms; and grime coated every surface. Big Jock gave it the quick once-over and said, 'We're not staying here.' Nobody had unpacked so we got back on the coach and eventually found ourselves a nice hotel in the centre of Buenos Aires, where we could unwind after our 20-hour journey from Glasgow.

The Argentinian police went everywhere with us, but their very presence was intimidating because you wondered why it was necessary to be protected by so many armed police. Some of us went to church one day and the police even came in and sat round about us. We habitually went on a lot of walks whenever we were away, and in downtown Buenos Aires we were, of course, accompanied by police. It made for a noticeably large group of people to be traversing the streets of that bustling city and we were shouted at by passers-by. On one of those walks, I saved Jimmy Johnstone's life. There are a number of seriously wide avenues in the Argentinian capital and as we went to cross one of them, Jimmy took a look to his right, saw nothing coming and stepped on to the road. He had forgotten, momentarily, that the Argentinians drive on the right side of the road and not the left, as in Britain. As he took to the tarmac, a collection of cars came screeching towards him, from his left, and he was saved only when I saw what he was doing and swiftly yanked him back on to the pavement. Jimmy's wellbeing was in the balance at that moment, for sure, but what was to come on the field of play was almost as much of a danger to his health.

On the day of the match, when we arrived at the stadium, thousands of Argentinians surrounded us and began trying to rock the bus. Argentinian police on horseback, with whips, lashed out at the culprits to get them away. Other policemen used dogs, on long leashes, to try to keep at bay the Racing supporters, who were already out of control. Once the bus got near to the door of the players' entrance, the driver eased it forward and back several times so that when he did open the door, there was not the slightest chink through which anyone could reach us or throw anything at us. It had become a test of nerve even before a ball had been kicked. It should have been a scary experience but we were just young guys, so on the bus we had been laughing and joking, drawing each other's attention to the wildest instances of behaviour from both fans and police.

Matters became less funny once we were inside the stadium. The feeling of being constrained and restricted proved to be well founded when we emerged from our dressing room for the match. The tunnel to the pitch was an extremely long one – about 40 to 50 yards – and very narrow with an extremely low ceiling. We were kept waiting in the tunnel for so long that it began to feel really claustrophobic and Billy began yelling at officials to let us out on to the pitch. Racing Club were using a tunnel on the other side of the pitch and when we did get out, we felt like the Christians in the Colosseum. The crowd were baying for our blood. As we were warming up, Ronnie Simpson, our goalkeeper, got hit by an iron bar and, with blood pouring from a gash in his head, he had to concede his place in the side to John Fallon before the match could start. The whole occasion, at that point, even before kick-off, had become a farce.

Early in the game, Jimmy Johnstone wiggled past several of their players and clipped the ball into the net only to be adjudged offside – a ridiculous decision. Once again, the Argentinians were flying in at us with studs up, spitting and niggling at us continually but midway through the first half, the first break of the day went our way when Jimmy was tripped inside the box and a penalty was given. Augustin Cejas, the goalkeeper, came racing off his line and towards the ball as Tommy Gemmell began his run to take the kick. By the time Tommy made contact, the goalkeeper was almost on the edge of his 6-yard box. He got his hands to the ball but the power of Tommy's shot beat him. Shortly before half-time, the Argentinians equalised with a header that was almost comically offside. Photographs taken from several angles later showed that two Argentinians were on their own inside the box as the ball was crossed. The referee, though, would have had to have been extremely brave not to have given it. There would have been a riot if he had disallowed that one.

On returning to the dressing room at half-time, we discovered that the water had been cut off, there were no oranges, no juice, no tea. We had been sitting in the dressing room for some time, discussing the game among ourselves, when Neilly Mochan, the trainer, came rushing in and told us that Racing were already out on the park and had been awaiting us for some time. We had to pelt down the tunnel and this time the fans were in a real fury at our lateness. The reception we got from them was infernal. That still didn't get to us, although playing in front of such a het-up crowd did mean that when you won a corner kick you took it quickly because all sorts of stuff was being hurled at you. Shortly after the interval, Racing went 2–1 ahead and that was how the match concluded. Since the aggregate over the two legs was 2–2, we now faced the prospect of a play-off in neutral Montevideo, Uruguay, four days later.

There was a lot of talk among the directors and the manager about whether we ought to contest a third game after the way in which Racing Club had demeaned the competition with their brutal approach in the home and away legs. The consensus among the players was that we should play them again. We were still thinking about matters in a purely footballing sense and were of the belief that we would beat Racing and show that we were the finest team in the world at that time. That may seem naïve but a deep attachment to playing positive, entertaining football had guided us in everything we had done under Jock Stein and a couple of bad experiences against a cynical side were not enough to shake that belief. I, for one, was quite glad to play Racing again. I felt that if they let us play football, we would triumph.

There were 75,000 inside the Centenario Stadium, Montevideo, for the third match and we believed that most of the Uruguayans, being a rival nation to Argentina, would be behind us, so we took to the field with a Uruguayan flag, thinking that this would help galvanise the crowd in our favour – only for the Racing players to come out after us with a Uruguayan flag that dwarfed our one. The match proved to be just as nasty an encounter as the two that had preceded it. The Argentinians were again at their sly spitting and fouling. They would give you a fly kick or offer a dunt with the shoulder every time they went past you. In the face of such provocation, our boys were now leaving the foot in after the ball had gone away. During the first two games, we had not really become involved in the nasty stuff but that changed in the third game as our patience with the Argentinians finally snapped. Our main aim had still been to get the ball down and beat them by passing it around. When it became clear that we were once again going to be thwarted in our attempts to do that, we became determined that we would not be messed about in this match as much as in the previous two encounters.

After much of the first half had been characterised by sporadic scuffles, Rodolfo Osorio, the referee, a Paraguayan, called the two captains together and told Billy and his Racing Club counterpart that the next time there was an incident, number eight of the greens – that was me – and number six of the blues, Alfio Basile, would be dismissed. It had certainly become a difficult match to referee but this was an illogical reaction – to threaten with dismissal, almost as if hostages ready to be sacrificed, two named players even if the next incident of on-field violence had nothing to do with them. I couldn't believe it. The referee was making up his own rules as he went along.

Within minutes, Jimmy had been whacked by an Argentinian. Pushing and shoving and then a brawl ensued. The referee semi-sorted it out, then simply said to number six of Racing and me, 'Off.' I walked off and Jock said, 'What are you doing?' I told him I'd been ordered off and he said, 'It's not you.' He ordered me to go back on to the field, which I did, noticing that their number six wasn't going off, either. One of the Argentinian forwards had taken a knock and Racing Club were trying to get the referee to agree to send him off rather than the number six. It was chaotic. The referee then spotted me and told me, again, to leave the pitch. I pleaded with him but he was adamant, so I walked back off and Jock, really infuriated by now, grabbed me again, turned me around and told me to get back on the park. I did as I was told and walked back on to the field, where Basile was still seeking a reprieve. The referee, seeing that neither of us was leaving the field, signalled to the sidelines and a soldier advanced on to the pitch and drew his sword to persuade me to leave the field of play. He was only a couple of feet away from me. When he told me to get off, he didn't have to do too much persuading. If it was a question of facing either an angry Jock or a soldier with a sword, there was no contest. I just walked off and went straight up the tunnel.

That was just before half-time. I was sitting in a corner, distraught at having been dismissed for the first time in my life, when the players came in at the interval. It was only once they had gone back out that I started to get myself ready and as I was walking up the tunnel towards two big, green doors that opened on to the park, one of the doors reverberated with a tremendous thud and burst open to reveal Jimmy, furious at having become the second Celt to be dismissed that afternoon. Jimmy Johnstone was without doubt the star in that Celtic team, as he had shown time and again, especially on that night in Madrid when he lit up Di Stefano's testimonial. People say Jimmy was a great dribbler but there was a lot more to him than that. He could see a pass, make an opening and score a goal. He was terrific, a unique individual who stretched and extended the boundaries of what was possible for a winger – but that also made him a target for desperate defenders.

I went back into the dressing room with him and when we came out, we found that Celtic were a goal down and then saw John Hughes being sent off by the referee after an incident with Cejas, the Racing Club goalkeeper. Bertie Auld was told by the referee, close to the end, that he too was being sent off but Bertie refused to go and remained on the park, which raises the question of what would have happened if, in the final minute or so, he had scored a goal. It was a farce, a fiasco. Jose Luis Cardenas scored the only goal of the game, for Racing, with a 35-yard shot, but theirs was a supremely hollow victory. They had had two players dismissed. I don't remember Jock Stein saying very much to us in the aftermath of that match. I do remember that we sat in the airport for a very long time before our flight left, which was pretty depressing, especially as stories were filtering back from the UK, via the press, of sensationalised reports of the goings-on in South America.

A couple of weeks after our return to Glasgow, a meeting with the players was arranged by Robert Kelly, the Celtic chairman, in the table-tennis room at Celtic Park. It was scheduled for a saturday morning in late November. We guessed it was to do with the South American excursion but we were not concerned because we felt we hadn't done too much wrong. We were due to travel to Fife for a League match against Raith Rovers, so we had come into the ground early in the morning to be addressed by the chairman. Mr Kelly told us that we had let the club down in the encounter with Racing Club in South America – not only the guys who had been sent off, he said, but the whole team. He started mentioning fining us and I thought to myself that he was going to fine us a week's wages. We were on about £45 per week at the time. I felt, sitting there, that that would be a bit harsh but as he finally wound his way to a conclusion, he informed us that the fine would actually be £250 – each. At that, needless to say, there was complete consternation among the players.

The money, Mr Kelly told us, would not be coming out of our pockets. Instead, the club were simply going to withhold the £250 bonus that we were each due for having beaten Dundee in the League Cup final prior to leaving for Argentina. That money would now be going to charity. Everyone was stunned as Robert Kelly turned on his heel and walked out. It seemed to me a harsh, unfair and unnecessary action on his part. Nobody had had a chance to say anything in response. Playing Racing Club in those three matches had been enough of an ordeal without him exacerbating it by fining us the equivalent of five or six weeks' wages. His point of view, as a man of principle, was that the players had let the club down but perhaps he failed to understand just how intimidating it had been to be on the same pitch as those Argentinians. That episode caused a lot of resentment among the players and it took a number of weeks for that to lift. It was a sour note on which to end the most remarkable year in Celtic's history.

The New Year began with an episode that left me even more disheartened and feeling that I was being edged out of Celtic. I'd been playing pretty well and scoring regularly for the team, so I was a bit disillusioned when Jock Stein left me out of the line-up for a Scottish Cup tie with Dunfermline Athletic at Celtic Park on 27 January 1968. I'd hurt my foot and been given an injection on the previous

Wednesday, but I was fine on the Thursday and trained really well on the Friday. Then, when I went in on the Saturday and heard the team being announced, I discovered that I had been left out. I couldn't believe it – and the team was subsequently beaten 2–0 to be eliminated from the Cup in the third round.

Afterwards, at home, I said to my dad that I believed I was being messed about. Confrontation is not in my nature but I was desperate to challenge the manager face to face. I told my dad that I was going in to see Jock Stein the following week and that I could be leaving the club. I believed that the manager had decided I was no longer his sort of player. So I plucked up the courage to go to see him on the Monday morning. I approached the window at reception, where you could ask Irene McDonald, Jock's secretary, or Jim Kennedy, the club's liaison officer, if you could have a meeting with Jock. As I neared that window, my nerve failed me and, instead of asking to see the manager, I slipped past, telling myself that I would do it on the Tuesday. The same thing happened on the Tuesday and the Wednesday. I ducked out of asking to see him but all that week I was feeling extremely frustrated, even though I got on with my work as normal.

On the Friday, after training, I'd changed and was heading for my car when Jock shouted after me to come back. 'I need to speak to you, Lemon,' he said as I followed him, slightly apprehensively, into his office. My nickname, 'Lemon', came from a misprint of my name in a newspaper. Willie Wallace spotted it, started using it as a joke and it simply stuck with me.

'You were really disappointed, weren't you, last Saturday?' Jock began.

'I really, really couldn't believe it,' I replied.

He told me that he had left me out because he had thought that, having had a problem with my foot, it was a chance to give it a bit of a rest. That observation and the build-up of dissatisfaction that I had felt in the preceding days provoked me into challenging him, one of the few times I ever did.

'I told you my feet were fine,' I said, quite sharply.

Jock wasn't exactly sheepish but he didn't come back at me the way he sometimes did. He explained that he had thought the boys would defeat Dunfermline without me and admitted it had been a mistake not to play me.

'Anyway,' he concluded, 'you'll be in the team for the match tomorrow.'

We faced Partick Thistle at Celtic Park the following day and after half an hour I had scored our first two goals in a 4–1 victory. Everything was back on an even keel for me at the end of a week that I had thought might possibly be my final one at Celtic Football Club. After that, I went on a tremendous scoring run, ending the season with my best-ever goal tally. That little glitch seemed to spur me on to do even better than I had done before.

Rangers had led the League from the start that 1967–68 season and were still unbeaten as we reached the early spring of 1968 and the crucial closing fixtures. We too were in the midst of a superlative run of form – we had won every single one of our League matches after drawing 2–2 with Rangers at Celtic Park on 2 January 1968 – and we finally went top for the first time that season in mid-April, beating Dundee 5–2 to go one point ahead of our great rivals. Our 102 goals, combined with our excellent defensive record, also provided us with a much better goal average than Rangers, but the fly in the ointment was that Rangers had three games still to play while we only had two.

The first of those games for Rangers, away to Morton, was played on the Wednesday night on which we faced Clyde in front of 25,000 in the final of the Glasgow Cup at Hampden Park. By half-time I had scored a hat-trick and we were 7–0 ahead, but even better news awaited us in the dressing room. Jock, who almost always tried to keep the news of other matches away from us, told us that Morton were winning 2–0 at Cappielow. We scored just once more in the second half of our game, possibly because we were spending so much time asking those in the dugout for the latest score in the rapidly changing Morton–Rangers match. That game concluded 3–3, which meant that if we won both our final fixtures, we would take the title for the third consecutive time.

It was not going to be easy. Both matches were against top six sides – Morton, who had given Rangers such a hard time, and Dunfermline Athletic, who had reached the Scottish Cup final after knocking us out of that tournament. Willie Wallace scored early in the first of those matches, at home to Morton in front of 51,000 at Celtic Park, but right on half-time, Morton equalised and, despite having laid siege to their goal, we had been unable to score again by the time the match entered the final minute. I had heard from the dugout that Rangers were 2–1 up at Kilmarnock, so if we were unable to do better than draw with Morton, Rangers would be back in front with one game left for each of us. With seconds remaining, I made a final foray into the penalty area. A cross came into the box and was flicked across goal. With Morton defending desperately deeply, the penalty box was as crowded as a post office on pension-payment morning but I managed to get my foot to the ball and knocked it under the goalkeeper. I was concerned there might be shades of offside about it, so I looked neither right nor left and was back at the halfway line before the linesman could even think about raising his flag. If there was any doubt in his mind, I was determined that my actions after the goal would help persuade him not to consider it. The goal was given, the ball was centred to restart the match and, seconds later, the referee blew for the end of the match. We were still in front with a game to go.

We went down to Seamill on the following Friday because we were anticipating that our match on the Tuesday night at Dunfermline – postponed because the Fife club were in the Scottish Cup final – would be a League decider. On the Saturday we were at Hampden Park to see Dunfermline defeat Hearts and lift the Cup. Afterwards, Jimmy Johnstone, Bobby Murdoch, Willie O'Neill and I were travelling down the Barrhead Road, back to Seamill, when we heard on the radio, 'We'll go to Scotland now, where Rangers have just suffered their first defeat of the season . . .' They had lost at home to Aberdeen. We were champions again. Our car screeched to a halt and we all bounced out and started jumping around like men possessed.

On the Tuesday night, we went to Dunfermline, where the two teams came out together, which was unusual in itself. Dunfermline paraded the Cup and went on to score first, which pleased their fans in what was given as a record crowd for East End Park of almost 28,000. So many people were desperate to see the game that some were standing on the roof. They were the fortunate ones. Thousands of others were locked out of the ground. As we sought an equaliser, I cut in along the byline and cracked in a shot that rebounded off a post and swerved away. The crowd behind the goal had swayed to catch what was happening and in doing so had spilled on to the turf in considerable numbers. The referee, seeing that, took us off the pitch to allow order to be restored. That was the first of three occasions that evening when we had to leave the field. During the second half I scored twice to give us a 2–1 win, which meant we had won the League on points and not on goal average. It had been the tightest title race in all of the Jock Stein years at Celtic.

I had scored in every one of our final 12 matches, hitting 20 goals in the process, to conclude the season with 44 goals in all competitions – League championship, European Cup, League Cup and Glasgow Cup. I should actually have had another one in the Glasgow Cup but Jimmy Johnstone stole it off me. That season, Jock had played me through the middle, unlike other seasons, in which I tended to find myself being used on the left wing. That central role made it easier for me to score goals. It was reward in itself to have scored so often for Celtic but, unbeknown to me, my successes in the League had made me the third top scorer in European football and duly eligible to receive the Bronze Boot. At that time, though, the local Scottish media were not tuned-in to the wider picture in terms of continental football, so I saw nothing in the press about this and was not alerted to it by the club. I remained blissfully unaware of my achievement for months afterwards.

Early in the following season, we travelled to St Etienne, a town in east-central France, for a European Cup tie against the local club. We were having our meal on the Tuesday evening, the night before the game, when James Farrell, one of the Celtic directors, walked in carrying a box, and made his way to the table at which I was sitting.

'That's for you, Bobby,' he said, handing me the box. 'I got it last night, in Paris.' It had my name on it so I opened it up and it turned out to be a bronze boot.

'What's this?' I asked him.

'You were the third-highest goalscorer in Europe last season, so I went to collect that for you last night,' he said.

That was the first I knew about it. Later, I discovered that Eusebio of Benfica, who had won the Golden Boot, had been at the ceremony in Paris to receive his award. Anton Dunai of Ujpest Dozsa, winner of the Silver Boot, had also attended. Celtic had been represented by Mr

James Farrell. Perhaps Eusebio and Dunai were wondering how a rather refined, middle-aged lawyer had managed to score so many goals for Celtic in the Scottish League. Meanwhile, I had been relaxing in our St Etienne hotel, unaware that such a ceremony had even been taking place.

I don't know why the club did not let me go to collect the trophy. I understand that we were preparing for a European Cup tie but surely the club should have had as much trust in me as Benfica had in Eusebio and Ujpest Dozsa had in Anton Dunai. I'm sure Jock would have known that I was not the type of player to be unprofessional and abuse the privilege of being allowed to attend such an occasion. I should have been told in advance that I had won the Bronze Boot and given the option of going to collect it. Maybe I would have decided it was better to remain in St Etienne to prepare for the match, but I should have been given the choice. A club director should not have taken my rightful place without my knowledge. It's not often that a player enters the élite among Europe's goalscorers and a lot of the goals I had scored the season before had been of huge importance to the club. The one against Morton, after all, had booked our place in the 1968–69 European Cup and without it, we wouldn't have been in St Etienne at all. For someone to walk into a dining room and present you with a box, telling you they had collected the award on your behalf, was pitiful and the other players were of the same mind. That episode was all too typical of the way in which Celtic was run at that time.

CHAPTER 8

BRITAIN'S BEST

The pre-match shenanigans in St Etienne were far from my mind as we neared the end of the match the following evening, with disaster impending. My thoughts were concentrated on Salif Keita, who appeared to be on the verge of presenting Celtic with the unwanted status of being one-season wonders in the European Cup. We were not quite ready to be consigned to football history but Keita had our fate at his feet. It was September 1968 and we were in the Stade Geoffroy-Guichard, 2–0 down to the French champions and staring in the face a second successive first-round exit from the Continent's greatest tournament. That would have made our victory in Lisbon a one-off rather than establishing us among Europe's élite. Defeat loomed large as Keita, a big, powerful player, rolled lithely through on goal in the final minute of the match. Before he could pull the trigger, though, Billy McNeill sent him tumbling and St Etienne were able to do little with the resultant free-kick. Our hopes of retrieving the tie in the second leg remained high, thanks to that cool professional foul from Billy.

The encounter with St Etienne began to turn our way in that instant. Back in Glasgow, the French side again showed that they were an excellent passing team but we got a penalty seconds before half-time, and Tommy Gemmell thumped it into the net to open the scoring in the match. Their players protested long and hard about the validity of the spot-kick and when they took the field for the second half you could see that some of them didn't want to know, while our players were really determined to press home their newly established advantage. The noise from our crowd was deafening, a few of our opponents went missing, and we smoothed our way to a 4–0 win. A goal changes everything in football. If we had gone out to St Etienne, it might have indicated to Jock Stein that he had to refresh and rebuild the team, and the side that had won the trophy in 1967 could have been broken up at an unfortunately early stage.

That victory took us into a second-round tie against Red Star Belgrade of Yugoslavia, a game that turned our way in another key instant, although this time the moment of inspiration took place away from the field of play. The score was 1–1 at half-time in Glasgow when Jock Stein drew Jimmy Johnstone aside in the dressing room and promised him that if we won by four clear goals, Jimmy would not need to fly to Belgrade for the second leg. Jimmy had had a deep-rooted fear of flying ever since experiencing a turbulent flight from the USA to the UK in 1966. Turbo-driven by that promise, Jimmy was a man on fire during the second half, making two and scoring two. He set up one for me, cutting a ball back which I put in the net from about six yards to make it 3–1. When he scored our fifth goal, ten minutes from time, he was running about shouting like a madman, 'I'm not going! I'm not going! I'm not going!' Nobody knew what he was on about. It was only when we went back into the dressing room that we found out about the pact between Jock and Jimmy, which had spurred us on to our 5–1 victory.

During the fortnight in between that game and the return in

Yugoslavia, Jimmy employed, off the field, the type of dodging and weaving that made him such a successful player on it. Once we had finished training, Jimmy would use all his elusive skills to stay clear of Jock so that Jock could not get to work on him with his powers of persuasion to try to convince Jimmy that he should travel to Belgrade. It did seem, with our sizeable advantage from the first leg, that his presence was probably superfluous but, as it turned out, we could have done with him once we experienced the force that Red Star unleashed in an attempt to retrieve the tie. After the opening 20 minutes, we should have been 5–0 down. What a roasting we got! It was as big a trouncing as we ever suffered from any team but they were unable to capitalise on it and score. The boys at the back were heading the ball off our line and desperately blocking shots from close range. One shot flashed past John Fallon, hit the bar and rebounded back into his hands.

Fifteen minutes from time, with the score still amazingly 0–0, Willie Wallace scored from about 30 yards to put us in front, but Red Star equalised with the last kick of the ball. They won a corner and when the ball was played into our penalty area, everybody switched off and they nicked it into the net. We were all really disappointed to see it finish 1–1 even though we were through.

The game had got off to a rather comical start. During the warm-up before the match, Billy McNeill slipped and got to his feet covered in mud from head to toe. When he tried to go back to the dressing room to change into a clean strip he was told by the referee that there was no time, so Billy, who always liked to be neat and well presented, started the match with mud dripping off him. It was a disgraceful sight, an embarrassment – he really let us all down that night.

Defeating St Etienne and Red Star took us into the quarter-finals and another testing tie, against Milan. On the evening before the first leg, in the San Siro, we left our hillside hotel in Varese and went down to the stadium in Milan to have a look at the pitch. It was a fair old jaunt. The bus driver, an Italian, took us there, dropped us off and then swiftly drove away. We quickly discovered that we could not get into the ground and only after waiting for a very long time did we find someone able and willing to allow us inside the stadium. The sight that greeted us that February night was quite incredible. The pitch and the terraces were entirely white due to heavy snowfalls in the area. When we reconvened outside the stadium, in minus-zero temperatures, at the appointed time for the bus driver to return, he wasn't there and it was ages before he and his bus appeared. The boys were ready to kill that driver. I think this was a bit of gamesmanship on the Italians' part. If so, it didn't work. We played very well to get a 0–0 draw on an evening when Milan had people constantly brushing the steadily falling snow off the touchlines to keep them clear.

The return match proved one of the biggest disappointments of my career. I took a knock in between the two games and was struggling to be fit. If we had been playing Morton and not Milan, I would probably have ruled myself out the day before, admitting I simply wasn't ready. The match was so immense, though, that I was down at Seamill, bathing my leg in the sea, hours before the match in a desperate flurry to try to convince myself and everyone else I could play. I didn't make it. The highlights programme on television later that evening began with a shot of me bathing my ankle in the shallows. It focused in closer and closer as I battled away to prove my fitness – unsuccessfully. I was forced to watch from the stand as Pierino Prati scored a fortunate goal after 11 minutes, which proved to be the winner. Although our guys played well enough, they couldn't equalise and we were out of Europe for another year. There was really nothing between us and Milan and they went on to the 1969 final, defeating Ajax Amsterdam 4–1. That told us that we were still among the élite of European football and but for one unlucky bounce of the ball in the quarter-final, it could have been us and not Milan contesting the final.

As a player, you don't really analyse whether your team is improving or standing still or going backwards, you just play – but ten goals in two cup finals during the month of April 1969 suggested strongly that, two years after Lisbon, Celtic were still a formidable side. The League Cup final with Hibs had been due to take place in autumn 1968 but on the morning of the match we had been sitting down to breakfast at Seamill Hydro when we were told that the match had been postponed because of a fire in the stand at Hampden Park. The delayed game was played on 5 April 1969 and we were 3–0 up by half-time, with the game over, then 6–0 ahead with 15 minutes to go before Hibs pulled back two late goals. We were whirring like clockwork that day. Bobby and Bertie were pulling the strings in midfield and Jimmy was up to all his usual tricks. I chipped in with a hat-trick.

Three weeks later we were back at Hampden for an Old Firm Scottish Cup final, having already wrapped up our fourth consecutive League title. Jimmy Johnstone was suspended and John Hughes was injured, which helped to make Rangers strong favourites. That was without reckoning on the innate ingenuity of Jock Stein, who changed the team around a bit, telling Stevie Chalmers and me to run into the channels, with George Connelly, a young midfield player, instructed to remain a bit deeper. We were again at our best. Billy McNeill scored with a header from my corner in the first minute and an early goal such as that one settles everybody because you know Rangers have got to start chasing the game. It proved to be a really good, tight game right up until almost half-time. Then I scored our second and George Connelly added another before the interval. It had been 1–0 and a close match shortly before the break but when we walked in with the scoreline at 3–0 everyone was very excitable and Jock's main task was to calm everyone down rather than motivate us. We went on to seal it with 15 minutes to go when Stevie Chalmers slipped the ball into the net to make the final score 4–0.

Many people have a vision of Jock putting the tactics board up in front of the players before every match. That wasn't the case. He did use a board before some games but not always, and nor did he take us through a detailed tactical talk prior to every fixture. If we were going through a sticky spell, he would be at his most talkative, going over and over how we could improve, and if we were down at Seamill preparing for a European tie, he would go through the opposition in detail. For normal League games, though, if things were going well, on a Friday all he would do was come into the table-tennis room after training, where we would all have gathered, read out the team and tell us to play the same as we had done the previous week. He would then disappear.

If the game against Milan in 1969 was one of the biggest disappointments in my career, our fifth Scottish Cup final under Jock, against Aberdeen in April 1970, proved to be one of my most bitter experiences. The memory of that match still makes me bristle with anger. It was well understood among those inside the game that Bobby Davidson, the referee, did not exactly favour Celtic and almost half an hour of the match had been played when a cross into our penalty area struck Bobby Murdoch high on his chest. Davidson couldn't point to the penalty spot quickly enough and Joe Harper, the Aberdeen centre-forward, stroked the ball into the net. Minutes later, Bobby Clark, the Aberdeen goalkeeper, dropped the ball at my feet and I knocked it into the net but when Clark claimed that I had knocked it out of his hands, Davidson, who had been in the centre circle when this had happened, was warmly receptive to Bobby's version of events and the goal was ruled out. The goal had been quite legitimate. Bobby had come up to me and had tried to take the ball across me but in doing so he had knocked the ball against me and had dropped it. There was a bit of background to that. Seven months previously, in a League Cup quarter-final at Celtic Park, in a similar situation, Bobby had claimed that I had knocked the ball out of his hands to score our winning goal and the press had made a big sensation out of it. That may have been in Davidson's mind when he disallowed my goal in the Cup final. The referee continued in the same vein when Martin Buchan, the Aberdeen centre-half, swiped me with his boot and sent me tumbling to the ground after I had taken the ball past him inside the Aberdeen penalty area. It was a clear penalty but Davidson waved for play to continue.

Aberdeen went 2–0 ahead in the latter stages of the match but, with only a few minutes remaining, I scored to make it 2–1. The scoreline was unbalanced in their favour. We had applied almost incessant pressure and I was sure, even at that late stage, we could still get a draw, but Aberdeen scored a third within seconds of the ball being centred for the restart. I couldn't believe it, and the manner in which the trophy was snatched away from us still irritates me enormously.

It was some compensation that we had already comfortably won our fifth successive League title and were once again *en route* to the final of the European Cup, having eliminated Basle, Benfica and Fiorentina – the last two being top-quality sides. That had taken us into a semi-final with Leeds United and there, it was widely predicted in the English press, our little sortie in the 1969–70 European Cup was destined to end. The English press and television people, with supreme arrogance, claimed that Leeds United were unstoppable that season and were champions of Europe in all but name. Those media people failed to consider whether some other teams in the competition might rival the talents of the club they were championing.

Following our two-legged victory over Fiorentina, the Italian champions, we had all been sitting in the bath a couple of days later, awaiting news of the draw, when Billy McNeill came through and told us that it had pitted us against Leeds. 'Oh,' said Jimmy Johnstone, 'another f****** easy one!'

At Elland Road, the playing surface was in terrible condition, as we discovered when we arrived at the ground. Jock, who was always adept at mind games, told us that we were to pretend to the Leeds players that our pitch in Glasgow was even worse. An hour or so prior to the match we were standing in our suits inside the tunnel when Billy Bremner, the Leeds captain, came up to us and said, 'What about that pitch of ours? What do you make of it?' You could see the shock on his face when we said to him, 'It's fantastic. We're looking forward to playing on that after what we've been used to back home. Compared to our place, this is like Wembley.' We started the game really well, scoring a goal after only a minute, through George Connelly. He also scored a really good second goal that was disallowed and 1–0 was how it ended on a night when we had shown ourselves to be far superior to Leeds.

When Leeds came to Glasgow for the return on 15 April 1970, there were 136,505 at Hampden Park, a record crowd for any European Cup contest, and the cacophonous noise that cascaded down the terraces was in keeping with the greatest British cup tie there has ever been.

Before that second encounter with Leeds, Billy McNeill had been struggling to be fit and on the Monday and Tuesday the prognosis for him was bad but on the Wednesday lunchtime, at the Hydro, he was declared ready to play and that was a great boost for the boys going into the game.

Billy Bremner scored a great goal to open the scoring in the first half but we got back into it with a goal from Yogi shortly after the break. Five minutes on, Bobby Murdoch got our second and after that there was no way back for Leeds. We were in a second European Cup final. It would not be true to say that we had proved the English media entirely wrong. They were correct in believing that Leeds were a great team – what they hadn't realised was that we were an even better one. Murdoch and Auld were fabulous against them and everyone, throughout the team, played to the best of their potential. We had been desperate to prove how good we could be and that had further cemented the togetherness in our team and had pushed us to pull off two excellent performances against the English champions. Norman Hunter, Jack Charlton and Billy Bremner would intimidate players in opposing teams in English football but they had not intimidated us for one moment. Additional to all that, we simply had more ability in our side than Leeds could even dream about.

A lot was said about the Scottish League being inferior to the English League but at Celtic we were forced by Jock Stein to maintain a set of specific standards. He never allowed us to slacken off in our attitude and commitment to the game, so there was never any possibility of us being lulled into lassitude by facing lesser opposition in the Scottish League. We certainly handed out the occasional thumping to teams, which gave ammunition to those south of the border who claimed our League was less competitive, but then Leeds did the same to some teams in England. I always carried a car-key ring with the slogan, 'Preparation is as important as playing.' If Leeds had thought they were coming up against an amateurish mob from an unprofessional League, they had been proven wrong.

Feyenoord Rotterdam were to be our opponents in the 1970 European Cup final and, in contrast to Leeds, they were a team about whom we knew little. We weren't even certain where the final would be played. It had been planned for Milan but strike action was hitting the northern Italian city and there were whispers that the game might be moved to Rome. Eventually, the San Siro in Milan was confirmed as the venue and we flew out to stay in the same hotel in Varese, close to Lake Como, in which we had been billeted prior to the European Cup quarter-final the previous year. It was about an hour and twenty minutes' drive from Milan and I felt that it might have been better if we had stayed closer to the city. I felt we were too far from the venue for the final but Jock liked the fact that it was lovely and relaxed and calm there. Jimmy and I went into Como to have a proper shave at a barber's and it was nice to see the aqua-planes landing on the lake – but it wasn't Milan.

Our preparations were the same as for any big match. There was talk of an agent being involved with the squad to maximise the commercial potential of the occasion and maybe one or two of the boys spoke to him but I can't remember any such dealings. Nothing was going on that could be said to have the effect of distracting us from the task in hand. We had our usual team-talk and the gaffer stressed that if we played at our best on the night, we would win the trophy. He said that Feyenoord were not as good as some of the teams we had played and beaten in the competition. On weighing up the abilities of the two teams, he had come to the conclusion that we would win the game if both sides played to their potential.

On reflection, we must have taken things a lot easier during the match than we should have done. I'm not saying we didn't prepare properly but I think we must have thought we could beat Feyenoord comfortably. On arrival at the stadium we went down a long tunnel to the dressing rooms and discovered that the Feyenoord players were already there, standing outside their quarters. As we walked past them, we could see them looking at us with what seemed to be a certain degree of awe, as if we were stars. We had, after all, by then become established as one of the leading powers in continental football whereas that Feyenoord side were new to the latter stages of European competition. I felt really confident before the match and most of the other boys, I believe, felt the same way. That was maybe not such a good thing.

The Dutch were more than a match for us. They started well, whereas we didn't, and we never improved, although Tam Gemmell put us ahead after half an hour through a free-kick that he swiped past Eddie Pieters-Graafland, the Feyenoord goalkeeper, from just outside the penalty area. If we had kept the score at 1–0 at half-time, it might have unsettled the Dutch because, although they had played extremely well, they hadn't created an awful lot of chances. If Feyenoord had gone into their dressing room at half-time without anything to show for their efforts, it might have left them slightly demoralised. For our part, keeping the lead may have allowed us to stabilise, become more organised and go on from there, but we didn't get the chance. Within three minutes of Tam's goal, Rinus Israel had headed an equaliser for Feyenoord and you could see them growing ever more confident.

For all that we didn't play well and they did, the score was still level at the end of 90 minutes. Then, with only two minutes of extra time remaining, Ove Kindvall, the Feyenoord striker, lifted the ball over Evan Williams, our goalkeeper, to give Feyenoord the winner. If the game had gone to a replay, chances are we could have been better. If we had seen out those final two minutes, we could have regrouped sufficiently well to get ourselves back on track to do better in the next game. We would also have gone into that game fully aware of just how exceptionally good Feyenoord were. A lot of 'ifs', I know. The truth is they deserved their victory because they had proved themselves a top-class team. A lot of their players performed very well on the night, which surprised us. Wim van Hanegem was particularly outstanding. He pulled the strings. He was on the ball a lot, as was Wim Jansen.

It is true to say that, in assessing Feyenoord before the game, Jock Stein had conveyed the clear impression that the Dutch were not anywhere near as stellar a selection of players as he had described the Internazionale side prior to our great victory over them in the 1967 final. It is also equally true that Jock's team-talk did not win the match in Lisbon, and nor did his team-talk cause us to lose the game against Feyenoord. The difference was that the players excelled against Inter and fumbled against Feyenoord. You can't use the manager's team-talk as a reason for losing a European Cup final.

I didn't play well in the final. Almost always, when playing for Celtic, you would find that your team-mates provided you with several options whenever you had the ball. On that night, Feyenoord were so efficient that when you got the ball, you felt isolated. There were not as many passes available for you to make as there would normally be when playing for Celtic. Our players were looking for space, searching for good positions, but Feyenoord's work-rate and intelligence meant that they were constantly closing off opportunities for us. There was no breathing space for us as they stifled and smothered our style. Having said all that, I put the ball in the net, during the first half, at a time when the score was 0–0. Pieters-Graafland parried a shot from Willie Wallace and I slipped the rebound past the goalkeeper. Concetto Lo Bello, the referee, disallowed it and it's never really been discussed since. I'd like to see it again to discover whether or not I was actually offside. I probably was, to be honest. I think I heard the whistle before I put the ball in the net, but I still wish the decision had not stood. Yogi also missed a great chance in the first minute of extra time, when he went right through on the goalkeeper but failed to score. It happens. You can't use that to blame Yogi for the defeat. Pieters-Graafland saved it but if Yogi had scored then, the game might have had a different outcome. There is such a fine margin between winning and losing in matches at the highest level.

At time up, I remember we all stood as a group on the halfway line, utterly dejected, while Feyenoord paraded the Cup on the far side of the field. With the floodlights reflecting off it, the trophy looked absolutely magnificent. That was the lowest point in my entire football career, by far.

Afterwards, Jimmy and I walked out from the dressing room towards the team bus, clutching our bags and our boots, and the first people we encountered were Kathryn and Jimmy's wife, Agnes. Kathryn was wearing red and white because she hadn't realised those were the colours of Feyenoord, so that gave us a wee smile. We went back to the girls' hotel, where Jimmy and I had a couple of beers, and I do mean only a couple. We were not in the mood for anything more than that. Then we took a taxi back along the long and winding road to the team hotel in Varese. Jimmy and I were so dumbfounded at the result that all the way back we were barely able to speak. All we could do was shake our heads, stare at the floor of the taxi and say, repeatedly, 'F****** hell!' We felt sick.

We came back to Glasgow only to fly out to North America almost immediately for a close-season tour. We played Manchester United on the Monday night, five days after the final, losing 2–0. Throughout that tour we played like losers. Teams were beating us that should not have been beating us because we were so dejected. A tour was the last thing we needed at that time. It would have been fine if we had had the European Cup with us. Then it would have been party time.

Instead, those were the most difficult days of our lives. We were all down.

Looking at it positively, we had reached the European Cup final, which is an achievement in itself, and we had given it everything. It's not as if anyone was less than exhausted by the end of the 120 minutes. It was quite a feat to have reached two European Cup finals in three years but, at the time, losing hurt. Having done so well to reach a platform on which we could show the continent of Europe how well we could play, we had let ourselves down badly. The feeling of despair was so great that it made me believe that I had to get out of a game that could drag you down to the depths so quickly and so mercilessly. That defeat from Feyenoord had been so devastating that it had made me want to quit football.

CHAPTER 9

BACK ON TRACK

It did not take Jock Stein long to recover his naturally fiery approach after our defeat at the hands of Feyenoord in the 1970 European Cup final. On tour in the summer of 1970, we faced Bari, the Italian club, in Toronto and found that the Italians were in no mood to consider our encounter with them as a friendly match to be played in a mood of end-of-season enjoyment. Instead, they hacked their way through the match as relentlessly as explorers scything their way through the jungle. Before the game their right-back had given me all the verbals about how he was going to leave me in pieces and, sure enough, when I tried to go past him late in the first half, he decided his time to act seriously had come and he cracked into my knee with his boot, leaving the joint to swell up into an egg-shape. There was a lot of bad feeling already flying around among those on the field and as I lay in pain on the ground, players from both sides began shoving each other around angrily. Next thing, Jock was on the park, furiously pushing Italian players around before heading for their dugout, where he gave their coach some terrible stick. The togetherness was back among our players and management after the deadening defeat from Feyenoord, and for that we owed enormous thanks to the thugs of Bari.

That was a strange game for other reasons. We had been trailing 2–0 to Bari but had levelled it at 2–2 when we were awarded a penalty kick with only a few minutes remaining. Three Bari players had been sent off by that time and when we were given the penalty, the Italians capped the farce by walking off the pitch, *en masse*, and heading for their dressing room. Bobby Murdoch stroked the ball into the empty net and, after waiting a while to see what would happen next, we eventually made our way to our own dressing room, where we were discussing the situation when the referee entered and told us that Bari would resume the match if we would re-take the penalty but miss it. We told him there was no chance of that happening. After a further 20 minutes we were told that Bari had gone back on to the park so we wandered back on, too, only to find that an essential ingredient was missing – the referee had by now left the ground. So both teams had to leave the field again.

I was not the only one to suffer at the hands – and feet – of that 'friendly' Bari defender. Eintracht Frankfurt were on that tour as well, sharing a hotel with us. After their game with Bari, one of their players came back to the hotel in a wheelchair. We asked him what had happened.

'Ach, the right-back of Bari,' came the reply from the German.

Sadness and disappointment had been my foremost feelings on that North American tour as I thought back continually to the defeat by Feyenoord. I still knew that, come July, once I'd had a holiday and was back for pre-season training, enthusiasm for the game would once again seep into my being and that my love of football would return. That had to happen to ensure that I remained on top of my game and stayed in the team. Jock would be quick to spot any player whose drive and commitment had waned and he would quickly let them know that he had no use for them.

There was a new look to the Celtic team for the start of the 1970–71 season, with young players Danny McGrain and Lou Macari, both in their early twenties, being given extended runs in the side, and Victor Davidson, a young player whom Jock rated particularly highly, also appearing in the team. It was clear that, following the Feyenoord defeat, Jock was planning to rebuild for the future. It was pleasing to me that I retained my place amid all this new competition.

Our reputation as Britain's top team meant that we were asked to travel to London to provide the opposition for West Ham United in Bobby Moore's testimonial on 16 November 1970. The rain cascaded down on a match marked by top-quality football. It ended 3–3, which put Jock in a great mood. Afterwards, in the dressing room at Upton Park, he told us of an upcoming treat.

'Lads,' he said, 'we have had an invitation to go to the Bahamas in February to play Santos, Pelé's team. We'll go out after our match on the Saturday, play the match on the Sunday and then have two days in the Bahamas before flying back in the middle of the week.' Everybody was immediately enthused by this and talking about what a great break it would be, when Jim Brogan, a centre-back, piped up.

'Well, obviously the club's going to make money,' he said, out of the blue. 'What will the players get out of this?'

'What?' said Jock.

'Why are we to fly to the other side of the world to play, unless there's some money in it for us?' Jim responded. Jock was having none of that.

'We're not going,' he immediately retorted, and with that, he walked out of the door, slamming it behind him. Jim took some stick from the boys for that and Chelsea went to the Bahamas in our place. Our chance to play against Pele had gone.

In our third final of 1970, we met Rangers in the League Cup that autumn. We received a boost before the match when we heard that John Greig was not in the Rangers side, but the confidence that news gave us may have backfired. John was a great player for Rangers and we may have been lulled into thinking that they wouldn't be able to summon up the same sort of impetus to their game that they had when he was at the helm. I don't know if that ultimately was a factor – all I do know is that, even without Greig, Rangers proved to be as committed as ever and Derek Johnstone headed the only goal of the game to win the trophy for the 'Gers.

Little more than two months later, we met Rangers again, this time in the traditional New Year match, at Ibrox Park on 2 January 1971. With one minute of the game remaining, and with the score at 0–0, I shot for goal only for the ball to hit the underside of the bar and bounce down. Jimmy Johnstone swiftly connected with the rebound to put us ahead. We felt the game was won but immediately after the restart, Rangers were awarded a free-kick after Jim Craig had fouled Willie Johnston midway inside our half. When the cross came into our box, Colin Stein got his foot to it to put it into our net, and the match ended 1–1. Losing such a late goal was a big blow for us because we were striving to remain close to Aberdeen, the League leaders, in pursuit of our sixth League title in a row.

Later, sitting in our team bus outside the ground, we were still mulling over how we had allowed victory to slip away. We had to wait for the directors before we could leave, and they were mingling with their opposite numbers in the boardroom, while we sat on the bus for however long it took them to exchange pleasantries and enjoy the last of the hospitality on offer. That January day, they took even longer than usual and we waited on the bus for what seemed an eternity. Eventually, Jock Stein stepped on to the coach and told us that we would be leaving without him and the directors. That was the first indication we had that something was wrong. Word soon trickled through to us that there had been a disaster at the match. Something had happened on a stairway leading from the terracing to the street at the end of the ground where the Rangers supporters stood. We heard that five or six people had been killed. That was shocking enough but by the time we reached Parkhead, it was being said that 15 or 20 people had died. On the journey back to Saltcoats, I switched on my car radio and heard the death toll rise and rise. The eventual figure was sickeningly high – 66 fans lost their lives that day.

Initially, it was thought that supporters going down that stairway to the street had heard the roar following Colin Stein's goal and had turned to try to get back on to the terraces to see what all the excitement was about. The resultant havoc, it was said, had been created when those trying to turn back collided with those still intent on leaving. People lost their footing and some fell and were trampled. It seemed to me that the cause of the disaster had been the maelstrom of despair quickly followed by celebrations among the Rangers supporters caused by those two late, late goals, but a subsequent inquiry reached the conclusion that that was not what had been at the heart of the problem. The steel barriers on stairway 13 had given way and that was what had caused the chaos and the crushing of people to death, along with many more being injured. It transpired that the supporters had all been heading in the same direction.

Regardless of the cause, it was a most dreadful tragedy and it was one that affected Jock severely. He was down for a long while after that. It got to him that people had lost their lives after having come to a football match to be entertained. It hurt him. Jock possessed a hard-faced exterior but he was a deeply emotional man and the events of that day at Ibrox stirred his soul. It was shocking to think of families awaiting their menfolk's return from a football match, only to be told that never again would they come back in the door. It was a real tragedy and it cast a pall over football for a long time afterwards.

Aberdeen continued to be our closest rivals for the title that season but although they led the League for many months, our 1–1 draw at Pittodrie in mid-April 1971 tilted things our way. We duly went on to win our games in hand on Aberdeen and collect our sixth successive Scottish League title, equalling the record of the great Celtic side in the opening decade of the 20th century.

Matches against Aberdeen and trips to Pittodrie, in particular, were always special. Every summer, when the season's fixtures were published, we were keen to know when the Aberdeen game was scheduled to take place. The Dons would almost always give us a good, close game up there and the trip itself was distinctive. We would meet at Queen Street station and take the ten o'clock train from Glasgow on the Saturday morning, have lunch on the train and get off at Aberdeen station to walk to Pittodrie for the match. There would be thousands of people on the streets, walking to the game, and we would join them in strolling up to Pittodrie. There was a genuine closeness between players and supporters.

We notched a record score for Celtic in Europe that season when we defeated Kokkola of Finland 9–0 at Celtic Park but I was not a particularly happy man at the end of that match. If your team wins by scoring nine goals and you are a forward, you want to have notched at least one of the goals but I had failed to do so that night. That was also the first time we had ever played in yellow – we changed colours because Kokkola played in dark green with a big 'K' on the front of their shirts.

The return match, in Lapland, was equally memorable. The temperature was well below freezing even though it was still September. A big fire blazed away in the dressing room but that made it feel all the more cold when we took to the pitch for the match. Jock left out Billy McNeill, Tam Gemmell and one or two other established players, so on the day of the game they hit downtown Kokkola and had 'lunch' – they weren't feeling the cold at all by the time they rolled up to watch us win 5–0. At the end of the game, the Finns announced two men of the match and Stevie Chalmers and I, having just started to warm ourselves up at that fire, had to return to the pitch, shivering, to receive our awards. Stevie was presented, appropriately, with a fur hat and I was given a shirt.

Jimmy Johnstone was scheduled to go on that trip to Kokkola, even though he hated flying and even though the second leg was little more than a formality. On arrival at Glasgow Airport, we discovered that our aeroplane was a tiny, fragile-looking turbo-prop – the airport at Kokkola was not big enough to take a jet.

'Have you seen the plane?' Jimmy said to me anxiously, adding, 'I'm feeling really rotten. My throat is killing me.' I was laughing away because I was sure he was, once again, attempting to get out of flying. Jimmy proceeded to tell Jock how bad he was feeling. If it had been Billy McNeill or Tam or me, Jock would undoubtedly have shouted the doctor over, but because it was Jimmy and because his dislike of flying was so well known, Jock just growled at him, 'You get on that plane, you little midden.' When we reached our hotel in Kokkola, Jimmy took to his bed and, on the orders of Doctor Fitzsimmons, the club doctor, didn't emerge again until the morning after the match, when we were flying home. He really had had a severe dose of influenza.

Trips such as that one to Finland were a lot of fun. When we had a big lead, training was easier and the mood among the players was relaxed. Once we were out on the field of play, though, we had to perform to the utmost of our abilities. Anything less was unacceptable to our manager. Even in testimonials, we had to play flat-out. If we didn't, we would get a rollicking at half-time. The English clubs, in contrast, tended to flannel a wee bit in testimonials or friendlies.

Another hefty victory, by 7–0 in Dublin against Waterford, the Irish champions, set us up nicely to win 3–2 at home and ease into a quarter-final against Ajax Amsterdam. We were doing well over there – it was 0–0 after an hour – until Johan Cruyff turned on a wee bit of magic and scored a goal. Barry Hulshoff then found a gap in our defensive wall, which wasn't set up too well, to make it 2–0 and in the last minute, Piet Keizer came streaking along the byline and rifled a shot into our net. Ajax ran out 3–0 winners. It was a strange tie because we had been very much in the game throughout and the score seemed slightly unfair, considering how close we had been to Ajax overall. Jimmy Johnstone scored in Glasgow after half an hour of the second leg but Ajax did not allow us to capitalise on that. We held on to the lead but the 1–0 victory was not enough to prevent us being eliminated by a side who were as good as any team we played in Europe over the years. Ajax had shown that they were a better side than us and we could not dispute that they deserved to win the tie, even though we were close to their level. They would go on to lift the European Cup three times in succession.

Excitement always pulsated within me before a match, home or away. Every match-day morning, I would take a short stroll down to the harbour in Saltcoats, just to fill my lungs with good, fresh air. Whether that actually did me any good at all in relation to the match, I don't know but I felt that it did, which was benefit enough. I would always think positively before a match. I'd tell myself that if a chance came to me, I was sure to put the ball in the net. I'd never think negatively. I'd never consider what might happen if I missed a good chance. Negative thoughts produce negative deeds. Forwards do miss chances but that just means you've got to try harder the next time.

There is a difference in being confident of scoring if the chance arises, and being absolutely sure of scoring in a particular match. The latter prediction is something that players tend naturally to avoid. I made it just once during my whole career. The occasion was the 1971 Scottish Cup final with Rangers. We were down at the Marine Hotel in Troon preparing for the game and on the Saturday morning I was lying in bed chatting to my room-mates, Jimmy Johnstone and Bobby Murdoch. The banter was good and there was a lot of kidding on but I was quite serious when I said to them, 'Listen, I'm going to say something I shouldn't say. I'll score today.' Both of them were really buoyant on hearing that. Five minutes before half-time, I zipped on to a ball that had been played through the middle for me and sent it shooting past Peter McCloy, the Rangers goalkeeper, for my third consecutive goal in Scottish Cup finals. I don't know why it came to me that I would score that day but I was delighted my hunch was correct. Late in the match Derek Johnstone equalised for Rangers but we won the replay 2–1, a result that, on the balance of play, flattered Rangers enormously.

We were winning the Scottish Cup regularly by the early 1970s and the post-match atmosphere tended to be more restrained than the delirium that had greeted our first Cup victory, the win over Dunfermline Athletic in 1965. In 1971, even though the crowd had numbered more than 100,000 that Wednesday night, only a handful of supporters gathered outside Hampden to acclaim us afterwards, in contrast to the thousands who had greeted us after the Dunfermline victory.

Matters proceeded less smoothly for me in another Old Firm

match, a League Cup tie at Ibrox in August 1971, when, despite all my efforts, the ball just would not run the right way for me. We were playing towards the Celtic end in the first half and, although the chances were there to be had, I couldn't take them. Jimmy Johnstone set up one particularly good opportunity for me, cutting the ball into my path only for me to smack it past the post. Another fine pass freed me to take on the goalkeeper but, unlike in the Cup final, Peter McCloy got to the ball and snatched it away when I could maybe have done more to get round him. The score was 0–0 as we walked down the players' tunnel at half-time, and my mind was churning away at the thought of missing those chances, when someone suddenly jumped on me like a mugger up an alleyway. I struggled to shake him off but it was Jimmy, who was in a fury with me, digging into me and clambering all over me like a demented monkey.

'Are you not trying to score?' he shouted in my ear repeatedly. 'What's wrong with you today?' He was really agitated and seemed temporarily unhinged.

'Get off me!' I yelled at him. 'Get a hold of yourself.'

It was a wee bit unnerving to find him in such a mood. We went two up in the second half, through Kenny Dalglish and Tommy Callaghan, and with around ten minutes remaining, John Greig tried to clear the ball only for it to rebound off me and fall nicely for me to sweep it into the corner of the net. At that, Jimmy planted a big kiss right on my cheek.

That victory over Rangers helped push us on to the 1971 League Cup final, which resulted in a 4–1 defeat by Partick Thistle, one of the greatest shocks in the history of Scottish football. People say to me that I was lucky to have been omitted from Jock Stein's team for that match, but my answer is not really – I'd have probably won it for us . . . Joking aside, Celtic had a lot of chances, especially in the second half, which the team had started 4–0 down. Kenny Dalglish got our goal with about 20 minutes remaining. Jock had fielded a lot of young players that day, such as Kenny and Lou Macari. He had also named Jim Craig as his substitute. That seemed fine, but when Jimmy Johnstone got injured right at the start of the game and had to come off, Jock had to replace him with a right-back, which entailed changing round the whole team. It left us a forward short, which was not good because, eventually, we needed to score a lot of goals.

A superlative seventh title came our way at the end of the 1971–72 season. Aberdeen were again our closest challengers but finished ten points behind us. There was nothing to indicate that our dominance of Scottish football would end any time soon because a group of good young players had come flooding into the first team during the early 1970s. Kenny Dalglish was a great all-rounder who could both create and score goals. It was always a treat to play alongside him. The same was true of Danny McGrain, who became as good a right-back as any in world football and who also made things easy for you if you were playing in front of him. David Hay was a combative but skilful central midfield player who did much to knit the team together. Lou Macari was a nippy goalscorer. The youngsters were complemented by the remaining Lisbon Lions – Billy McNeill, Bobby Murdoch, Jimmy Johnstone and me – and with our experience we helped ease those younger players into the team. That rich blend helped us to reach the semi-finals of the European Cup in April 1972, in which our opponents would be Internazionale of Milan, our old rivals from Lisbon. As with us, their team had undergone several changes in the intervening years but Giacinto Facchetti, Tarcisio Burgnich and Sandro Mazzola, stalwarts of 1967, were still in the side.

It proved a tight match in the San Siro and it was 0–0 with half an hour remaining when Jim Brogan suffered an injury that necessitated him being replaced by another of our young players, Pat McCluskey, a 19-year-old who had made just a handful of appearances in the first team. Within minutes of him entering the fray at left-back, an Inter player went racing past him and although Paddy recovered to tackle him perfectly cleanly, a huge roar went up from the crowd to demand a penalty. Sometimes all it takes is for a big surge of sound to go round a stadium such as the San Siro for a referee to cave in and provide a penalty for the home side but, fortunately for us, our referee that night refused to be swayed and the game ended 0–0.

The opening 20 minutes of the encounter in Glasgow produced so many goalscoring openings for us that we could have had the tie won well before half-time. We failed to score, though, and with the Italians defending in depth, the match became more of a stalemate the longer it went on and eventually ended goalless, which took us into our first-ever penalty shootout. Jock asked who would like to take our penalties and when five other guys volunteered, I was quite happy. It says a lot about those guys that they were willing to stand up and be counted. Dixie Deans, a striker whom we had recruited from Motherwell earlier that season, missed the first one but these things happen. I think he was going to crack it hard and low but at the last second decided to sidefoot the ball and it went narrowly over the crossbar. With Inter scoring all five of their penalties, we were out of Europe. Penalty shootouts are always a lottery – it's equivalent to being put out on a technicality. People still say to Dixie, 'What about that penalty you missed against Inter?' That can be annoying at times for him and for his pals. If I'm in his company, I respond by saying, 'What about the couple of hundred goals he did score in his career?'

Prior to facing Inter, we had played Ujpest Dozsa in the quarter-finals and I remember clearly, in the approach to the game, being described in the press as 'the veteran forward Bobby Lennox'. I was all of 28 at the time. Jock had a laugh about that. It just shows you how, if you start early and stay at the same club, you are regarded as having been around almost forever, especially when there are young guys such as Macari and Dalglish bursting into the team.

It's also funny how matches that seem routine can turn out to be deeply significant for a footballer. Early in 1973, chasing our eighth successive Scottish League title, we travelled to Methil to play East Fife. We were after a win in the hope of reducing a four-point gap that Rangers had accrued at the top of the table. East Fife had a decent side and were progressing well in mid-table but we were definite favourites. That encounter at Bayview proved an odd one for Celtic and significant for me, even though I did not feature in the action, having been selected as a substitute that day. We were awarded three penalties, which was notable in itself, but, even more notably, we missed them all. Bobby Murdoch, Kenny Dalglish and Harry Hood all failed to find the net from those spot-kicks and, in the closing minutes, East Fife were leading 2–1.

When we missed our third one, Jock turned to me on the bench and said, 'If we get another penalty, you're going on and you're taking it.' It's understating it wildly to say that was a surprise. I'd never taken a penalty before – I actually shied away from doing so – but my nerves were spared by the referee, who opted not to award any more penalties. Dixie Deans scored with a header to make the final score 2–2. The following weekend we went to Motherwell for a Scottish Cup tie and in the dressing room the banter was going well when Billy McNeill came up to me.

'They tell me you're on the penalties today, wee man,' he said. I thought he was at the kidding so, in a spirit of fun, I joked back.

'Aye, just give me the ball, I'll take it. I'm your man,' I boasted.

Unbeknown to me, Jock was standing behind me. I hadn't seen

him. Sharp as a tack, he rattled out, 'Well done, Lemon, glad to hear you'll take the penalties for us. It's good to hear someone taking on a bit of responsibility.' I was left standing there, wondering what I had done.

We never got a penalty that day at Fir Park, a game that we won 4–0, but a week later at Celtic Park it was a different story. More than 40,000 were in attendance for a match with Aberdeen and after an hour or so of a very tight encounter it was 0–0; then Willie Young, the Aberdeen centre-back, handled the ball on his own goal-line after Bobby Clark, the goalkeeper, had gone down injured. We had won a penalty, one that could be vital if we were to overhaul Rangers at the top. So, having unwittingly nominated myself as penalty taker, I went and got the ball and put it on the spot. Bobby Clark was receiving treatment so there was a delay before the kick could be taken and during that lull, Jimmy Johnstone, my best pal, took the opportunity to come over and have a word with me. The crowd, I'm sure, would have been under the impression that Jimmy was doling out some positive encouragement to his friend as I prepared to take the kick. Instead, he was saying to me, 'Do us a favour, wee man, let somebody else take it. You don't take penalties and we need to score this one.' It wasn't exactly a vote of confidence, but I managed to stroke the ball into the corner to put us ahead, turning away afterwards in relief. We went on to win 2–0, Kenny Dalglish adding a second goal ten minutes or so from the end.

That night, the evening sports programme, after showing the football highlights, concluded by showing me stroking a penalty into the corner of the net and Peter Lorimer doing the same for Leeds United. They repeated the sequence several times. That made it look easy but it was a job I never particularly relished. If you scored with a penalty kick, it was what was expected of you. If you missed, you were a fool. A goalie is in a good position with penalties. He can take pot luck and it can hit him. He can even go the wrong way and find that the ball strikes him on the foot and he has saved what many people feel should be a certain goal. I don't think you can practise penalty kicks. You can score as many as you like in training but when you are presented with the real thing, you could be up against a goalkeeper who is moving around on his line or standing slightly closer to one post than the other and that raises an element of uncertainty in your mind. You can also have 60,000 people swaying and shouting while you're trying to conquer your nerves. It's not easy.

My sense of professionalism and love of Celtic occasionally worked against me. I think I was occasionally left out of the team for cup finals during the early 1970s because I was the easy option for Jock. There were occasional rumblings at the club among the young boys at that time. Celtic were falling further and further behind the major English clubs in terms of the money they were willing to pay players, and the manager and directors were finding that this was making the more outstanding young players restless. If a young player had become unsettled over money and wanted away, Jock might try to placate him by leaving me out of the team for a final so that he could play. Jock knew that I was happy at Celtic and that I was not the type to batter down his door to demand why another player was in the team when I was not. I just wanted to show what I could do if selected for the next game. It still felt terrible every time we got to Hampden Park and the team was announced and I was not named. My spirits would plummet dramatically and I would think it was quite unfair.

One aspect of Jock's management that I think he could have approached differently was the way he handled the situation when he decided it was time for a player to leave the club. Once Jock had reached the conclusion that a player was no longer of any use to him, he would turn off him, cut him dead. There was no soft landing for the player concerned. Jock would simply tell the player that he was going, another club was ready to sign him and it was time for him to pack his bags. That happened to a lot of players, including Lisbon Lions. The guy could, literally, be swept out of the club without getting the chance to say goodbye. Jock could maybe have helped players more when it was time for them to leave. Instead, he was brutally ruthless to both fringe players and those who had done an awful lot for him. There was no grace or ceremony, and little thanks, about it. In contrast, while you were at the club and doing the business for Jock, he made you feel great. He wasn't unique in his approach to the matter. Most managers are the same.

Billy McNeill, Jimmy Johnstone and I were in the Celtic team throughout the years when we won 'nine in a row' – a sequence of successive League championships that we completed in the spring of 1974 – so the side always had a core of players who knew how to win the title. Others of the Lisbon Lions, such as Bobby Murdoch and Tommy Gemmell, were there for most of those nine title-winning years. That imbued confidence and a winning mentality in the side. Kenny Dalglish, David Hay and others came into the team gradually, learned from those already in place and became really good players and winners. Our reputation helped us. Teams feared the prospect of playing against us, which gave us an advantage even before a match had begun.

Perhaps because he had so many excellent youngsters available to him, Jock had been slightly precipitate in breaking up the Lisbon Lions, although the process was probably hastened by the nature of our defeat by Feyenoord in the 1970 European Cup final, a match in which seven of the Lions had featured. If we had beaten Feyenoord, Jock would maybe have kept the team together for longer but by the following year, Yogi, Willie Wallace, Bertie Auld and Tommy Gemmell had all been shown the door. Tommy and Yogi were still only 28 at that time. It was only when the team began to break up that we truly began to realise just how good we had been together.

I still think that the Lisbon Lions could have played together for a year or two longer. Jock began to dismantle the side possibly because he was determined that the team would retain its status forever and would not be allowed to grow old together to sour the memory of what those players had achieved as such very young men. Jock's determination to guard jealously the reputation of that team may have meant he became too hasty in jettisoning players. I remember being unable to believe it when, in the early autumn of 1973, Bobby Murdoch told me that he was moving to Middlesbrough. You would sometimes hear rumours about which guys would be coming or going to and from the club but that didn't happen with Bobby. Jock seemed to work that way – a player would be moved on with no warning. Bobby had only just turned 29 and to me he retained all of his powers as a majestic midfield player. He did have a problem with his weight, which would fluctuate frequently, but he could still play. I also thought that if Bobby were to go, it would be to another club of enormous stature, certainly first division, but at the time Middlesbrough were in the second division of the Football League in England.

Bobby hadn't wanted to leave Celtic. The story goes that Jackie Charlton, the manager of Middlesbrough, rang Jock Stein one day to say that he was seeking a central midfielder who could pass the ball. Charlton wanted to see if Jock could recommend anyone. When Jock said that Bobby Murdoch was available, Charlton thought he was joking. It turned out he wasn't and Bobby was whisked away by Charlton before anyone else could get a sniff. Charlton had been looking for a scrap of advice from Jock and instead found himself stumbling upon a gem. As things turned out, Bobby was a huge success at

Middlesbrough, where he loved it, helping them into the top division in England and later becoming the Middlesbrough manager himself.

At one stage, Jock had said of the Lisbon Lions, 'This team won't be beaten.' He made sure that the team's reputation would survive intact because he started a match with the 11 Lions just five times after we had won the European Cup, all of those matches taking place before the end of 1967. Although we had good young players coming through in the years after that, you can't take players such as Bobby Murdoch and Bertie Auld out of a team and expect it to run quite as well. As soon as the players who had made the Lions tick were jettisoned, things could never be quite the same again.

The Lisbon Lions had been a tight-knit team. We had been very close to each other so when I saw members of that team leaving I knew I would miss them. Still, no matter the glamour that surrounds the game, when you are an employee of a football club, you are at your work and you've just got to get on with it. As a player, you didn't have any say in who was going to be there and who was not. I had a job that I loved with a club that I loved so although other people were leaving, I was happy still to be there. It was the same when the manager bought players for the club. You couldn't go into a wee shell because there was new competition for your place in the team. You had to be positive and make sure you did all you could to stay the number one pick. The changes in the team were very subtle because players left one by one and new players were introduced by Jock very gradually.

We pipped Rangers to the League title in the spring of 1973, winning it by just one point. A year later, we finished four points clear of Hibernian, giving us the famous nine titles in a row. An ankle injury in that 1973–74 season meant that I had been restricted to 28 starts but I had managed to score 22 goals, which is almost as good a goals-to-games ratio as you'll get. I always had problems with my ankles – I had to strap them up for every training session. It may have been a legacy from when I was a wee boy and once hit the ball wrongly while playing in the park, which resulted in a painful ankle, or it might just have been that I've always had weak ankles – who knows?

Our tremendous run of success under Jock seemed set to continue indefinitely. Another run to the semi-finals of the European Cup accompanied our feat of achieving nine in a row. The thumping of TPS Turku, a Finnish team, on a 9–1 aggregate in the opening round had taken us into a tie with Vejle Boldklub of Denmark but, although this was another Scandinavian side of whom we knew little, they proved a much more difficult prospect. In the home leg we passed up a couple of good chances to take a lead into the second leg and it ended 0–0. The return game was redolent with anxiety for us because of the prospect of going out of the European Cup at such an early stage to an unknown club – Vejle were not quite of the same standard as Ajax and Internazionale.

The tactics blackboard had been set up in a room in our hotel in Denmark prior to the return match and as we awaited the entry of big Jock, we noticed that the number seven had been placed in a wide position on the left-hand side. That was normally Jimmy's number so, when we saw that, we began to wonder how Jimmy, who had been made captain for the first leg, might deal with playing wide left. Jock breezed into the room and announced, 'Lennox will be number seven instead of Johnstone.' Jimmy would have no role at all in the game. He was delighted for me but furious to have been dropped for a European Cup tie. I had similarly mixed feelings – I was pleased to have been named in the side while being upset for Jimmy who, it was clear, was not taking the news at all well.

The match turned out nicely for me. Ten minutes before half-time, one of the Vejle defenders attempted to come out with the ball and I managed to nick it away from him on the edge of the penalty area before cracking a sweet shot with my left foot into the net. That was the only goal of the game but it was never at any point a comfortable victory. At time up, Jimmy, who tended to smoulder if he felt he'd been wronged, was still raging at the perceived slight of being dropped, even though he was really happy that we had gone through, and on our return to Glasgow, he was ready to explode at Jock. At the first opportunity, Jimmy hammered on the manager's door and demanded an explanation of why he had been omitted for the match in Denmark.

'What was the score?' Jock asked him.

'One nil to us,' said Jimmy.

'Who scored the goal?' Jock asked, before supplying the answer himself. 'Bobby Lennox – the man who took your place. Now, get out of my office.'

Things tended to be short, sharp and pretty clear-cut with Jock. As Jimmy reflected, there's not much you can say when things are presented to you in such a way.

Basle were eliminated by us in the quarter-finals, which slotted us into the semis, where we faced a tie with Atletico Madrid. I didn't play in the first leg, in Glasgow, where Atletico simply kicked lumps out of our players and ended the evening having had three of their side dismissed. Sitting in the stand, I was wincing at the punishment being doled out to the boys. Our team would normally be good enough to get a win once our opponents had had one or more players dismissed but we did not get the opportunity to do so in that game because Atletico disrupted the match incessantly, with their persistent, niggly fouling. Even the Atletico goalkeeper, Miguel Reina, was in on it. Every time he received the ball he would hold on to it for as long as he could before kicking it deep into the 'Jungle' terracing. That emphasised how little intention they had of making it a football match. They were well aware that for a free-flowing, passing team such as ours there would be nothing worse than having the game constantly interrupted. We could not get into any sort of rhythm and Jimmy Johnstone, in particular, was tanned black and blue by Atletico's ultra-violent ways. They were fortunate, by the conclusion of the 90 minutes, to have had only three individuals dismissed. It was a dreadful display from them.

It may seem as though Celtic were a bit naïve on those thankfully rare occasions when we faced the type of gamesmanship employed by Atletico and, in 1967, by Racing Club, but there really was not much we could have done. You cannot combat tactics like that unless you stoop to the depths of your opponents and at Celtic we were unwilling to do so. It was not in our make-up to behave like that. It is easier to disrupt a game of football than to try to play the game properly, and against Atletico the players had obeyed Jock Stein's instructions to keep their cool in the face of extreme provocation. Atletico's cynicism had been clear to anyone watching inside the stadium, such as the official UEFA observer, or scrutinising the television pictures of the match. We were sure, on that evidence, that UEFA would order the return match to be played at a neutral venue and when that did not happen we felt let down badly by the governing body of European football.

Ruben Ayala, an Argentinian with hair down to his bum, became synonymous with the viciousness of the Atletico players. He was one of those sent off and I heard later that police had restrained him after the game. There had been a brawl in the tunnel after the final whistle and someone had smacked Ayala after he had become involved with David Hay but it was the Atletico man whom the Glasgow police had 'lifted'. Word of that filtered back to Madrid and was used in the local press to inflame the feelings of the Atletico supporters.

Over in Spain, we had no sooner checked into our hotel, which was swarming with armed police there for our protection, than we received news that a threat of assassination had been made against Jimmy Johnstone and Jock Stein. The immediate response from Jimmy, with whom I was sharing a room, was to close the curtains – he had visions of a sniper with a rifle taking him out from the embankment in the grounds of the hotel. Those curtains remained closed from the Monday lunchtime until the Thursday morning, when we left for Glasgow. There was some fruit in the room and at one point he picked up an apple and was about to eat it when I asked him what he was doing. 'What does it look as if I'm doing?' he snapped at me. I responded that there were other ways of assassinating someone than with a rifle. At that, he dropped the apple, pronto. Jimmy didn't want to play in the match because he felt he would be too exposed as a potential target but Jock said to him, 'Listen, once you're out there, going this way and that, weaving away on the wing, they'll not be able to get you. I'll be a sitting duck, there in that dugout.'

Police ringed our coach all the way to the Vicente Calderon Stadium. There were cars in front of us, behind us and alongside, with a host of motorcycle outriders thrown in for good measure. As we got off the bus at the ground, the Atletico fans, on first sight of us, collectively let out an enormous, bestial howl. They were after our blood but, fortunately, a fence separated them from us. We weren't made particularly welcome by the Atletico officials, either. Whenever we needed anything from them, they made themselves scarce.

The crowd at that game was the noisiest I had ever heard as a player. They would have torn us apart, I'm sure, if they hadn't been kept at bay by moats, police with dogs and on horses, and a fence that surrounded the pitch. It was not a pleasant atmosphere in which to play but at least, this time, the proceedings on the park bore a greater resemblance to a football match than the first leg had done. Six Atletico players had been suspended after the events in Glasgow but that was no handicap to them. Juan Carlos Lorenzo, their manager, had packed his team with hackers for the first leg and had, all along, planned to fillet them from his side for the return in Madrid in order to replace them with ball players. The suspensions had simply done his job for him. The aim had been for the picadors to soften us up in the first leg before the matadors killed us with skill in the return. It didn't exactly work out like that.

We missed several good chances at 0–0 and at one point I was freed to go through on Reina, who was again in goal for Atletico. As the two of us simultaneously went for the ball, close to the Atletico 18-yard line, I got to it first and prodded it past him only to see it roll narrowly the wrong side of the post. With less than quarter of an hour remaining, Atletico opened the scoring and then snatched a second goal a few minutes before the end. They had won but they had never at any stage proved themselves a better side than us and the overall manner of their victory left a bitter aftertaste.

Three weeks later, in the final, Atletico were 1–0 ahead against Bayern Munich when, with the final kick of the match, Katsche Schwarzenbeck sent a 30-yard shot flying past Reina. I celebrated as though I had supported Bayern all my life and was deeply grateful when they thumped Atletico 4–0 in the replay two nights later. No club ever deserved to win a final less than Atletico Madrid at that time. They were disgraceful. I am convinced that if we had beaten them in Glasgow we would have gone through to the final. Once again, we had been so close to winning another European Cup – we could have beaten Bayern. Instead, the chance had been whipped away from under our noses by the most unfair means.

CHAPTER 10

LAST OF THE LIONS

Winning was so vital to me as a footballer and that may be why my memories of the mid-1970s have become a little bit hazy. It's easier to remember winning than losing and during that period, for the first time under Jock Stein, Celtic began to experience significant setbacks after a near-decade of ongoing success. I also became a bit less involved with the first team, so my recollections of those days are far less sharp than of events further back in time. I do know that we were top of the table at Christmas 1974, but we finished the season 11 points behind Rangers. That's about all I recall of that League season. I must have wanted to forget about that season as much as possible and I have succeeded pretty well.

One event I do recall clearly is our next European Cup tie after the debacle against Atletico, which was almost as jarring for me as the clash with the Spaniards. Facing Olympiakos Piraeus of Greece, in the autumn of 1974, was memorable because it produced the second dismissal of my career, which was as unjustified as the first one against Racing Club in 1967. We were 2–0 down in the second leg, played in Olympiakos's Karaiskakis Stadium in front of a frenzied crowd, when

I was sent on to the park with 15 minutes remaining, as a substitute for Jimmy Johnstone. I had been on the field for a few minutes when Olympiakos were awarded a free-kick. I was standing in front of the ball while they made a substitution, and their inside-left and I were smiling at each other as he waited for the game to resume and the opportunity to take the kick. Suddenly the referee shot across the park and reached my side, where he booked me. I pointed out to him that as a substitution was being made, the ball was not in play so I couldn't have been infringing on my opponent. 'I decide the substitutes,' the referee responded. Two minutes later, the Olympiakos right-back went to cross the ball, I blocked it, it went over my shoulder and the referee again zipped across to me and dismissed me. I still don't know why.

The rest of that season is pretty much a blank up until the Scottish Cup final. The significance of that match is, unlike most of the events either side of it, etched firmly in my memory. We faced Airdrieonians in early May 1975 and I remember going to Hampden on a beautiful sunny day and coming out on to the park half an hour before kick-off, expecting to see a huge Celtic support only to find that it was the Airdrie fans who were making their presence felt. Their end was mobbed – the whole of the town must have been at Hampden that day and they provided the match with a great atmosphere. Paul Wilson, another exciting young Celtic forward of the 1970s, put us ahead early in the first half but Airdrie equalised, from a goalmouth scramble, a couple of minutes before half-time. From the restart, we switched back into attack and Paul scored our second with a neat header from my corner. I think that really deflated Airdrie, losing another goal so swiftly after having equalised. Shortly into the second half, I was brought down inside the penalty box and Pat McCluskey's successful penalty kick completed the scoring and clinched the Cup for Celtic.

Winning was important enough in what otherwise had been a poor season by Celtic's standards but the truly momentous part of that afternoon, in my view, was still to come. After the game, I reflected that, having made a worthwhile contribution to the victory, I might expect to play a greater role in the first team the following season but Billy McNeill, the only other Lisbon Lion to feature in that 1975 Scottish Cup-winning side, had decided he had had enough. That very day, once the trophy had been lifted, he told me that he was quitting as a player. I was shocked because I had no inkling that Billy was thinking along those lines. Everyone was elated at winning the Cup but I was sitting there stunned at Billy's news. He had been a great captain and I had seen no tailing-off in his performances at the heart of the team. I tried to persuade him to check in for pre-season, when he would be able to see whether he felt differently, but he insisted that he had made his decision. It was a major loss. Billy had been central to everything at the club since I had joined in the early 1960s, and walking into Celtic Park of a morning without Billy being around the place meant that the old ground would never be the same for me.

Jimmy Johnstone was released by Celtic that summer and I remember him telephoning me, distraught, after he had been given the news. The promise of a joint testimonial for Jimmy and me, against Manchester United at Celtic Park the following season, helped soften the blow.

Before that, Jimmy took the option of making a fresh start with the San Jose Earthquakes in the North American Soccer League – and decided that he wanted to take me with him. Kathryn and I were at a function in Glasgow in the early summer of 1975, and a few drinks had been consumed, when Jimmy suggested that I join him Stateside.

'Why don't you come?' he said. 'It will be great for the families to be together over there.' Jimmy was a gregarious guy among his own people but I think he was maybe a wee bit apprehensive about going to the USA and being surrounded by a whole lot of new faces at a football club he did not know.

This was only a couple of days before Jimmy was due to fly out to San Jose. I pointed out to him that I was still a Celtic player and committed fully to the club and could not just drop everything and go to play football in North America. Jimmy would not give up, though, and suggested that as it was the summer, the close season, Jock Stein might be amenable to the idea. I insisted it was not plausible. Early the following morning, I received a phonecall from a raging Jock Stein, asking me just what I was up to, wanting to go to play football in the USA. Jimmy, with his date of departure rushing towards him, had wasted no time in phoning Jock to ask permission for me to join him in his new adventure. I had to explain to Jock that the entire plan had been dreamed up by Jimmy and that I had had no part in it.

Another shock shuddered through Celtic that summer of 1975 when Jock Stein was involved in a terrible car crash that left him hovering between life and death. We were all hugely relieved that he survived. He was absent from the club for several months, though, leaving Sean Fallon to step in as caretaker manager. Kenny Dalglish had been told by Jock that he would be captain after Billy had decided to retire but when we returned to training that July, Sean announced that, as the manager was in hospital, there could be no firm decision taken on the captaincy and that, in the meantime, I was to take the armband. It was an enormous thrill to lead the team through the opening matches of that season.

After leaving hospital, Jock was told that he must rest in order to recuperate, and he did subsequently take a year out from hands-on management at the club. Being Jock, though, he could not keep away entirely and as early as 6 September 1975 he was back to watch our first ever home Premier Division match, against Dundee, a 4–0 victory in which I notched the first hat-trick in Scottish football's new top division. Jock's influence behind the scenes was soon being felt and, shortly afterwards, Kenny was named the captain of Celtic. Again, I was delighted because he was a great player, probably the best in the world at the time, and a good choice for captain.

We were in the European Cup-Winners' Cup that 1975–76 season, and defeated Valur Reykjavik and Boavista to reach a quarter-final against Sachsenring Zwickau of East Germany, a match in which my concerns over taking penalties were fully realised. To practise spot-kicks I would take a couple of canes up to my local park, set them apart as if they were goalposts, and spend time repeatedly sidefooting three or four balls as close as possible inside each of the canes. That was how I aimed to take my penalties – placing them as far away as possible from the goalkeeper by hitting the ball hard and low inside the post. It wasn't that unusual for me to practise in the park. I loved my job and I enjoyed training for it – if I was on the bench for a match, the following day I would go up there and put myself through a session to make up for the exercise that I had missed.

There were almost 50,000 inside Celtic Park for the first leg with Sachsenring Zwickau and when we were awarded a penalty midway through the first half, a sense of anticipation coursed through the crowd like a surge of electricity. Practising is all very well but, as I've said previously, nothing prepares you for the real thing. On my approach to the ball, I was planning to stroke it inside the post, just as I had done in my practice sessions, when I thought I noticed Jurgen Croy, the great German goalkeeper and a giant of a man, move slightly in the direction I was about to send the ball. That made me change my mind at the last second and strike the ball differently, less convincingly, allowing Croy to make the save. If I had slotted it inside the post, he would not have been able to save it because he was a big guy and he wouldn't have been able to get down quickly enough. As soon as you miss a penalty such as that one, you wish they would give you the ball back and let you take it again right away. Second time around you would have had your mind concentrated by the miss so would be less likely to worry about the crowd or anything else. If I had carried out in the match what I had been doing in training, I would have scored the penalty against Zwickau but, in a match situation, distractions are present that aren't there in training. That's why taking a penalty in a match situation is such a difficult thing.

The game ended 1–1. Over in Zwickau, I did not get the opportunity to make up for that missed penalty – I had a muscle injury and had to sit it out. Zwickau scored after five minutes and held on to their 1–0 lead to eliminate us from the competition. A few weeks later, we were playing Rangers at Celtic Park and the Celtic supporters began chanting 'St Etienne! St Etienne!' Rangers had been eliminated from the European Cup that season by the French club. I expected the Rangers supporters to respond to the chant but there was nothing but the loudest of silences from them. Sandy Jardine was marking me and I turned to him and said, 'Sandy, the only reason your lot aren't chanting anything back is because they can't pronounce Sachsenring Zwickau.'

It had been an interesting run in the European Cup-Winners' Cup and it was disappointing to lose to a side such as Zwickau, who were no better than we were. It did indicate, though, that we were just not good enough that year to progress all the way to the final and take the trophy. Zwickau, in the semi-final, were trounced by Anderlecht and sent out of the competition on a 5–0 aggregate. Early the following season, we were eliminated in the opening round of the UEFA Cup by Wisla Krakow of Poland, another eastern European side who were no great shakes. They, too, tumbled out of the competition in the following round. It showed that Celtic had by then lost something. We had slipped down the pecking order in European football. It was puzzling, in the middle of it, for me to try to put my finger on why we were now failing against sides who were clearly nothing special. Changes at the club had taken place so gradually that it was only when we suffered disquieting defeats such as those that reality was brought home emphatically – we were no longer quite as good as we had been.

Celtic's slackening of standards in the second half of the 1970s may have had much to do with the effects of the car crash slowing down Jock Stein. He returned as manager in the summer of 1976 and it was great to see him back but he no longer seemed to have quite the same zest, drive and spark as before, and he did not seem quite as desperate about winning and being the best. During the next couple of years, from 1976 to 1978, the team was chopped and changed a lot whereas previously Jock had characteristically been much more consistent in his team selections. A lot of players arrived at the club in those years who were short of the standard that Jock had previously set for his sides and who drifted in and out of the team. They were good players, of Premier Division standard, but they would not have looked out of place at Dundee United or Motherwell. Celtic need more than that – players with something extra, to make sure the club wins League titles and reaches Cup finals. Jock appeared to be neither sure of his best team nor confident in a number of the players whom he had introduced to the club. There seemed to be a lot of turmoil at the park. Things were not running as smoothly as they had done previously.

Celtic remained the cornerstone of my life and I was just as happy to be involved with the club as I always had been, even though the autumn of my career had arrived. I had turned 32 in August 1975 and, although I was the last of the Lisbon Lions at Celtic Park, there still wasn't the slightest thought in my mind of retirement. I remained extremely fit and as a mature player you are better equipped to cope with the demands of the game. Prior to matches, you are calmer – you are past the stage where over-excitement, stress or nerves might affect your game. I was back involved in almost every game that 1975–76 season but when you are in your early thirties a terrible phenomenon kicks in, a general consensus of opinion in the press that you are now nearly finished. In actuality, I was fitter than I had ever been but that does not deter those who want to pigeonhole you because of your age. Then, when I broke my leg in late 1976, aged 33, I was written off by the media and it was said that I would never again pull on a Celtic jersey. In contrast, I was telling myself that I would definitely play again and that my fitness would carry me through. The press didn't know me, didn't know how fit I felt. Journalists are really bad for glibly writing off a player on the grounds of age.

The injury was the most serious of my career and I can still picture exactly how it happened. I was through on Stewart Kennedy, the Rangers goalkeeper, that November night at Ibrox, had taken a touch to steer the ball to my right and was about to clip it into the goal when John Greig tackled me from the back and I went down. It was a particularly sore one but I did not think my leg was broken, and there was some compensation in knowing that I had won us a penalty. The referee had pointed immediately to the spot. The linesman, though, was flagging for offside and the Rangers players surrounded the referee and helped him to change his mind. There were many offsides given against me in my career – some right, some wrong – but I was convinced that one was wrong. I still don't understand how the linesman could have come to such a decision but, anyway, the referee bought it and Rangers restarted play as I was being helped off the park at the

Celtic end of the ground. I stamped on the leg a couple of times and signalled to the referee, who allowed me to come back on to the pitch. After a couple of minutes, I realised I had a fracture. Greigy came down to Saltcoats to visit me a couple of days later – just to make sure that the leg was broken.

The soft sands at Stevenston aided my rehabilitation enormously. They had plenty of 'give' and, once I began jogging lightly, they provided the perfect surface on which to run. Jock was great, allowing me to take things at my own pace. He trusted me enough to allow me to rest and train gently at home as I eased my way back. My first match back, five or six months later, was a reserve game against Ayr United at Somerset Park. 'Spud' Murphy, the Ayr full-back, a very good player but one who liked a kick at opposing wingers, came to see me beforehand and told me he would ease off when I was in his vicinity. I was grateful to him for that gesture. It rebounded on him slightly when I scored early on in the game but I had a laugh with Spud about it afterwards.

As part of my recovery programme, I participated in a memorable testimonial match for Tommy Smith, the Liverpool centre-back, in the spring of 1977. A Bobby Charlton select was to play Liverpool on the Friday evening of 27 May, only two nights after Liverpool had won the European Cup for the first time by defeating Borussia Moenchengladbach 3–1 in Rome. I travelled down to England and Bobby took me over to Liverpool for the pre-match meal. I didn't know any of the other players particularly well, only by reputation, so when it was time to get on the bus, I sat on my own, the only Scot among all these England internationals. Bobby Charlton wasn't there because he was driving his wife to the match. There I was, sitting about halfway down the aisle when, next thing, Bill Shankly, the former Liverpool manager, appeared.

'Did I see Bobby Lennox getting on this bus?' he inquired in his distinctive Ayrshire rasp, halfway between a growl and a greeting. I made my presence known to him and as he approached, he said, 'I thought I saw you.' He came and sat beside me all the way to the ground and that gave me quite a boost. He had come on to the bus, specifically seeking my company. I scored a hat-trick that night and thoroughly enjoyed the game.

For the trip back to Manchester, I got a lift with Bobby Charlton and his wife. We were chatting away when I asked him to give me the name of Celtic's most-capped international player. He suggested Billy McNeill, Tommy Gemmell, Jimmy Johnstone and one or two others. After a couple more attempts, he gave up and asked me to tell him the answer. 'Bobby Charlton,' I said. He had registered for Celtic to play in one game, a testimonial for Ron Yeats, and he was pretty proud when I offered him that statistic.

The broken leg restricted me to six first-team starts that 1976–77 season but, although I was fully fit for the beginning of the following season, I made even fewer first-team appearances, starting just five matches. It was clear that Jock had decided I was no longer part of his plans. Billy McNeill had become manager of Aberdeen in the summer of 1977, following Ally MacLeod's departure from Pittodrie for the Scotland manager's job, and early in 1978 I received a phonecall from Billy asking me if I would be keen on a move to the north-east. Arthur Graham, the outside-left, had left Aberdeen for Leeds United. Billy really sold me the idea of going to Aberdeen. I didn't even need to worry, he said, about buying a house because the chairman had plenty of properties in the city and that would take care of our accommodation. As it was obvious to me that I could not get into the Celtic team, I told Billy that I would go to Aberdeen. Billy conferred with his chairman and got back to me to tell me that he had also spoken to Jock and everything was arranged to take care of my transfer. It was then a case of waiting for Jock to notify me officially that I was to move to Aberdeen.

A few days passed, during which I heard nothing from Jock. Billy phoned me to ask what was happening. I told him that the manager hadn't spoken to me so Billy phoned Jock again. Within minutes, Billy was back on the phone to me.

'What's wrong with you?' he asked, irritatedly. 'Why don't you want to come to Aberdeen? Jock told me that he's already spoken to you about the move and that you don't want to come to Pittodrie.'

'Billy,' I replied, 'he has not said one word to me about it.'

Next morning at Celtic Park, Jock summoned me.

'I want a quick word with you, wee man,' he said. 'Listen, there are three American clubs in for you and it would be great for you and Kathyrn and the kids to get away to America for six months. You get away and enjoy your six months in the sunshine.'

Jock was full of enthusiasm for the idea and told me to come back the next morning to discuss it further with him, which I duly did.

'There's a new club starting up in Texas and I think they would be ideal for you,' Jock told me. 'There's a guy from the club arriving in Glasgow tonight and he'll be at the airport for you to meet him and talk things over.'

Jock held all the cards. I could not mention to him that I knew of the interest from Aberdeen because that would mean I had been 'tapped' – approached independently of my club – and as that was entirely illegal it could have brought serious repercussions for Billy McNeill and for me. It would mean I had been complicit in trying to arrange a transfer. Under SFA rules, once I had heard from Billy I should have gone to Jock and told him I had been approached by Aberdeen. I was supposed to notify my club of any illegal approaches for my services. All contact was supposed to be made initially between the clubs before the player was approached. Jock had used this rule, which was routinely abused, to cover himself when he had told Billy that he had spoken to me because Jock knew that if Billy or I were to challenge him on that, we would be exposing ourselves. Now, out of the blue, he was presenting me with the opportunity to try something special. It was clear to me that Jock was intent on blocking Billy's attempt to take me to Aberdeen and had decided that he would quickly move me elsewhere as a means of killing Billy's plan stone dead.

Jock never told me why he had not been playing me so much that 1977–78 season. I was as fit as ever and the leg that had been broken was probably stronger after coming back from the injury than it had been before. The team had won the League and Scottish Cup double in 1977 without me, so perhaps he felt I was superfluous to requirements and it was time to give younger guys a chance, but that's speculation on my part. Jock never clarified the matter to me. It does seem, though, that Billy's request for my transfer stirred Jock into action and he decided the USA was where I should go. Perhaps the thought of me facing Celtic with Aberdeen or another Scottish club and doing some damage to Celtic made him think that it would be best for him to ship me across the Atlantic. If I had done consistently well in what was a very good Aberdeen side – one that was doing much better than Celtic at that time – it would maybe have caused people to question Jock and his judgement in letting me go.

Timo Liekoski was the man I was to meet in the Excelsior Hotel at Glasgow Airport that evening in spring 1978, representing Houston Hurricane, newly of the North American Soccer League (NASL). He was a chatty, forthcoming fellow, a Finn who had married an American and settled in the States. The NASL had been formed a decade earlier but it was really taking off in the late 1970s, by which time greats such as Pelé and Franz Beckenbauer were among its stars. In 1977, a record crowd of 77,000 had attended an NASL game featuring the New York Cosmos. America seemed like the place to be and a lot of British players aspired to a move to the USA.

Within 20 minutes of being in Timo's company, I liked the guy, and Kathryn liked him, too. I agreed, then and there, to take the family to Texas and play for his club during the American soccer season, which stretched over the summer months. Houston Hurricane had been the final new franchise awarded in the NASL that year and Timo had been given less than three months to find a team, so he was probably pretty pleased with my swift agreement to his proposition. Two other American clubs were keen to sign me but I never discovered who they were because I had decided to commit myself to Houston. I knew I would be happy there after talking to Timo. Within a week of Billy instigating the conversation about me going to Aberdeen, I was en route to America. Billy was not disappointed in me – although he maybe was in Jock – because he knew there was nothing much I could have done to make a move to Aberdeen happen.

The day on which Jock informed me about the possibility of the move to the USA was also the one on which I sat for longest in his office. I must have been in there for about an hour and it was actually quite a sad occasion. We talked about what we had gone through together at the club over the years and how it would help me to go away and make a new start in the sunshine, enjoying my football. It was sad because I was the last link to the great team he had inspired after his arrival at the club more than a decade earlier, but although it was a wrench to leave, I had no choice in the matter. The manager had told me it was time to go and I knew I wasn't going to get back into the team. A new world and a new experience were on the horizon.

A week remained before I was due to fly out to join the Hurricane in March 1978, and on the day before I was due to depart, Celtic had a reserve fixture against Motherwell for which I was selected. We were 3–1 down before I scored twice to make it 3–3. Scoring those goals meant that I left Celtic in high spirits. It was a low-key final appearance in the green-and-white hoops after 17 years of unbroken service for the club, but that was how players tended to leave Celtic under Jock Stein and, in the end, I had proved to be no exception to that rule.

CHAPTER 11

THE STEIN SCENE

Jock Stein ruled with iron-cold calculation and control so you feared him and that fear was at the root of everything he achieved with his players. He could laugh, joke, sing and be playful but even in his lighter moments, it paid to be slightly wary when you were around him. Still, if Jock sat down beside you in the dressing room, gripped you on the shoulder with one of his shovel-like hands and told you how well you were doing for him, you would walk away feeling like a million dollars. He liked to give guys a lift from time to time. I remember standing inside the tunnel area at Celtic Park one day in the late 1960s along with Bertie Auld, Bobby Murdoch and two or three other boys when Jock strolled up, started to chat and then said to the boys, 'Who would we miss most from this team if he was unable to play?' The boys offered one or two suggestions before Jock said, 'Bobby Lennox.' I felt ten feet tall when he said that. Weeks after he said something like that, you would still be walking on air. Conversely, he would be sending a message to the other guys present that they could maybe look at improving their game. He knew exactly when to praise you, when to criticise you and, just as importantly, when to leave you alone.

You never knew where you stood with Jock. When we reached the League Cup final of 1971, in which we faced Partick Thistle, I had scored four times en route, including one in a 3–0 victory over Rangers at Ibrox. We arrived at Hampden for the match with Thistle, strolled into the dressing room and when Jock announced the team, I wasn't included. Only one substitute was allowed and he named Jim Craig. I really couldn't believe it. As Jock finished reading out the team, I placed the match programme that I had been holding on the nearest table. Jimmy Johnstone and Bobby Murdoch came over and told me how they couldn't believe I wasn't playing. I left the dressing room, really disappointed, and watched the match from the stand along with Billy McNeill, who was injured.

After Thistle had walked off with their astonishing 4–1 victory and the Cup, Billy and I turned up in the dressing room minutes after the final whistle, to find Jock ranting and raving. If I thought I would be excused, given my absence from the team, I was wrong. He turned on me, saying, 'Your attitude before the game was stinking. Your pals should have been concentrating on the game but you distracted them by throwing magazines about and then having them round about you.' It wasn't true. I hadn't thrown the match programme down in a temper or with bad grace. I had laid it on the massage table, that was all. It wasn't in any sense a gesture but that moment had stuck in his mind. His interpretation of what had gone on was wrong but his reaction was typical of the man. He would get utterly infuriated after defeats and he would chew over any detail that had displeased him and which he thought might have contributed to being beaten. It was hard being on the end of it but that was Jock and he was right much more often than he was wrong.

On a happier occasion against Thistle, Jock had been equally quirky. It was 1–1 at the end of the first half of a match played at

Right: Jimmy Johnstone, Tommy Gemmell, Me, Bobby Murdoch, Willie Wallace and Lou Macari at the opening of Bobby's Bar in Saltcoats in 1970.

Bottom left: In action against Eddie Gray of Leeds in the European Cup semi-final, 15 April 1970.

Bottom right: Celebrating scoring against Rangers in the 1971 Cup final.

SCOTTISH DAILY RECORD AND SUNDAY MAIL

ACTION IMAGES

HERALD & TIMES

HERALD & TIMES

Scoring on my debut for Scotland against Northern Ireland, Hampden Park, 16 November 1966.

And making headlines in Denmark scoring for Scotland, 16 October 1968.

Beating Gordon Banks to put Scotland 2–0 up at Wembley, April 1967.

The whole team celebrating that goal. From left: Eddie McCreadie, Billy Bremner, John Greig, Me, Denis Law, Ron McKinnon, Willie Wallace, Jim Baxter, Tommy Gemmell, Jim McCalliog.

Right: Rest and recuperation from my broken leg, at home with Kathryn...

ACTION IMAGES

... and on the beach at Seamill with Jimmy.

Right: Arriving onto the pitch with Jimmy – as Sir Matt Busby looks on – at our joint testimonial against Manchester United in 1976.

Staff Photo

Bobby Lennox (11) of the Houston Hurricane takes the ball away from San Diego's Axel Neumann during the first overtime period at San Diego Stadium last ni[illegible] Hurricane won the shootout, 1-0.

Above: In action for Houston Hurricane against San Diego's Axel Neuman.

Right: Enjoying the pool in the Texan sunshine with Gillian, Kathryn, Jeff and Gary, May 1978.

SCOTTISH DAILY EXPRESS

SNS GROUP

Left: Challenging Rangers' Ally Dawson in my final competitive match for Celtic; the Scottish Cup final against Rangers at Hampden Park, 10 May 1980 which we won 1–0. A good way to sign off.

Right: With my MBE after the ceremony at Holyrood, 1981.

Below: On the other side of the fence, as reserve-team coach with first-team players Paul McStay, Tommy Burns, Roy Aitken and Frank McAvennie in 1988.

HERALD & TIMES

Above: With some exalted company in 2002, on being named by supporters as one of the greatest-ever Celtic players. From left: Me, Henrik Larsson, Kenny Dalglish, Paul McStay, Jimmy Johnstone, Bertie Auld, Billy McNeill, Tommy Gemmell, Danny McGrain, Ronnie Simpson.

Right: My grandchildren Calvin, Zack and Nicole at the Scottish Football Museum Hall of Fame, into which I was inducted in 2006.

Below: Golfing with Stevie Chalmers, Billy McNeill and Bertie Auld.

GOAL

BOBBY LENNOX
Celtic

One of the speediest forwards in Scotland. A real flyer, Lennox helps to create many of Celtic's goals, but also has a knack for turning up in the right spot when a scoring opportunity arises

BOBBY LENNOX
CELTIC

JHFW

BOBBY LENNOX
Celtic

Bobby Lennox
CELTIC

Firhill in mid-October 1967, and Jock gave me a pasting at half-time. I had been through on the goalkeeper a couple of times but he had dived at my feet and had snatched the ball away, so Jock forcefully told me that I had to be more clinical and that if the goalkeeper dived at my feet, I shouldn't be frightened to go right through him. By the end we were 5–1 winners and I had scored every one of our four second-half goals but Jock never said a word to me after the match. The rest of the boys couldn't believe that he had given me such a dressing-down at the interval but had not remarked on my goalscoring achievement during the second 45 minutes. All he had done was give the team a general, 'Well done.'

Half-time was when Jock was often at his most decisive and effective. Substitutions had been introduced to Scottish football during the 1966–67 season, early on in Jock's time at Celtic. We were playing Airdrieonians one day, shortly after the rule was established. Initially, just one substitution was allowed and a player could be replaced only if he had been injured. I went in for half-time during that encounter with Airdrie knowing that I wasn't having a particularly good game and Jock said to me that early in the second half he would give me the nod and I was to go down as if I was injured so that they could take the opportunity to replace me. I duly received the signal, so the next time the ball was played through to me, I ran and jumped between two Airdrie defenders, flicked the ball on and then took a tumble and went down as if I had been hurt. The ball went through to Joe McBride who ran on to it and scored to make it 1–0 to Celtic. Neilly Mochan, our trainer, ran on to the park and began attending to me. I was groaning away, pretending to be injured, and Neilly said to the referee, 'We'll give him a few more minutes and see how he gets on with his injury.' Three minutes later, the ball got played to me and I went through to score and make it 2–0 so the word came from the dugout just to leave it. Then, in the final minute, I scored to make it 3–0. Jock, as always, had been ready to adapt to changing circumstances.

If he could be canny with the substitution rule when it was introduced, the new development in the game also offered another insight into Jock Stein the man. Once substitutions became optional, and not only in the event of injury, if you were the sub and the crowd started chanting your name, demanding that you be brought on, you might as well just have packed up your gear and headed home. There was no way Jock was going to allow anyone to infringe on his right to pick and choose whom he fielded and whom he kept on the sidelines. He may have greatly appreciated the Celtic support but he was the man in charge and everyone had to be reminded of it.

Jock constantly chivvied us to maintain the standards he expected from Celtic footballers. After any cup final, it was accepted practice for players to be allowed to keep, as a souvenir, the strip that they had worn in the match. With Celtic, most of the time, that meant we would be keeping a winning team's jerseys. On those occasions when we did lose finals, though, one or two players would still want to keep their strip and if Jock saw them stashing away a Celtic jersey in their bag after a defeat he would go absolutely loopy. 'You want to keep strips to show your children and grandchildren you accept second prizes, do you?' he would roar at them, like a bulldog with a sore throat. 'If that's what you're wanting, you shouldn't be here, at this club. Get those bloody strips back in the hamper.' He'd grab them off the players and, if he could, I think he would have burned those jerseys there and then. I'd throw my strip straight down on the floor on the occasion of defeats, never in my bag.

You never had to try to work out what Jock Stein was thinking because he told you, right to your face. On those occasions when his temper was up, it was simply mayhem – mental. If you were the one on whom he was fixed, he would just eyeball you and get stuck right in. If the whole team were the subject of his ire, he'd stand in the middle and shout and bawl. He filled the whole dressing room when he was angry. You didn't want to see it, I can assure you. Most of it would be constructive. It would be about what you should and shouldn't have done and how you weren't working hard enough in certain areas of the park. He would get more and more uptight if a game wasn't going our way. It never felt as though he was going to become physically violent so when I say he ruled by fear, the thing that concerned you was whether he was going to leave you out of the team for a month or two. It was as well that he never threatened to lift his hands because he had a big left paw and if he had used it, he would have broken your face. His bulk did, though, help to make him an imposing figure.

One miserable, wet evening at Celtic Park we were playing St Johnstone and leading 1–0 at half-time. Although I had scored our goal, I had also missed a couple of chances and when we came into the dressing room, he laid right into me for the way I had passed up those opportunities. After that, he turned to the rest of the team and said, 'I've left him without a name but at least he's willing to get into the box to miss two or three chances – the rest of you aren't getting into the box at all.' He then laid right into everybody else. We ended up winning 4–0. So he was hard but fair and he was clever with it. When he gave you stick, you tended to deserve it.

If you made a mistake in the opening ten minutes of a match, you knew that no matter how the match had gone, Jock would have a go at you about it when you walked into the dressing room at half-time. He wasn't the type of manager to remember only the last thing that had happened in a match, and nor did he consider it worthless going over something that had happened early on in a game. That could also work in your favour – if you had done something well in the first few minutes, he would tell you how pleased he had been to see it and that it was the type of thing he wanted to see all the time. You were well aware of his presence in the dugout and as soon as the half-time whistle went, you immediately started thinking, 'What did we do right? What did we do wrong?' You knew he would have something to say about it. That was unless you were winning convincingly, in which case the big face would be all smiles, he'd be rubbing his hands together and saying, 'You're doing great, lads. Keep it going.'

If you had been playing well for four or five games, he would come to you and give you some really good, quiet encouragement to keep it going. Conversely, if you were going through a period when you were getting positive press, he would come to you and say, 'By the way, don't think you're playing as well as these guys think. I'm the man you have to please.' He could bring you down as easily as he could praise you.

One pre-season, we had just returned from our summer break when I got a rash inside my groin. I thought that it was blisters but it stayed for a few days and when I went to the doctor he told me that I had shingles down my leg. It was tended to but I was unable to train for a couple of weeks. It cleared up just as the season was beginning. On the morning I returned to training, Jock whipped me. He gave me a really tough session. Afterwards, he told me to go and get my lunch at the Beechwood on the south side of Glasgow and then come back to the park for another hard session. I was dreading it but while I was at the restaurant, a call came through from Jock, telling me to go home, have an hour in bed and then put on a shirt and tie and come back to Celtic Park for a match with Ayr United reserves that evening.

I scored a goal in the first half and really threw myself into the game. With about 25 minutes to go, I got the order to come off. My legs were hanging off me by then and I was wondering whether he was happy with me, having substituted me with a fair amount of the match still to go. As I headed towards the bench, I saw him leaving his seat in the stand. The thing about Jock was that you never knew what was going to happen. He came down and as I walked towards him, the big hand shot out in congratulation. He shook my hand and said, 'We whipped you in training this morning and some guys would have taken it easy in the match tonight. You didn't. You were great. I'm delighted with you.' Then he went back up to his seat. I stood there for a while, so content at receiving such acclaim. I'd be ready to do anything for him on the park after something like that.

When Jock arrived, the squad consisted of very good players, ready and waiting to be moulded into a team, but it was Jock who transformed us. We had quick players, skilled players, good tacklers. The elements were there and he was the alchemist who made them into something magical. He would be out training with us almost every day although, with the limp from the bad ankle that had forced him to quit football as a player, he couldn't actually join in games or go running. That limp of his was quite pronounced and when he got irritated, it would become even more visible, and he would clench his left fist. You knew when he was angry. Willie Fernie, the coach, or Neilly Mochan, the trainer, would take the training and Jock would be in the middle of the field. He'd get the goalies warmed up and when you were participating in shooting exercises, someone would play the ball in to him, he'd lay it off and you would have a shot at goal. If the original ball in to him was not so good, he would boot it away and tell the offending player to fetch it – he could be a big midden. Everything had to be right. 'How can I pass the ball to him if you can't pass it to me properly in the first place?' he would bellow, bristling with anger at the man who had mis-hit the pass.

Sometimes, Jock would be busy in the office when it was time for training to begin so he wouldn't be there when Neilly was taking the warm-up, but as soon as we saw Jock's car pulling up, we would put a bit of extra effort into what we were doing. That was nothing to do with Neilly – we loved Neilly and would train our backsides off for him but no matter how quickly we were jogging or sprinting we always seemed to be able to find an extra yard from somewhere whenever the gaffer's car loomed into sight.

Celtic, under Jock, were a good team, a fine ball-playing team, and that sometimes disguises just how fit we were. Although Jock liked to use the ball a lot in training, he never lost sight of the need to keep us in prime condition so that we would have the wherewithal to use our skills. If no midweek game was scheduled, he would send us on to the running track on a Tuesday and absolutely hammer us. We worked our socks off – over hurdles, in and out of sticks, 12-minute runs, sprints. If Jock told you to do a 50-yard sprint and people were slowing up after 45 yards, he would make you do it again. He'd say that slowing up was cheating and if you were cheating in training, you would cheat on a Saturday. Those sessions were tough when you were being put through them – and beforehand, we would all look at each other, knowing just how demanding and difficult the following two hours were going to be – but it was always great to finish off and lie in the bath afterwards with a real sense of satisfaction at having come through such a test of endurance. That fitness work translated into us having the ability to win a lot of games late on in the proceedings. Even in the final 20 minutes, we would still be taking the game to the opposition at a ferocious pace. We never came up against a team that was fitter than us.

It is true to say that Jock was a great motivator but he wouldn't spend ages talking to players on a one-to-one basis. He would speak to you individually from time to time but mostly he addressed the players in a group, telling us what we should anticipate from opponents and expect from each other. Whatever Jock said, we treated as gospel. If he told us to do something, that was what we did. I don't think he was often wrong but when anything did go awry, he would be of the opinion that it was because the players hadn't carried out his instructions on the pitch.

As with Sir Robert Kelly, Jock went out of his way at social functions, and our Christmas dinner, to make the players' wives feel welcome and comfortable. He would be highly attentive and would know all about everyone's family. We were all young guys and it was easy for him to keep track of who was getting married, and the arrivals of our children. One day, I remember, we were having a light training session behind one of the goals at Celtic Park when Jock announced through the Tannoy system, in a kindly, lilting voice, 'John Clark has just become the father of a bouncing baby girl . . .' That was a side of Jock that the public didn't often see.

The friendly face that Jock showed to our wives did not, however, extend to him welcoming the women to the ground when there was a match to be played. That was something to which he was resolutely opposed. He would never arrange for the women to have seats at a game. If Kathryn or any of the other wives did decide to come to a match, even a European Cup tie, at Celtic Park, there would be nothing provided for them in terms of hospitality. Afterwards, they would have to remain outside, in pouring rain if necessary, until we came out with the keys of the car. The lads would have the keys because we'd have travelled to the ground, left our cars there and then got on the coach to Seamill for our pre-match preparation. Half an hour or 45 minutes after the game, I'd exit Celtic Park to find Kathryn standing there in the rain, with her brolly up for protection against the elements. She never complained about it. Celtic Park, in the 1960s and 1970s, was almost entirely devoid of anything approaching facilities for extending hospitality to visitors but some shelter would have been nice for the girls. Children were also unwelcome in the vicinity of the dressing room.

Jock would say, 'If you were a plumber, would your wife come and stand watching you while you installed somebody's sink? If you were a joiner, would she come and watch you fit a window?' We were at our work, to Jock's way of thinking, and that meant there was no place for women. He also felt that if you accommodated women, they would start to bitch – one would complain that another was in a better seat and so on. We players felt, even then, that they should at least have been let in the front door after a big game, if only to allow them to stand inside out of the rain.

It would have been difficult to approach Jock Stein on a matter such as that, although Jock was never a remote figure to the players, because you had to watch when you approached him. You would have to judge when the time was right if you wanted to speak to him and it could end up messily if your judgement was slightly off. If a player asked to see Jock and he was not in the mood for it, he would simply tell the guy to go away, not always politely.

I was always wary of approaching him about anything. I couldn't even pluck up the courage to confront him when I felt I was being edged out. On one of the rare occasions on which I did go into his office, it was because I knew I hadn't been playing well. The goals had dried up completely for me, so I chapped on his door.

'Boss,' I said, 'I'm really struggling.'

'You are, actually,' he replied. 'I'm glad you came in because I'm leaving you out of the team tomorrow. At least you know that you're not doing it and aren't kidding yourself.' The next day, I was sitting in the stand and the team banged in seven goals . . .

We prepared for the League Cup final of October 1969 against St Johnstone at the Marine Hotel in Troon. My ankle was sore, although I was still hopeful of making the match, but after a light session beside the golf course I knew that I was not ready. I told Neilly Mochan that I was struggling. We went up to see Jock, who was sitting in his bath, and he was full of praise for me having told him the day before the final that I would be unfit. He knew it was not an easy thing for a professional to do – you're always tempted to believe that you can get away with carrying an injury into a game, especially a big game. Jock told me he was delighted with my professionalism and honesty on that occasion and that there would be plenty of other finals for me to enjoy in the future.

Our pay was improved by Jock on his arrival at the club but it didn't improve too much after that. We were on about £40 per week when we won the European Cup, which was quite good money at that time in comparison to the average working man. It made us comfortable without being particularly well off. The bonuses for a good run in Europe were also fairly handsome, increasing generously with each round, all the way up to £1500 for winning the trophy in 1967, which compared favourably to the £1000 that each member of the England squad had received for winning the World Cup the year before. As time went on, though, we became more and more aware that players at clubs in England, less successful clubs than Celtic, were on better terms than us. At Fulham in the early 1960s, Johnny Haynes, a great player, was famously the first in Britain to earn £100 per week, but Fulham never won anything. A lot of players with similar clubs in England were on similar money during that decade. English players' pay continued to increase into the 1970s and if any of us had left to go to England, we would have doubled our basic wages, at least. On the other hand, we were earning good bonuses through winning consistently, so that brought our pay up quite a bit and kept me, for one, quite happy.

I think Billy went to Jock a couple of times to ask for some improvement in our basic pay but we never obtained any gargantuan increases. Most of us who were at Celtic Park when Jock joined, played for the club for such a long time because we were Celtic supporters. Had we been somewhere else, we would have thought sooner about moving on and cashing in on our commercial value as European Cup winners. We would maybe have moved to England and to less prestigious clubs for better rewards.

Two or three times, I was actually sounded out by other clubs who wanted me to move but their overtures never interested me at all. I could have gone to Tottenham Hotspur, Everton or Arsenal during the late 1960s but I was never even slightly tempted to do so. Tottenham, a fine side that included players of the calibre of Terry Venables, Dave Mackay, Alan Gilzean and Pat Jennings, tried to tempt me to north London. They talked to me about it while Celtic were on tour in North America in 1966, after we had won our first Scottish League title. We played Tottenham three times on that tour, beating them 1–0 in Toronto, where I scored, and 2–1 in San Francisco, where I scored the winner. Vancouver was the venue for our third meeting and we and the Tottenham party were all staying at the same hotel. On the day of the match, one or two of the Celtic boys and I crammed into the elevator, which was already quite full, only to realise, once in, that we were squashed up against some of the Tottenham players. I found myself face to face with Alan Mullery, who had been marking me in our first two matches. His team-mates started to give him stick at finally being able to get close to me. Mullers, staring at me from a couple of inches away, muttered, 'This will be the farthest you'll be away from me all night. I will not let you out of my sight tonight.'

After ten minutes of the match, I had scored our goal. We drew 1–1, Tottenham equalising with the final kick of the ball. Afterwards, two or three of their players asked me how I'd fancy going to White Hart Lane. They'd obviously been told to sound me out. I told them there was nothing doing.

Everton contacted me repeatedly to try to persuade me to go to Goodison Park. On one occasion Celtic met up with the Everton squad on tour in Israel, and Alan Ball, their midfield player, Jimmy Johnstone and I had a really good night out. When we got back to the hotel, Alan spied Jock Stein hoving into view in the lobby.

'Our manager would kiss his arse if he would let you join Everton,' Alan said to me, within Jock's hearing. 'Harry Catterick loves him.'

'Aye, well, he'll no' be joining you,' Jock grunted, as he was passing, Then he walked off.

It was always good to know that clubs of a high stature wished to sign me but I was where I wanted to be. I was in the Celtic first team, I was scoring goals and we were winning. Why go somewhere else? I was never tempted by any of these offers.

The funniest incident of all in relation to clubs hustling for my services came during the summer of 1977, when we were on a tour to Australia and the Far East. My first full game for Celtic since suffering that broken leg in late 1976 was against the Singapore national team. There were 70,000 inside the stadium, we won 6–1 and I played pretty well. On the evening after the match, we all went out for dinner and afterwards waited for our coach in a lounge where the television was showing highlights of the previous evening's match. I sat down on a wee two-seater couch and Jock plonked himself down beside me. The other boys were all sitting and standing around. The co-commentator on the match was Bertie Mee, who had been the double-winning manager of Arsenal in 1971, and the action switched to a shot of me letting the ball run through my legs, turning the right-back, taking the ball along the byline and cutting it back for Tommy Burns to hit into the net. Bertie Mee said, 'And there's Bobby Lennox, just back from a broken leg – what a great servant he's been to Celtic. In 1967, I bid a record British transfer fee for him but it came to nothing – Celtic just rejected it.' It was the first I had heard of it. I knew nothing of a record fee being bid for me, although Arsenal had tapped me at the time.

It should have been an embarrassing situation for Jock, having it publicly revealed that he had not told me about the possibility of such a momentous move, but all he did was stand up and say, 'Andiamo,' which meant, 'Let's go.' It had become his catchphrase inside the club down the years. 'Andiamo,' he said, 'let's get on the coach.' All the boys were hee-hawing and laughing but Jock said nothing about it to me and he never broached the subject at any point in all the years after that. Even when all the boys were kidding on about me being a wee Gunner and all that sort of thing, Jock never cracked a light.

The bids for my services from England did provide me with a certain feeling of security in the game. There was never any desire on my part to leave Celtic or Saltcoats but, with all those clubs keen on securing my services, it was in the back of my mind that if Jock at any time did decide to dispense with me, I would not have too much trouble finding myself another club – and a good club at that. When you're playing in Scotland, you tend to think that you're a bit out of the way and that you don't get the recognition that you are perhaps due. That wasn't entirely the case. On holiday in Majorca one year, someone shouted to me, 'Hello Bobby, how are you doing?' It was Joe Harvey, the manager of Newcastle United. We had a good blether, so it was obvious that these people did know and recognise players who were doing well in Scotland.

Jock had an obsessive need to keep tabs on everybody. He wanted to know exactly what was going on all the time. If we were in a room, say at Seamill, he would take a seat that afforded him a perfect view of every nook and cranny. He had to be able to see the door, the window, the bar, to make sure he saw who was coming in and out and what everybody was doing. If you were sitting in the best place, he would say, 'Just move yourself a bit and let me sit in there.' He wouldn't stand on ceremony.

Jock enjoyed seeing the players relax and liked being in among them but he was always wary about the boys drinking and he had a good idea who would try to bend or break the rules in relation to that. Sometimes, when we had been told we weren't allowed a drink, one or two of the boys would order a vodka and Coke in the belief that Jock would be duped into thinking they were merely refreshing themselves with soft drinks and nothing else. Jock, though, would wander into the room, go up to them and say, 'I'm feeling a wee bit thirsty tonight – give me a sip of your Coke.' He'd lift the glass to his lips, take a taste and start spluttering with rage at the miscreants in question. On other occasions, he would take a sip and it would indeed be a non-alcoholic drink. Eventually, the boys became as fly as he was. If they wanted a drink, they would have one in a place where they could be sure he wouldn't see them.

Jock had a deep and genuine hatred of drink. He loathed it with real and severe feeling. He had no time for it at all – not even in moderation. It would outrage him even to think about one of his players having a pint of beer. Needless to say, he was a teetotaller. He never drank – he thought it was a bad habit. Sometimes, the boys would sneak off and have a few pints out of his sight and maybe go too far whereas I feel that if Jock had been slightly more liberal in his attitude towards drink and had said to them that they could have a beer at the bar, they would have stuck to that. They'd have been fine and they probably would have been more restrained in the knowledge that they were in the presence of the manager. He hated seeing any of his players standing with a pint in front of him, although he would know that if he gave the players permission to go out for an hour they would invariably take the opportunity to have a few drinks. That did not prevent him glowering on the players' return and scolding them, 'Been drinking, have you, eh?' Jock wanted his players to be above drinking. He wanted them to be above everything – well disciplined and professional.

I remember one evening on which he did, out of character, actually say to the boys, 'Go to the bar and have a drink.' They had been there for just a few minutes when he came bowling up and started laying into them. 'Look at the state of you, standing there drinking.' The boys reminded him gently that he had told them that they could have a drink. 'Ach, never mind that,' he replied. 'Look at the state of you there.' He more or less told them to get to their rooms, as if they had breached his code of discipline without his permission.

The Celtic team of that time has been labelled with the reputation of being a hard-drinking one. It is true that some of the boys liked a good bevvy but, on the whole, they drank at the right times, on a Saturday night or on a Sunday – not on the Tuesday night or Friday night before a match. One guy who wasn't a drinker under Jock Stein during the early years was Jimmy Johnstone. When we won the European Cup, neither he nor I had a drink afterwards. There's a great photograph of the two of us wearing sombreros and holding two bottles of champagne after the game in Lisbon but those bottles were empty. We had been handed them as props for the photo.

Utter ruthlessness was another of Jock's hallmarks. One Saturday in late November 1972, we were winning 3–2 at Falkirk when, with a couple of minutes to go, I collected the ball close to the touchline in front of the dugouts and was immediately confronted by Stuart Kennedy, the Falkirk right-back and a very quick and skilful player. I was dragging the ball with my right foot, waiting for the right moment to go past Stuart, when the booming voice of Jock Stein assaulted my eardrums. 'Go up the line! Go up the line!' he was yelling. Well, Stuart Kennedy was a clever player. I knew he was hearing this and maybe expecting me to follow my manager's wishes, so I opted to cut inside. It proved the wrong thing to do – Stuart nicked the ball off me and Falkirk took it away up the park. We still won 3–2 but at time up the first thing Jock Stein did was haul me over the coals.

In the dressing room, I remember, he called me all the names under the sun for my disobedience. Then, in that calmly terrible way he had about him when he was angry, as if he resented having to waste valuable breath on you, he said to me, 'You were told to do something and you failed to carry it out. If you can't listen to instructions, you won't be in the first team for the next two or three weeks.' He was as good as his word – I was missing from the team for the following three matches, including the League Cup semi-final with Aberdeen and the final with Hibernian. Although I returned to action as a substitute three weeks later, it was another two months before I was in the starting line-up.

When Jock made a decision, I doubt if he gave any thought to sparing a player's feelings. I imagine his thoughts were entirely connected to the team as a whole and what was best for it. He would not always be happy just to have won, either, unless we had done so in some style. When we defeated Rangers, it was different. He would always have a big smile on his face then, and it did not matter how we had played in achieving that feat. That was one match that was out on its own so a victory was a victory. He would maybe have a wee go at you for not playing well but his irritation would be tempered by the fact that we had won.

Against any other team, if the performance hadn't been up to scratch, he would not be happy, win or lose. We'd troop into the dressing room and he would lay into us. 'That's not the way we play,' he would say. 'We get it down on the ground and we pass it quicker and we move off it quicker and we defend better and we push up to the halfway line . . .'

Often, before a match, he would say, 'There are forty thousand people out there today. They've worked hard all week and saved their money to come and watch you, so you had better entertain them today.' Supporters were really, really important to him. At cup finals he'd say, 'These guys are here today, full of hope. They've got to go to their work on Monday morning and I want them there full of pride in their team. It's OK for you. You only have to face each other on Monday morning – those guys have to face their work-mates and I want them facing them with their heads held high.'

The rivalry with Rangers engaged Jock intensely and he would use all means at his disposal to gain an advantage in games with them. If we were playing at Hampden, he would maybe tell us to wait around in the foyer until the Rangers lads disembarked from their coach and then to greet them and ask them how they were. We were to be as friendly as possible. Next time we played them at Hampden, he would lock us in the dressing room and tell us that when the referee knocked on the door for the teams to come out we weren't even to look at the Rangers players as we walked towards the pitch and that not one of us should say a word to any of them. Every time it was different. Another of his favourites was to wait until the Rangers players were standing in the tunnel while we were still in the dressing room. The referee would chap on the door and say, 'Rangers are ready.' Jock would say, 'OK, thanks.' He'd then close the door and say to us, 'Right, everybody sit down for a couple of minutes.' The referee would be chivvying him but he would just keep them standing for a bit longer.

He would perform a similar trick when we travelled to face the other Glasgow clubs – Clyde and Partick Thistle. Shawfield and Firhill would always be packed to capacity when we came calling, with most of the crowd comprising Celtic supporters. The referee would knock on the door to tell Jock that the other team were ready but Jock would hold us back until they were on the park. He would say to us, 'Right, we'll now get a big Celtic cheer.' We'd trot on to the field and the opposition would find themselves engulfed, at their own ground, in this huge roar for Celtic, immediately overturning their advantage in being at home. It was radical at the time to employ such thinking. He would do anything to upset the opposition, and to keep them on tenterhooks.

Jock Stein was a very brusque man. He could be dour at times, or he could be full of the joys of spring. I think he was actually a really shy man if he wasn't among his own people, working-class people, with whom he felt most comfortable. If everything was going well, he had the most expressively happy face. If things weren't going well, he was the last person on earth you wanted to see. He could be friendly but there was no way in this world that any of his players would be allowed to pass the time chatting to him about this or that in his office, and there was no question of Jock seeking advice on tactics or anything else from his players.

During his final two or three years at the club, although he had some good players, Jock didn't have half as good a team as he had during the late 1960s, and I think he found it difficult to be no longer dominating Scottish football with Celtic in the manner to which he had become accustomed. I'm proud to say that I was the only player to be there the whole time Jock Stein was manager. I served him from his first season to his last. He must have known a half-decent player when he saw one, mustn't he?

CHAPTER 12

HOUSTON CALLING

A number of European players regarded it as a breeze to play soccer for a club in the USA and that had me in trouble even before I had kicked a ball for Houston Hurricane. I was lining up for my debut, away to Los Angeles Aztecs at the Orange Bowl in Pasadena, facing Charlie Cooke, the former Aberdeen, Dundee, Chelsea and Scotland winger. Charlie greeted me cheerily and said how pleased he was to see me. I was on the left wing for us and Charlie was on the right wing for the Aztecs.

'I'm really looking forward to playing out here,' I said to him. 'It should be a great wee holiday as well.' Immediately, Charlie was on my case.

'What do you mean, "a great holiday"?' he fired back at me, raising his voice, clearly riled. I had to calm him down and persuade him that I was not treating the entire enterprise lightly. I had merely meant that, along with the football, it would be a nice change for the family to be out in the sunshine of Texas all summer.

After the game, Charlie explained that I had touched a raw nerve. He told me that he was aware that I would be completely professional in my approach to soccer in America but that a lot of players from

Europe had been joining clubs in the North American Soccer League and taking it extra easy, and that irritated players such as Charlie, who was determined to do all he could to help association football establish itself as a serious sport in the USA. I admired Charlie's attitude. I thought he was one of the great ambassadors for Britain in America.

We lost a goal in the opening minute of that match in LA. Ron Davies, the Welsh international, headed the Aztecs in front and in the first minute of the second half he repeated the feat to make it 2–0. We pulled one back and then equalised late in the game. I had heard all about how drawn matches in the NASL were settled by shootouts in which a player ran from a 35-yard line, one on one against the goalkeeper, and was allowed to take a certain number of steps with the ball before shooting. I said to Timo Liekoski, our coach, 'I'm knackered after the game and all this travelling. I'd rather not take part in this shootout.' I had arrived in Texas only three days earlier and had met the players on the Friday, before flying out to LA on the Saturday and playing on the Sunday.

'That's fine, Bobby,' Timo said, 'but before there is a shootout, we play thirty minutes of extra time to see if we can get a winner.' I panted through that and, with no further scoring, the match duly went to a shootout. The Americans must have a winner.

Keeping goal for our side that opening day of the season was Dario Maranovic, a Yugoslav who had arrived at the club even later than me. He had flown directly from Europe to Los Angeles on the morning of the match and he spoke no English. Radomir Stefanovic, our Yugoslavian centre-half, was faced with the task of explaining to Dario all about how the 35-yard shootout, a concept unique to American soccer, operated. It seemed unlikely we would come through the shootout successfully but Dario, who had been at fault for both of the goals we had conceded, came into his own. Every time the opposing player took possession of the ball and began his run at goal, our goalkeeper would simply launch himself at them, springing from his goal and whisking the ball away from them. His efforts won the shootout for us and we got six points for winning the game and two points for scoring two goals during the 120 minutes. Every goal up to three gave you a point. The Aztecs themselves got two points for their two goals, even though they lost the match.

Houston Hurricane were fined after that game because we had played in our training gear – the club was so new that we had kicked off in our first-ever game without having a set of strips to our name. There had been a delay in adidas, the kit supplier, sending them. Even our training kit was really smart, though, so it was no drawback. One of the questions I had asked Timo on meeting him at Glasgow Airport was, 'What colours will the team play in?' Timo drawled, 'Bobby, we'll play in the pastel shades.' Various colours went swirling through my mind as I tried to conjure up an idea of what he might mean. When the strips eventually arrived, they consisted of red shirts with a white band across the midriff and an orange hurricane in the centre, red shorts and orange socks. It was smarter than it sounds.

The drama of my high-speed introduction to the USA was not yet over. I found, after the match, that I was suffering from a poisoned toe, and as soon as we arrived back in Houston, Ian Anderson, the team captain and a fellow Scot, who had played for Dundee, sped me from the airport to hospital where Dr Matsu, our Japanese club doctor, gave me an injection in my toe and pulled the nail out completely. It had been quite a welcome to America.

We shared the Houston Astrodome, an enormous bowl of a stadium, with the Astros, the local baseball team and, sometimes, if I arrived particularly early for a match, I would be able to watch the stadium being converted from a baseball set-up to one for football, with seats and pitch being shifted around to suit the dimensions of a different sport. The Astrodome had been dubbed 'the eighth wonder of the world' when it was built in 1962, and its structure was influenced by the Colosseum in Rome. It had been designed as a domed, indoor, air-conditioned stadium, originally with a grass pitch. However, the dome blocked the sunlight and the grass had died, so they designed an artificial surface with which to replace it and invented the substance known as Astroturf. I didn't mind playing on it, although I do believe it did lasting damage to my knee. The defensive players liked it less than I did. If they performed a lot of sliding tackles they would come off with their thighs seared by friction burns. Playing away from home wasn't always such a bad thing as the pitches were usually grass.

We never came near filling the stadium. Our average crowd was slightly under 6,000. That was reasonable for a first season in the city, considering the sport was alien to North America, but the crowds could have been larger, I felt, if the Hurricane had co-opted a couple of boys from the Mexican community in Houston. For some reason, those who ran the club did not want local Mexicans in their squad. I would often go to watch the Mexicans play matches that they had organised among themselves in Memorial Park, and at their annual dinner, they presented me with a plaque for showing an interest in their football – a gesture that made me feel very honoured.

Very few of the NASL clubs' stadiums were full. They are so massive that it was always going to be difficult to bring in enough people to fill these vast arenas, even though some clubs attracted decent crowds of 20,000 or 30,000. The stadiums had been built for the more popular native sports of American football and baseball. Soccer was seen as a more relaxed, family-orientated sport in the USA. Before matches, outside the ground, you would see families sitting on the fold-down tails of their cars and participating in copious picnics. The warm weather, particularly in the South, suited that. I found that it wasn't too much of a problem to play in the heat, once I became accustomed to it, but it could still surprise you. Away to Tampa Bay Rowdies, we had a nice, air-conditioned dressing room and while having a laugh among ourselves before the game, we forgot about the heat outside. When the door of that cool room was opened for us to go out for the match, we walked into a wall of heat so intense that you felt it could almost have knocked you over. Some opposing players found Houston's Astrodome, with its closed roof, to be oppressive, but I enjoyed playing there.

That season, we played 15 matches at home and 15 away. Travelling to away games – or going 'on the road' as they called it – was great fun as it meant a visit to a different state and a different city. Every player in the League was given a Toyota. Mine was splashed with red and orange and had 'Bobby Lennox – Houston Hurricane – 11' emblazoned on the side. With encouragement from the children, we also put several 'Scotland for the World Cup' stickers on the car that summer of 1978 in support of the Scottish national team at the World Cup in Argentina. The stickers were there for about four days before Scotland made an unexpectedly early exit from the tournament.

Kathryn and Gillian, Jeff and Gary, our children, had a great time in the States. There was always plenty to do – going to see the Beach Boys in concert at The Summit in Houston, for instance, basketball at the same venue, and Barnum's three-ring circus, which must have held about 10,000 spectators. The club could always help out with tickets for such events. The weather was lovely – you never really needed a warm-up before a game because the heat meant that you were warm anyway. At training, if we were practising free-kicks, the guys who were not involved could sit in the shade until it was time to move on to the next thing. It was a nice contrast to the winter mud and rain of Barrowfield.

Not everything went without a hitch, though. At a big meeting one day the American boys at the club said that they felt the European boys were bullying them a bit. There were some good American players in the team but there was a difference in culture between them and the Europeans. The Americans always wanted praise. If they did something well, they wanted their team-mates to pat them on the back and tell them, 'Well done.' That wasn't really part of the culture of European footballers, but a bigger sticking point was when the Americans were not doing so well. They did not like people pointing out their mistakes, but if a European player sees a team-mate making a mess of something, such as fluffing a corner kick, he's unlikely to say, 'Well done.' It would be more like, 'What the f*** did you do that for?' The Americans didn't like shouting and swearing on the park. The big pow-wow was to discuss the difference between the two footballing cultures.

A lot of the American boys had become very friendly with my family. We would often have them round to socialise and I liked them. I tried to explain that when European guys had a go at them on the park, we were not saying that they were useless. We were merely using industrial language to sharpen their senses, to get individuals moving and performing better for the team. We didn't feel that giving someone a pat on the back when they were failing to help the team was particularly productive. The meeting helped both factions to understand each other a bit more. One thing about the American players was that, coming from a sporting culture that favoured baseball, American football and basketball, they were very useful with their hands. If we won a throw-in close to goal, they could deliver a ball to the back post with supreme accuracy. It was almost as good as winning a corner.

Howie Charbonneau, the left-back, and Nicky Megaloudis, the right-back, were the two young American guys who were particularly notable for their ability at throw-ins. The Americans, in the late 1970s, were pioneers in putting players' names across the back of their strips and I thought it was quite an achievement that they had managed to fit Howie's name across the width of his shoulders. Nicky, a New Yorker, was one of the American boys who took it hard if you were a bit sharp with him on the pitch but I liked both him and Howie a lot. Nicky would sit on the team bus and imitate the noise made by an American police-car's siren and you would see people genuinely looking around to try to spot the cops. John Stremlau, the American inside-forward, asked me one day why I always sang 'The Star-Spangled Banner' so heartily before matches. He would look at me slightly oddly as I belted out the national anthem of the USA. I told him that, since I was taking their money, I felt obliged to show gratitude to the nation that was hosting my family and me.

Timo was an excellent coach. His varied training routines kept things alive during the week and he knew how to pace it so that we had plenty of energy left for the match at the weekend. In truly American fashion, he would produce extensive dossiers on the opposition before every match. These dossiers contained information on every one of the players in the other team and noted who they would pick up at corners, with drawings of how they operated their marking system and the type of runs each of their players tended to make. The dossiers also explained in detail your own task in the forthcoming game. We were all supposed to study them carefully. The American boys loved it and would devour them from cover to cover. Their sporting culture was based on a strict adherence to detailed tactics.

On one occasion we travelled to play Chicago Sting and on the evening before the match, as was habitual with our team, we went for a walk and a beer. It was light beer and we would always restrict ourselves to one only. Timo and the club fully approved of this practice. It was a traditional American thing to have a beer on the evening before a game, in the same way as a European might have a soft drink. The venue for our pre-match relaxation in Chicago was a place called Flanagan's Bar. On the following morning at breakfast, Timo asked me where we had been and I told him Flanagan's. Timo told me he had been in a place called Mooney's.

We then proceeded into the room where we were to have our pre-match tactics talk. Timo began with a surprise. He flipped over the tactics blackboard so that it was out of action. He told us how it cost the club $500 per match to compile the dossiers that contained the tactical information, before holding up his copy and throwing it into the bin.

'Today, we're just going to go out and play,' he went on. 'I'm not going to fill your heads with stuff about who does this and who does that. Today, just use your instincts. Now, does anybody want to know anything about Chicago?'

You could see that the American players were in a state of worry and confusion about how to approach a match without extensive tactics being mapped out, so they were probably pleased when I raised my hand in response to Timo's question.

'Yes?' said Timo.

'How do you get to Mooney's Bar?' I asked.

The European guys all thought this was funny but the Americans just looked blank. Timo was laughing himself as he said, 'Right, lads, we'll just go out and enjoy ourselves tonight.'

The American players were unwilling to leave it at that. They coralled Timo and told him that they couldn't play the game without tactics. In the event, we played well – I scored a good goal off a one-two – but got beaten 2–1.

After every one of our home fixtures, a notice would be displayed on the massive electronic scoreboard at the Astrodome, informing the fans that they could meet the Houston Hurricane players and their opponents after the game and telling them the name of the hotel at which we could be found. If we had been beaten at home, you would walk in expecting the fans to be looking at you sideways. Instead, they'd be as cheery as ever, ready to greet you with open arms, saying 'Good job, Bobby!' I'd be sick at the defeat we had just experienced but the fans would be saying things such as, 'Great corner you took there today.' It was strange because that, to me, is not a winning mentality and yet the Americans love winners. It may simply have been that the Texans were really nice, friendly people. When they come out with 'Have a nice day' it's not insincere – they really mean it. Soccer was more of a family game over there, so less likely to attract the more rabid type of supporter. It may also have been the case that soccer fans in the USA were so grateful to be able to watch live action in their own city that they were unwilling to be too critical of the players who were providing it for them.

When we played a home game against the Fort Lauderdale Strikers, George Best, who had moved to Fort Lauderdale from LA during that season, shouted over to me after the game that he would see me back at the post-match reception at the hotel. Warning bells might have sounded for some people, in view of George's reputation as a seriously heavy drinker, but I was fine with it. When I arrived, slightly late, I was told that my pal Barry Radcliffe, an Irish doctor who had emigrated to Houston, Kathryn and the kids were already with George. Gary was wearing a Scotland strip and George was signing it and talking away to Kathryn, Gill and Jeff. All evening he sat peacefully there with us – not the sort of nightlife associated with George but you could see he was really enjoying himself. I asked him a couple of times, 'Do you not want to go back and sit with your team-mates?' I didn't want him to feel obliged to stay. He said, 'No, I want to sit with your family.'

It was nice to meet fellow British players in the relaxed surroundings of the USA. Away to the Memphis Rogues, we came out of the dressing room and were lining up in the tunnel when Eddie McCreadie, the Rogues manager, spotted me. I had always greatly enjoyed Eddie's company when we had played together for Scotland, so when we saw each other we had a big, long hug. It must have looked strange to the other players to see a manager and an opposing player hugging each other tightly before a match. The bonhomie with Eddie didn't prevent me scoring my first goal for the Hurricane.

The system in the NASL allowed a club, if they no longer fancied one of their players, to trade him to another club, without consultation with the player. A player with the Houston Hurricane could receive a phonecall telling him that he had been traded to, say, the Vancouver Whitecaps, he was booked on a flight to his new base the following morning and to make sure he was on it. It wasn't too far away from the system Jock Stein employed at Celtic, except even more streamlined and endorsed officially rather than, in the case of Jock, a means of working the system to best advantage. I had made it clear to Timo, though, when we met initially in Glasgow, that if there was any prospect of me being traded from Houston Hurricane to another club, I would be coming straight home to Scotland. He gave me the necessary assurances and it was never a problem for me.

Most of the players from Europe were desperate to do well but one or two had drifted into the NASL and were not interested in making a contribution – only in the money that was on offer. I certainly wasn't one of those. That sort of approach wasn't in my make-up. I played for the Hurricane to the same level and at the same pace as I had done for Celtic. It had been bred into me always to play to the best of my ability, and you could see that other imported players were doing the same – Charlie Cooke, George Best and Bobby Moore among them, who were all playing in the USA at the same time as I was. Those guys had pride in their performances and, as players who had won top honours in football, reputations to maintain. I was also determined to do my best for Timo Liekoski, who had come all the way to Glasgow specifically to invite me to join his team.

Guys who kidded on did not remain at NASL clubs for very long. A couple of British boys – I'd rather not mention their names – who came over from an English club treated their recruitment by Houston Hurricane with a massive lack of respect. They saw it as a big lark, ran a club car off the road and every day came in late for training, which they treated as a joke. A player would be fined a dollar a minute for being late for training, up to $50, and after that would be barred from training that day. These two would brazenly turn up, accept their fine and go home. It wasn't long before they were being transported back to the lower divisions in England.

Others made the most of their new opportunity. Mark Lindsay, a London boy who had played for Crystal Palace, had been in the USA, with Tampa Bay Rowdies, for several years by 1978, when he joined the Hurricane. He was a great player and a really good lad but he got injured after four games of the season in which I joined the Hurricane and proved to be a big miss for us. Radomir Stefanovic, our centre-half, was another character and a great guy to have around the dressing room. He would say after matches, 'Number nine didn't score a goal.' We'd maybe have been beaten by a couple of goals but he would be proud that the guy he had been marking had failed to score. We'd suggest to him that he might have done well to have tried to pick up the other forwards but at Hajduk Split, which is where he had come from, the culture was that you had done your job if the man you were marking had failed to score.

Part of our remit as Houston Hurricane footballers was to attend 'soccer clinics', at which we passed on advice on football to children. On one occasion, a child, troubled by my Scottish accent, asked, 'Hey, is that guy a Russian?' This was during the Cold War. Another time, I participated in a radio promotion for the Hurricane. The message I recorded for broadcast was, 'Hi, my name's Bobby Lennox and I'm number eleven. I'll be down on that field tomorrow night and you can have the shirt off my back. Tomorrow night, we welcome the Detroit Express.' They used that quite a lot, merely changing the name of the opposition to make the message relevant for the forthcoming home game. Those who got down to the stadium early did indeed get the shirts off our backs – before the game, every player gave the training top they had worn for the warm-up to a spectator. The tops bore the slogan 'I named a Hurricane', a reference to how the people of Houston had chosen the name 'Hurricane' for their new soccer team.

When I recorded that advertisement, two American players and I had gone along to the studio. I was conscious of my Scottish accent, especially as the ad had to be snappy, and said to the guys at the radio station, 'You'll not understand me. This will be a waste of time.' The American players went into the recording booth before me and with each of them, there was a lot of re-recording and huffing and puffing. I went in and recorded my words in one take. The radio people were completely satisfied with the first attempt I made. I must have been so determined to speak as clearly and crisply as possible that I had come across well – either that, or I was a media natural.

Prior to going to Houston, we had been told that it was the most violent city in America but that the violence tended to affect people only tangentially. On the night of the Mexican dinner and dance, at which I was awarded my plaque, there was a murder across the road, in the car park of a club called The Rabbit Habit, a huge place. The Piano Bar was where people would go to play backgammon, which was just becoming popular, or to listen to a singer accompanied by the piano promised by the name of the establishment. Kathryn and I occasionally visited there and we came out one night to see one guy passing a pistol to another. We jumped in the car and scooted off as quickly as we could. That was the closest we came to seeing the city live up to its violent reputation. We never saw any raw violence or even so much as anyone arguing with someone else. Unlike in Glasgow, we didn't even see any drunks wandering about. It was a very different world, over there in the Texan sunshine.

Houston Hurricane were keen for me to remain with the club for longer than a single season, and I think that if I had wanted to stay, Kathyrn would have been quite happy to do so. The sun shone almost every day and we had a good way of life. I'd get back from training in the afternoon to join the family around the swimming pool, and we would, more often than not, choose to eat out. Little novelties helped make the time there special. We'd find shops open until 11 in the evening for instance, whereas in Scotland, in the late 1970s, they would close at five o'clock. We were invited to lots of picnics and barbecues, and every Monday evening we would go up to Memorial Park to watch Houston Hurricane's second team. Kathryn and I and the children were among the first people to go up there to lend them our support, and that started a trend. By the end of the summer, all the players' families were up there of a Monday, relaxing on the bleachers beside the pitch. We watched as our children grew and developed in Houston. They were out at the pool every day, with the sun on their backs. When we first arrived, Jeff, who was four years old, needed to be wearing armbands before he could go in the water with us but by the time we left, he was diving into the pool from the top diving board.

Within hours of our arrival in Houston, I had taken the children round to the pool and playground at our complex. A big Texan came wandering over to us and drawled slowly, 'Hi, are you Bobby Lennox?' I was taken aback at such instant recognition and said, 'As a matter of fact, I am.' He went on, 'Hi, I'm Bill. I'm your next-door neighbour and my wife is from Ecclefechan in Scotland.' Here was this genuine, ten-gallon-hat Texan telling me that I had come all the way across the Atlantic to discover that I was living next door to a Scots girl. We became very friendly with Bill and Alison, his wife, and Ryan, their little son.

The children went to Askew elementary school and Gary, then eight years old, came back from school on his first day quite upset because the teacher had told him that he had contravened school rules by wearing short trousers. From then on, he had been told, he would have to wear long trousers. That prompted Kathryn to go to the school to find out the facts. She was told that the children could not wear short trousers because if they fell and cut their knees, a claim could be made against the school – the usual American thing. She replied that in the sweltering heat of Texas there was no way Gary was wearing long trousers, and if Gary fell and hurt his knee, it would be his own fault. Within weeks, a number of his class-mates were following this new Scottish trend.

Roy Aitken and Tommy Burns, my former team-mates at Celtic, were our guests for a month that summer, and they both came along to a few training sessions. Timo was absolutely desperate to sign them. 'Could they not just stay and play?' he would ask. I told him these two young guys were future Scotland internationals, highly prized by their club. We managed to cram all four adults and three children into the Toyota as Tommy and Roy accompanied the family all over Texas. Kathryn's parents also came out to stay for a month. People who knew us could not believe that we had opted to go to Texas, because they knew of our love of the seaside, but Galveston and its beach was only an hour's drive away from Houston and we frequently packed ourselves into the car and headed down there. We also visited NASA at Cape Kennedy. I couldn't have worked any harder for the team or in training but I enjoyed all the benefits that life in America offered away from the game.

The season was good for me individually but less so for the Hurricane overall. The NASL system seemed a bit strange to European eyes. The League was divided into the National Conference and the American Conference, both of which comprised three divisions of four teams each. We were in the American Conference, and shared a division with Detroit Express, Memphis Rogues and Chicago Sting. We had to play these three home and away, but we also played matches against other clubs from both Conferences. Some we would play at home but not away and others we would face away but not at home, and some we didn't play at all. After playing a total of 30 fixtures, the order of clubs in each division was decided by the overall points tally, not just points won by playing the other clubs in the same division. The top two clubs progressed to the play-offs for the Soccer Bowl.

I didn't score as many goals as I would have liked to have done but the Hurricane weren't the best of teams and I played for them more in midfield than I did up front. I did feature in all 30 of our matches. In the final game we faced Tampa Bay Rowdies, needing not only to win but to score three goals if we were to make the play-offs for the Soccer Bowl. It was a tall order but by half-time we were, you might say, two-thirds of the way there at 2–0 ahead. We needed just one more goal and to remain in front to clinch our place. Our dressing room was buzzing during the interval, but it was a different scenario at the end of the match – we had lost three goals and failed to score another. Our chance had gone. Houston finished fourth in our division, with 96 points, well behind divisional winners Detroit Express, whose front players were Alan Brazil and Trevor Francis.

The Hurricane wanted me to re-sign for 1979 and were prepared to finance me to return to Scotland for the winter, train with a club to keep fit and do some scouting, but at the age of 34, I could not afford to go without playing for six months as the Hurricane wished me to do. More importantly, I never had any intention of remaining in Houston. We had found our stint there very enjoyable but I liked my home environment in Scotland far too much to contemplate spending any longer away. I was keen to get back. Before leaving, though, I promised that if I did return to the USA in 1979, I would definitely go back to Houston.

I had always seen our stay in the USA as short-term. Going there for the summer meant that the club would put you up in accommodation. If I had signed a long-term contract at the end of that summer, it would have changed everything. Houston would have become more of a home to us and I would have had to buy a house. Additionally, the general manager of the club could decide to trade one of its players, on a whim, and if I was on a long-term contract I might not have been exempt from that, as I had been in the summer of 1978. The boys at the club used to talk about it a lot. If they were traded to a club in, say, New York, they would be on the same salary but $100 in Texas would be worth about $60 in New York because that city was so much dearer.

People thought that players who went to the NASL were paid

fortunes, but it wasn't true. We were well looked after, though. I knew that healthcare could be expensive in the USA, so before leaving Scotland I stipulated that the club would pay any medical bills for the family. They agreed on the basis that I did not tell any other players about it. I also told Timo that I did not want any other player to be earning more than I was and he agreed readily to that. I suppose you could say that I was there as their star man. I did make a few bob from my stint in Houston but I was far from super-rich on my return. I came back from America with a fair amount of money but the American boys at the Hurricane were earning just a few dollars a week – some were on peanuts and often came round to our apartment to get a meal.

Our time in America had been an energising experience and we all look back on it with great fondness. We returned tanned and refreshed after the change in lifestyle, but as we touched down in Scotland that August of 1978, for me there was a degree of uncertainty about what the future might hold. The season was about to start and I had neither employment as a footballer nor knowledge of any British club that might be interested in me. Fate had always been kind to me but I had no way of ascertaining whether I would be allowed to finish my career in style or whether it would peter out ignominiously.

CHAPTER 13

SECOND HELPINGS

A gentle descent into the lower levels of football seemed my possible destiny as we settled back into our house in Saltcoats on our return from the USA. I soon discovered that a couple of first-division clubs – Kilmarnock and Ayr United – were interested in acquiring my services but I wasn't too keen on signing for either of them, especially as Ayr were part-time and that was not a route down which I wished to go. The season was just about to start so I spoke to both of those Ayrshire institutions within hours of my return from the USA. I was pretty keen to get fixed up with a club but hoped to hold out a little bit longer to see if anyone thought I was still up to playing at Premier Division level. Interestingly, a couple of English clubs inquired after my services and I was still pondering my next move while simultaneously combating some severe jetlag, when I took a call from Jock Stein, asking me to turn out for Celtic in his testimonial match against Liverpool. He was about to sway my career in a new and unexpected direction, yet again.

The match against Liverpool was to mark the conclusion of Jock's 13 years as Celtic manager. A few weeks after I had left Celtic, Jock had been replaced by Billy McNeill. I told Jock I was far too jetlagged and exhausted to do myself justice against Liverpool. I had arrived back in Scotland on the Saturday and the testimonial was on the Monday. He asked me to come along on the night anyway. Jock then mentioned, almost casually, that Billy was short of players and asked me if I would like to return to Celtic for a short spell, just to help tide Billy over and to be someone he could rely on as he began his work of bringing in new faces to the club. I responded that I would be delighted to do so. I never did find out why it was Jock and not Billy who phoned me with that proposition.

I was surprised that Billy would want me back at Celtic but it became more logical the more I thought about it – Billy had, after all, wanted to sign me for Aberdeen six months previously and Celtic were short of quality players when he took over as manager. The club had finished fifth in the new ten-team Premier Division at the end of the 1977–78 season, one of the worst performances in its history, and things had been happening during the final days of Jock's management of the club that he would never previously have contemplated. I remember telephoning Roy Aitken from Texas, a few weeks after arriving there, to ask him how Celtic had done the night before. The team had lost 4–1 at Hibernian. I asked who had scored for Celtic and when Roy said 'Mike Conroy' I had no idea who he meant. Mike had joined Celtic from Port Glasgow Juniors one week and gone straight into the first team the next. That was why I didn't know him – he had not even been at the club when I had departed. The younger Jock Stein, the man who had pushed us to the heights in Europe, would never have dreamed of signing a player from Junior football and pitching them into the team the following week. As it turned out, Mike Conroy was a very good acquisition for Celtic and I very much enjoyed playing with him during my second stint at the club.

On returning to Celtic, it was almost as if I had never left. In fact, when I turned up for the start of the 1978–79 season, I think a lot of the other players assumed that the plan had always been for me to go away and come back.

Billy was my third manager inside a year and I found it very difficult to call him 'Boss'. I could not do it at first, having known him for so long as a team-mate. Eventually, I got over it but initially I would refer to him as 'Cesar', automatically. Billy was very thorough in everything he did and training was carried out in a good atmosphere. He had always been a good speaker and had no problem standing in front of players and communicating with them. Additionally, he made good signings, such as Murdo MacLeod, the midfield player, and Davie Provan, the winger, to help the club regain the dynamism and vitality it had lost in the couple of years prior to his appointment as manager. Danny McGrain was still there and still great and youngsters such as Roy Aitken, Tommy Burns and George McCluskey were coming through. Peter Latchford was a useful goalkeeper.

I signed a one-year contract and close to the end of that 1978–79 season, when we played St Mirren, I scored with a header in a 2–0 win that kept us alive in the race for the championship. That helped to set up one of the great nights for Celtic, when, on 21 May 1979, we faced Rangers at Celtic Park, with the title at stake. Victory would clinch the championship for Celtic. Anything else would leave Rangers set to win it. It looked ominous for us when an Alex MacDonald goal had Rangers 1–0 up at half-time, and worse still when Johnny Doyle, our winger, was dismissed ten minutes after the break. We managed to equalise, through Roy Aitken, and shortly after Billy had sent me on as substitute in place of Mike Conroy, we went ahead when George McCluskey scored. Two minutes later, I was back in defence when Bobby Russell, the Rangers midfield player, sent in a shot that clipped the post on its way goalwards to make it 2–2 with little more than ten minutes remaining. The sound of that ball pinging against the post as it travelled into the net still echoes with me to this day. It looked as though Rangers might just have done enough but two Celtic goals in the final five minutes – a Colin Jackson own goal and a long-range shot from Murdo MacLeod – gave us the title. We had looked unlikely champions before Christmas but had won 13 of our final 17 League matches to make a late swoop for the championship.

The place was bouncing at the final whistle – we celebrated long and hard on the pitch and there were a number of ex-Celts in and around the dressing room afterwards. One of the first people I bumped into after coming off the field was Jimmy Johnstone. Everybody was really emotional about our success because of the way we had done it. That team had a strong will to win. It had a bit of aggression about it and was full of desire – a team built in the image of its manager. We won a lot of games with ten men around that time, which says much about the character of the side. 'Ten Men Did It Again' became one of the regular chants from the Celtic fans. Following that game with Rangers, Billy asked me to stay on for another year.

Winning the League allowed me another serious crack at the European Cup and in the autumn of 1979, we were drawn against Partizani Tirana of Albania, which proved to be the strangest country I ever visited with Celtic. When we got there, they kept us waiting at the airport for ages, looking at our passports and checking our faces against the photos displayed in them. Albania at that time was a communist country, almost entirely isolated from the outside world, and the authorities held a deep distrust of foreigners.

We went to train at the ground on the day before the game and 10,000 people came to watch us – Albanians are fanatical about football. As we boarded the coach to return to our hotel, many of them rushed over, desperate for souvenirs. One uniformed security man was doing his best to keep the mob away but, being daft lads, we were on the bus gesticulating at him and making faces behind his back, which had the Albanians laughing away. The security guy would turn round to see what we were doing but we would all look away and put on innocent expressions. He may have been the butt of the joke but that one man managed to keep the crowd away from the bus simply through carrying a big stick and by exerting the authority that his blue uniform gave him. We stayed in a big, old 1950s-style hotel and at night, hundreds of men walked up the street, then back down again, then back up again. I think it was a display put on to show us how 'normal' life in Albania was.

We lost 1–0 in Tirana but beat Partizani 4–1 in the return to go through to a tie with Dundalk of Ireland. A 3–2 win in the first leg was preserved over there when the second leg ended 0–0 on a wet, wild, windy night at sloping Oriel Park, where they had still been putting up temporary stands when we were training on the pitch the night before the match. It was nervy at times. In the final minute, Dundalk got a free-kick, from which the ball skidded across the face of goal. Their striker needed just a touch to knock it into the net and eliminate us on away goals but the ball went between his legs.

Those tricky ties led to a quarter-final with Real Madrid in March 1980. We gave ourselves a great chance of progressing by winning a rousing first leg at Celtic Park to take a 2–0 lead to the Bernabeu. This will perhaps sound blasé but by then I was used to performing in stadiums such as that. The Bernabeu was crammed with 110,000 people on the night but this was my 66th European match so the size of the crowd and the atmosphere inside the ground barely affected me. I think I would have noticed more if there had been empty seats and hardly anybody there.

We had a young team but they were handling it well until we lost a goal right on the half-time whistle. We had been defending for a spell and I volleyed a ball right up into the third tier to concede a corner to Real. I thought that by the time they got the ball back from the crowd and had taken the kick, the referee would sound his whistle for the break. Instead, the ball was played in and Carlos Santillana, the Real striker, got his toe to it and prodded it over the line. It was a fortunate, scrambled goal for them. You could see a change come over our team at half-time because of that, with the youngsters thinking, 'That's Real back in the game now.' If we had had more experienced players – Auld or Murdoch or players of that ilk – they might have been saying at that point, 'Come on, we're still in front here.' Instead, the boys looked a bit deflated and daunted by the prospect of the second 45 minutes.

We lost a couple of goals in the second half to make it 3–0 to Real. It was like that Ajax game back in 1971, when we were comfortable at 0–0 for an hour and then Cruyff scored a goal and we were suddenly under pressure before going on to lose 3–0. Santillana's goal had lifted Real's entire game and the crowd had got behind them again. It was especially disappointing because their opening goal had come immediately after the referee had penalised Peter Latchford for supposedly taking more than four steps with the ball, a decision that wasn't often given. From that free-kick, they had won the corner that had led to the goal.

Even at 3–0 down, though, we knew that if we nicked a goal in the late stages we would go through on the away goals rule. Late in the game, Billy switched me from wide left to through the middle and I got played in with my back to goal. I flicked it on and Uli Stielike, the big German, flipped the ball away with his hand. To me, it was a stonewall penalty but Karoly Palotai, the referee, waved for play to continue. He wasn't too keen on giving us much that night and one or two other dodgy decisions went against us. There were only three or four minutes to go and a goal then would probably have been enough to take us through to the semi-finals of the European Cup. That would have been quite a penalty kick for me to take – in the Bernabeu with 110,000 Madrilenos screaming at you to miss. It was hugely disappointing to lose that game because I thought that we had done enough to get through, and if you've knocked Real Madrid out of the European Cup, anything can happen.

That elimination by Real had a knock-on effect for the rest of the 1979–80 season. We had been eight points clear of Morton, our closest challengers in the League, at the time of the first leg with Real and with two points for a win, that was a considerable advantage. In the wake of the tie with the Spaniards, we began to falter. Aberdeen were coming up fast as our closest challengers and at home to them in early April, in front of 40,000, we were 2–1 down early in the second half when we were awarded a penalty. I had just come on as a substitute for Tom McAdam, who had suffered concussion, so I was not the nominated penalty taker for that game, but when the ref pointed to the spot, the rest of my team just walked away. By default, in effect, I was the man, and how I wish that hadn't been the case. It is the one penalty kick I wish I could take again. It had all happened too quickly and I wasn't too sure of myself. As I stepped up to strike the ball, I fluffed it and Bobby Clark, still in the Aberdeen goal at the start of the 1980s, saved it rather too easily. That miss proved vital, as Aberdeen held on to their 2–1 lead to move closer to us at the top of the table.

Dundee drubbed us 5–1 a fortnight later to set us back further, but although it may seem laughable, we could have beaten them that day. We were always in the game but it seemed that every time Dundee shot for goal, they scored, not least because their finishing was excellent on the afternoon. Every one of their goals was superbly executed, with deadly accuracy, and there is little that you can do about it when a team has a day such as that one. We were struggling and our lead was whittled away again after we lost at home to Aberdeen, for a second time, and away to Dundee United. As in the previous year, our final fixture was the decider. We went into the last day's games one point behind Aberdeen but could only draw 0–0 at St Mirren while Aberdeen won 5–0 away to Hibernian. So Aberdeen took their first title since the 1950s. That Aberdeen side, under the leadership of Alex Ferguson, was one of several great Scottish club sides that I saw down the years. It was still hugely disappointing to lose the title to them because it had been more a case of us losing the plot than them pegging us back.

We had to re-energise ourselves for the Scottish Cup final the following week, in which our opponents were Rangers. It was a good, open game and a match that could have ended 5–5 because there were so many chances created at both ends. Strangely, the score remained 0–0 well into extra time until Danny McGrain screwed a shot towards goal. George McCluskey deflected it, sending the ball veering away from Peter McCloy, the Rangers goalkeeper, and into the net. It was all we required to win the Cup. We had played that game without a centre-half. Mike Conroy was drafted in from midfield to play beside Roy Aitken. The worry for us was the danger presented by Derek Johnstone in the air but Mike and Roy played fantastically well that day and Peter Latchford dealt with everything that came his way. Mike, for me, was the best player on the park.

I was sitting in the bath afterwards, puzzled that not a single photographer had shown up in the dressing room to snap the Cup winners. Usually, the place was crowded with snappers. 'Where are they all today?' I asked my team-mates. Then somebody came in and said mayhem had erupted out on the pitch. A riot had developed after supporters of both sides had climbed over the pitchside walls to confront each other on the turf. Mounted police eventually pounded on to the turf as a means of breaking up the battle, but we were oblivious to that dramatic post-match action.

My 37th birthday was approaching but after that 1979–80 season I felt confident that I could continue to make a positive contribution to the Celtic team. I had, after all, featured in 47 of the club's 54 fixtures in League and Cup competitions that season, scoring ten goals, which wasn't bad for someone who had been described as a veteran almost a decade previously. Billy McNeill clearly felt I was a useful man to have around because I was signed once again for the start of the 1980–81 season and happily bounded on to the plane for our pre-season tour of West Germany and Holland in the summer of 1980.

The matches were low-key affairs designed to tune our fitness. An encounter with SV Wesseling, a low-level West German side, came first, followed by matches with Nijmegen, Go Ahead Deventer and Werder Bremen. It was always nice to get a goal, regardless of the opposition, and I was pleased with mine against SV Wesseling, a game we won 8–0. I received the ball 25 yards from goal and, as Danny McGrain ran outside me screaming for a pass, I took aim with my right foot and sent the ball streaking into the top corner. It seemed a good way to get back into the swing of hitting goals in preparation for the new season but that goal, notched by me on 16 July 1980 in a modest, tree-lined ground with a tiny stand, in a small industrial town on the Rhine, proved to be my final one for Celtic and the last significant act of my two decades as a professional footballer.

A groin strain had been bothering me, on and off, for some time and after that game with Wesseling, it became so aggravated that it prevented me appearing in the remaining, more high-profile encounters of the tour. I was struggling so badly with the injury that I could not even take a place on the substitute's bench. Back in Glasgow a number of weeks later, waiting for the injury to clear, I was playing in a bounce match with some of our youth-team players when I moved to make a run to the near post and found that my groin simply gave way. It was shot through with severe pain and my leg, above the knee, quickly turned black, blue and green. The discolouration even extended to my stomach muscles. The problem was clearly serious, and even more painful than my broken leg, but the resultant medical diagnosis was still shocking. I was told I could never play football again.

CHAPTER 14

IN RESERVE

Every footballer thinks he will play forever, including me, so when I was told to retire it was like taking the toys away from a baby. Everything about playing the game had been invigorating for me – even Sunday-morning soreness. It made you feel so alive to be involved as a player. My only compensation was my age. I was 37 when I was forced to quit and could at least look back on a rich and varied career. I had gone to the specialist expecting him to tell me to rest for three months. When he informed me that my time was up and there was no way back, it left me feeling down for a while. I did not get depressed, though, because I'm not a depressive type. There is no point in worrying about things beyond your control.

Before long, any feelings of disappointment at quitting as a player were supplanted by my wondering what I was going to do next. I did not have too much time to think about that because, within days, things were soon clicking into place, as they have tended to do throughout my life. Frank Connor, who had been the Celtic reserve-team coach, accepted the post of Berwick Rangers manager in early November 1980 and Billy McNeill asked me if I would like to take over from Frank. It was not difficult to decide to accept the job, but it was hard to make the transition from player to coach. I had always enjoyed the fun and banter of the dressing room and now I would have to take a step back from that and become more detached, especially as I had played with all of the reserve-team players, either in the first or second team or in training. I now had to get changed for training on my own and learn how to present a slightly more serious face to the players. Footballers are also slightly more wary of you once you become part of the management team. They may worry that you will report things they say back to the manager. That was something I would never have done but it is understandable that players think it possible and it was another reason for me to keep my distance.

I had previously had chances to go into management – during the mid-1970s a couple of clubs had approached Jock Stein to ask him if I could take over the reins. One club had wanted me to join them as player–manager but the first – and last – I heard of it was when Jock informed me of their approach when we were in Perth for a match against St Johnstone. He told me which club had been in for me and then just laughed and said, 'They wanted you to be player–manager but the last thing you want is to go there and do that when you can still be a player here at Celtic. So I just told them, "No." ' That was it. Jock had decided for me and I was quite happy to remain a Celtic player. Another good, mid-sized Scottish club approached me directly in the late 1970s with a similar proposition, but I declined.

Jim Lumsden, who was in charge of the youth team at Celtic, was of invaluable help to me when I took the job of reserve-team coach. I had been used to doing, rather than coaching, and he assisted me hugely in making the transition. I did not find it easy to become a coach and I leaned on Jim's shoulder a great deal in those early days.

Managing a reserve team is different from managing a first team. We won various Reserve League titles, Reserve League Cups and BP

Youth Cups during the 1980s but winning such trophies was never the major purpose of the reserve team, and anyone who thought otherwise was absolutely incorrect. The role of the reserve-team coach is to nurture players and prepare them for the first team. Billy McNeill would actually tell me that it didn't matter whether the reserves won or lost. Mind you, if we didn't win, he would ask, 'How did that happen? You've got good players there.' It was a bit of a cleft stick.

Although I was in charge of the reserve team, I never really selected the side. I would discuss the team in detail with Billy but he would have the last word and that was only right because, as I've said, the reserves were in existence purely to see who was ready for first-team action. It could be frustrating. If the reserves had played well for you in a match, you would maybe want to retain the same team for the next fixture but Billy might insist on three or four changes. We would go through the entire team, discussing every player, whether or not they should be in the side, which position they should play and how they should play it. David Hay, who succeeded Billy as Celtic manager in 1983, had a slightly different approach. He would simply tell me which first-team players he wanted to slot into the reserves for the next fixture and leave the rest to me. I must say that I found both Billy and David extremely easy people with whom to work.

Another quirky aspect of being reserve-team coach was that as soon as you had an outstanding player in your team, you would, without any question or argument, lose them immediately. Paul McStay had been in the side for my first match in charge, away to Motherwell, but it was clear even then, aged 16, that he was going to be a great player and he was, within days, whisked away from me to join the first-team squad. Other players who seemed to have great potential never did quite as well as expected. I used to love watching John Buckley, a winger who would change feet incredibly quickly and then zip away from his opponent. He made just one first-team appearance before moving on to Partick Thistle in 1983 – possibly a lack of consistency hampered him at Celtic. Similarly, Dougie McGuire, another wide player, left for Coventry City in 1988 after failing to find a place in the first team.

Sometimes I would recommend a player for the first-team squad because he had done well with the reserves, but the player in question would find it too great a jump and be unable to adapt and perform to the standard required. Some players would be fine in front of 200 or 300 people but in the first team, with the manager watching and many thousands of pairs of eyes on the game, they would find the situation too stressful, too much for them. That happened with a couple of players but I wouldn't like to mention their names. One boy, if he saw his name in the first-team squad of 16, would turn to me, pale as a sheet, and say, 'Oh, Bobby, I'd rather be with your team.' You are not, though, at Celtic to play with the reserves. You are there to make it as a first-team player.

The opposite would happen when a first-team player was drafted into the reserves when he clearly did not want to be there. First-team players were there because they were recovering from injury or were out of form and, realistically, they had their own agenda. Most first-team guys were honest pros and would come in and do you a turn – others would make it clear that they thought they should not be there, although they would never be big enough to say that to your face. Instead, they would just go through the motions. That drained morale from the young guys but, fortunately, at Celtic Park we didn't have many like that. It could also, admittedly, be difficult for first-team players coming into the reserve team, where the passes and the runs and the thinking are not quite so good and so quick as at the higher level. You can have a strange mix in a reserve team – you can have two or three internationals, slumming it, a few of your reserve regulars, a nervous trialist and one or two new players slightly overwhelmed at wearing Celtic's colours. It is unlikely that all of those players will be on the same wavelength.

One of my last games in a Celtic jersey had been in the reserves, up at East Fife, with Johnny Doyle and Charlie Nicholas as my fellow forwards. At half-time, Frank Connor had Charlie by the throat demanding to know why he, a boy of 18, was allowing Johnny and me, two experienced players, to do all the running while he waited for the ball to arrive at his feet in the penalty area. Charlie had so much ability and knew how well he could play with the ball at his feet that he was happy to have two senior players doing his running for him – he was so confident in his talent that he did not feel the necessity to show the coach a willingness to work hard. That led to friction between him and Frank, with Frank stressing that he had to complement his natural ability with hard work.

With Paul McStay, Charlie moved quickly into the first team but in mid-January 1982 he was having a spell back in the reserves when, on a night down at Greenock, against Morton, he went down in the penalty area. Since Charlie would go down in the box if he had broken his fingernail, no one thought he was seriously injured. I thought he would be up on his feet within seconds but, as it turned out, he had broken his leg and he missed the remainder of the season.

The job of reserve-team coach became easier and more enjoyable as time went on. One of the excellent things about Celtic is that the club is never short of invitations to youth tournaments abroad and, as part of my remit, I would go along with the under-18s. I learnt more about the young boys, both as players and as people, at those tournaments than I did in a month back home.

During one visit to Switzerland, we were enjoying a boat trip on

Lake Maggiore when I announced to the boys that when we landed on the other side of the lake, we would be in Italy so would have to have our passports ready for the customs people. This was completely untrue, of course, but there would always be one or two guys who would fall for such stories. When we reached the other side of the lake and began to disembark, one of the players, who shall remain nameless, could be seen crawling off the boat on his hands and knees, in the midst of a throng of young Celtic players, hoping that he could get across the 'border' that way without the customs people noticing him.

On another of those trips, our aeroplane was in the final stages of its approach to Glasgow, when I looked across at a couple of the boys, returning from their first trip abroad, and told them to make sure they had their seatbelts on for the descent. They made sure their belts were secure. I said, 'Good – now have you got your landing cards ready? You need a landing card, like a boarding card, for the final descent . . .' The boys, of course, did not have 'landing cards' so they undid their seatbelts and went running down the aisle to the stewardess, shouting, 'We don't have landing cards! We don't have landing cards!'

Often at those tournaments abroad, coaches from other clubs would seek me out to reminisce about the great Celtic teams of the 1960s and 1970s. That was interesting. We had always looked upon the players at Real Madrid, Milan and Internazionale as being the cream of European football but here were people telling me how we had been held in similar regard. In common with players from those clubs, we had won the European Cup and had reached the latter stages on numerous occasions. It sometimes takes an outsider to put things into perspective. We didn't realise it but we were as well known on the Continent as the continental stars were in the UK.

My son Gary, who was a promising footballer as a youngster, accompanied us on one trip. The tournament was held at Bellinzona in southern Switzerland, and we faced Napoli in the semi-finals. At that time, Gary was at Queen's Park and if Celtic were ever short of youth players we would go to Eddie Hunter, the Queen's Park manager, and ask if we could borrow two or three of his better players. The Italians were extremely confident of beating us and were not concerned about hiding the fact. Bellinzona is only a small town so it was hard to avoid the Italians swaggering around, as they do.

We played well against Napoli and won a penalty in the first half but the Napoli goalkeeper saved Alex Mathie's spot-kick. Alex was distraught at half-time, but we raised the boys' spirits before they went back out and they were still on top during the second half. However, they failed to score until five minutes from time, when David Elliott broke up the left, crossed one to the back post and Gary came crashing in to whip a volley into the net. We were all on the park in jubilation before, in the final minute, a quick clearance sent Dugald McCarrison through on the goalkeeper. Dugald, who was a great finisher, uncharacteristically knocked the ball against the Italian but it rebounded to Gary, who lobbed it back into the net. I was absolutely delighted at the boys' success, and that wee bit of fatherly pride came through as well.

In the final, we went 1–0 down to Internazionale but, unlike in 1967, there was no comeback and Inter won the tournament. Our showing, though, had impressed some Japanese officials who were watching the tournament, and it was the Celtic, rather than the Inter, reserves who were subsequently invited to tour Japan. That visit proved to be a great success and culminated in our reserve team defeating the Japanese national side by 3–0. Gary, whose goals had taken us to the final in Bellinzona, still gives me stick about how he was not invited on the trip to the Far East.

On principle, I would never have put my son forward to be signed by Celtic, even though Gary had done well in that tournament in

Switzerland. Celtic already had an awful lot of extremely good players on their books. Gary did well enough at Queen's Park to earn a move to Dundee when he was in his late teens. He enjoyed staying in digs but perhaps living away from home was more difficult for him than he had thought it would be, because we are an extremely close family. He played midfield, was a good passer and very fit but people thought that he should have been quick, like me, which was a bit unfair on him. He was certainly good enough for Dundee but for one reason or another he found it difficult to make progress there and moved on to Falkirk, whom he joined in 1991 and where he did well for a couple of seasons, alongside players such as David Weir and Kevin McAllister. He later played for Ayr United and then joined Dalry Juniors, a friendly club just over the hill from Saltcoats, where he was particularly happy.

There were myriad reasons why a Celtic reserve-team player might not make it into the first team. Charlie Christie, who became manager of Inverness Caledonian Thistle in 2006, was a really good player and a nice lad but would have been a better player for Celtic if it had been possible to shift Inverness south so that it was situated beside Glasgow. He was so attached to his Highland home that he frequently returned there and would always be asking me if it was possible for him to go home for a night or two. That not only hampered his contribution to the team but eventually led to him being released by Celtic. He was selected for a first-team squad, for a Monday night match, but had gone back to Inverness without permission. By the time I was able to track Charlie down and tell him he had been selected for the first team, it was too late and he was unable to get down to Glasgow in time. Needless to say, that did not go down well with Billy McNeill and Charlie was soon on his way out of the club.

David Moyes and Paul McGugan were good centre-halves but both needed to get away from Celtic to thrive because they could not displace Roy Aitken and Tom McAdam from Celtic's central defence. It was clear that David, who went on to have a good career as a player after leaving Celtic, and who became manager at Preston North End and Everton, was a leader and a great guy as well. On one occasion, we went down to St Joseph's school, in Dumfries, for a charity match, and they put on a lovely spread for us, which included a big plate of cakes. The boys knew they were not allowed to eat cakes before matches but I went away for a few minutes and when I came back I noticed an empty cake wrapper and asked who had eaten it. David owned up immediately. I said to him, 'So you decided that because the manager isn't about and it's only wee Bobby in charge of the team, you would just flaunt the rules.' He was really embarrassed and came to me four or five times to apologise.

When it came to whether or not a player got a break in the first team, luck had a part to play. Barney McGhee was a very good left-back in the reserves but when Mark Reid, the regular first-team left-back, was injured, Barney was injured too, so Derek Whyte, a quick defender and a good reader of the game, stepped into the first team and never looked back. Barney never got another chance to make it at Celtic and moved on to Partick Thistle while Derek played almost 300 times for Celtic and became a Scotland international. Jim McInally, another good left-back, also found his way blocked but he was a great lad and was always prepared to listen and learn. He blossomed on leaving Celtic, eventually becoming a Scotland international and, in 2004, manager of Morton.

Some boys would come into the club at 16 and start well but then fail to develop or perhaps be led astray and fall into bad habits. Others would maybe not start so well but would develop much more smoothly. One task that I am very glad I never had was that of telling those who were not going to make it with Celtic that they were being released by the club. I know that Billy and David hated it and I remember Jock Stein once telling me, on the morning on which he would be releasing players, 'This is the one day out of 365 that I hate the most.' It was always the manager's job to take the boys into his office and tell them that they would be leaving Celtic. That must be such a difficult thing to do – to destroy a dream that a boy has carried for years, possibly since he was four or five years of age and kicking a ball around for the first time. I would discuss the boys' chances of progressing with Celtic together with Billy or David but whether they stayed or left was always the manager's decision.

Physical fitness is something that has always been uppermost in my thoughts in relation to football. I've always felt that if you're not fit as a footballer, you will struggle. There is nothing worse in a game than being tired late on and the other team getting on top, and I don't think anybody could say that their team ever ran over the top of my reserves. Forcing players to test their fitness also made the boys mentally stronger. My favourite testing ground was Queen's Park, the extensive parkland on the south side of Glasgow, close to Hampden. I don't know why I chose Queen's Park but it was a great venue, with lots of hills and dips. We would go up one slope, then up another slope, then another until you could see the boys were suffering, groaning and thinking all sorts of things about me. It brought them to peak fitness and I take it as an enormous compliment that Stuart Balmer, one of my reserves, says he was the fittest he has ever been in his life during his time with me as his reserve-team manager. Stuart went on to have a lengthy career in England, playing in the FA Premier League with Charlton Athletic, so for him to say that he was at his highest level of fitness with the Celtic reserves speaks volumes.

It was enjoyable work with the reserves, especially as Billy McNeill and David Hay, guys with whom I had played, fully understood the club. Billy returned to Celtic for a second spell as manager after David moved on in 1987, but when Billy was dismissed in 1991 and Liam Brady became the new Celtic boss, it ushered in a less happy period for me. I found that life changed, and not for the better. Liam initially said that he had no intention of sacking any of the coaching staff, which was fine, but the climate inside the club, I felt, turned slightly frosty. With Billy and Davie, the manager's door had always been open to me. Now, under Liam, it was closed. You'd have to knock before you went in and if he was busy on the phone, he would often just wave you away.

I would have things planned for the reserve team at training and Liam, without consulting me, would simply tell me that the plans for the reserves were entirely different from how I had envisaged them. I'd be left trying to pick up the pieces and re-arrange things as quickly as I could. I didn't really know what I would be doing from one day to the next in terms of running the team. It began making me unhappy in my work. I couldn't get back to Saltcoats quickly enough at the end of the working day.

I don't think Celtic is the place for a manager coming into his first job. It is a much bigger institution than people down south imagine. You really need to be in and around it to realise just how big a club it is, how big a support the club has and how many people are interested in Celtic FC. Liam, I believe, had been in English football for so long that he probably thought the Scottish League was a bit Mickey Mouse and he could coast through it, but it's not like that. Maybe he thought Celtic would steamroller the opposition up here but that doesn't happen. When you go to Airdrie, for instance, you play on a wee, tight pitch against players who are desperate to beat you. It's not easy and you've got to be aware of that and of how to beat them.

I was on holiday in Cyprus with Kathryn in the summer of 1993 when the telephone rang at eight o'clock in the morning and it was Liam Brady.

'Hello Bobby, Liam here. I think you know what it's about,' he said.

I had a good idea why he was ringing me but I was determined not to make things easy for him because he had not made things easy for me at the club.

'No, Liam, I don't,' I responded.

He said he had had to let go a few of the coaching staff and mentioned who they were.

'So I think you know what I'm saying,' he went on. Again, I knew fine well what he was saying and I mouthed silently to Kathryn, 'I'm sacked.'

To Liam, I said, 'No, I don't know what you're saying, Liam.'

'Well, I'm letting you go, Bobby.'

Liam would have known before I went on holiday that I was about to be dismissed, so I thought he could have spoken to me about it face to face instead of doing it by telephone. I felt absolutely shattered and sickened. Thirty-two consecutive years of service to Celtic and that was it, concluded by an early morning phonecall during a summer holiday.

CHAPTER 15

DOMESTIC FIXTURES

Mercedes-Benz and Jaguar never enjoyed the benefit of my custom during my days as a footballer. It had never been my style to drive anything flash. Instead, I selected steady and durable vehicles, mainly Fords, to take me up and down to Glasgow from Saltcoats. The cars may not have been flash but they had to be comfortable. By the end of my playing career, though, I had conceded enough to style to drive an Audi, a make that had just come on the market at that time. Once the Lennox family suffered financial meltdown in the early 1980s, though, I had to trade in the car for a less prestigious and smaller model. I gathered the children round and told them that I had decided to exchange the Audi for a nippy, wee black sports car, in an attempt to mollify the blow. My ploy backfired. Following my little pep talk, the children told all their friends that their dad would be collecting them from school in this cracking little sports car but when I turned up in a Vauxhall Astra, a more than modest vehicle, the joke was very much on us.

It was shortly after I finished playing that things went belly-up for us, financially. Back in the early 1970s, I had started to invest money in some local businesses. I had always been aware that football, and the good earnings that came from it, would not last forever, so had been looking at other means of making a living. I did ask my father about the prospect of going into the bookmaking business but he advised against it, telling me that you had to be really well established to be a successful bookmaker, with three or four shops, each one in a different town. That way, if one shop took a heavy loss, the other three would keep the business afloat. If you had just one shop, he said, and it suffered a bad run, you could lose everything you had.

I ploughed money into some hairdresser's shops and a couple of pubs in Saltcoats. At the time, I had been too busy concentrating on football to pay much attention to the detail involved in running those establishments, and I entrusted the administration to a friend of mine from Saltcoats. One day in the early 1980s I received a telephone call asking me to go down to the office, which I was happy to do, expecting to deal with nothing more than a routine matter. Instead, when I got there I was greeted by the tax men. There was a huge hole in my business finances and they were looking for money that was due to them. These are not people with whom you can argue.

It turned out that the businesses had been leaking money drastically for some time and it had all now come to a head. Kathryn and I had a meeting with the brewers and they told us how much we owed them and how much it would cost us to pay them back in instalments. It was simply unaffordable with the way the business was going, so Kathryn, who had been a full-time housewife since the late 1960s, said that next morning she would start work, managing the pubs. Her aim was first to get their affairs in order and then to get them to turn a profit for us. I suggested that in swapping domestic life for the sharp end of business dealings overnight, she was making too hasty a decision, but she was determined to do what she had said. I've got to say she did an incredible job and our financial situation gradually started to stabilise.

The 1980s were still a very difficult decade for us. I was coaching at Celtic Park but, inevitably, my earnings took a big drop from when I was a player, and we had three young children to clothe and feed. The great thing was that we were able to hold on to our house at Winton Circus, Saltcoats, although we had to put on hold some little maintenance jobs that needed doing – door and window repairs, painting work, things that we, as adults, might notice, but which would not bother the children.

Kathryn has been at the centre of my life ever since we got married, on 14 June 1967, at St Mary's Star of the Sea in Saltcoats. It had been blisteringly hot on the Ayrshire coast during the opening fortnight of June that year and it remained so for our wedding day. Several of the Celtic players, and Jock, were there and hundreds of people were outside the church to wish us success. It was only shortly after the European Cup triumph and the crowds were so dense and frenzied that we needed a couple of policemen to escort us to our car. Following our reception, at the Queen's Hotel in Prestwick, we flew out to Ibiza, but even on honeymoon there was still no escaping the Lisbon Lions. After a few days on the island, I was finding that the hotel was too formal – jacket and tie for dinner is the last thing you want on holiday in Spain. A friendly local helped us to switch to a hotel in Majorca, where we bumped into Billy McNeill, who was there with Liz and the kids, and Tommy Gemmell and Anne, his new wife, who were also there on honeymoon. One evening, all six of us went to a barbecue and after a few drinks Tam ended up being persuaded to become a bullfighter. He stepped into the ring but any worries we might have had about his safety were dispelled when the animal that emerged to confront him turned out to be a donkey with a couple of fake horns attached to its head.

I was a Saltcoats boy to the tips of my toes and never had any intention of leaving the place, so we set up home in Argyle Road. Three or four weeks before Kathyrn and I got married, Jock had invited me to make a rare foray into his office where he had asked me if I would like to move to Glasgow. I told him I didn't fancy that at all, and that was the end of the matter. I think Celtic would have liked me to move but Jock knew it was better not to force me to do something I really didn't wish to do. 'That's fine,' he said, 'as long as you're happy.' I wouldn't have been any happier moving to Glasgow but it would have been a lot more convenient. Some winter mornings, it was a real trial having to drive up there. On three occasions, in snow, my car slipped off the road and into a field. Those minor mishaps were not too great a price to pay for my privileged existence – driving up and down to Glasgow to play for Celtic and listening to the car radio was better than digging the roads, which was exactly what I thought every time I saw a gang of guys doing just that as I passed them.

A couple of days after we returned from honeymoon, Kathryn and I were at my mother-in-law's house for a visit. To the rear of her home was an enclosed lane where, that day, some youngsters were kicking a ball about. Of course, I could not resist joining them for a game. Later, a knock on the door of my mother-in-law's house heralded the visit of a couple of policemen. A lady who lived in the lane had phoned them because of the disturbance the ball had caused by ricocheting off her back door. The police officers had a laugh about the matter with me while explaining that they had to come out because it had been reported to them. I think I must have been the only Lisbon Lion reported to the police for playing football that year.

New trends in the swinging sixties didn't influence me much although I did enjoy the music. Once, in the USA, John Clark pointed out a record in a store and suggested I buy it. If I didn't like it, he said he'd take it off me when we got home. It was the Mamas and the Papas, who combined male and female vocal harmonies to wonderful effect and epitomised laid-back California of the early hippy era. One year, on tour in Bermuda, we all came back with love beads. Drugs, though, were beyond my ken. They were not, at that stage, in any sort of wide circulation in the west of Scotland. I loved all the sixties music, the Beatles and all those groups, and saw most of the bands of that era in concert. On one occasion, Jimmy Johnstone got two tickets for the Beatles but a couple of days later he came into the park looking pretty sorry for himself. He had been picked for the Scotland squad and the match coincided with the night of the concert in Glasgow. Begrudgingly, he gave me the tickets. Kathryn and I went to see them and they were absolutely outstanding. We saw the Rolling Stones at around the same time. They had had one or two hits by then but weren't quite up there with the Beatles.

Marriage changed my life drastically, and for the better – I became Scotland's top goalscorer. I enjoyed being married. It's a great thing. You sometimes hear people making negative comments when they hear someone is about to get married but I always think it's a wonderful idea. We were quite young – I was 23 and Kathryn was 20 – but in the 1960s everybody got married at that sort of age. We were really happy in our new, terraced house and exactly a year to the day after our wedding, Gillian, our daughter, was born. That was the best anniversary present we could have been given. Gary was born on 6 December 1969 and Jeff was born on 30 July 1973. With the three kids, we needed a bigger house so we moved from Argyle Road to Winton Circus, down on the Saltcoats seafront. Buying that house was a very big investment for us. At one stage, we had had the chance to move to a very attractive house a couple of miles along the road, in Stevenston, but that was too far away for me. That's how much of a homebird I am. Ours was a happy household and if you're happy in your surroundings and in your life, there is nothing better.

One particularly joyous family occasion was when we all went to collect my MBE in July 1981. I had received a letter from Margaret Thatcher, the prime minister, the previous November, asking if I would like to be included and whether I would accept it. I was pleased to do so and my name appeared on the honours list on New Year's Day 1981. I felt it really was a big honour. You are not told who had nominated you for the award; it could be anyone. I have never discovered who it was that put my name forward for my services to Celtic and Scotland.

It was a lovely day when we went over to the palace of Holyroodhouse in Edinburgh for the ceremony. The Queen came to me, in Scotland, to save me going to her. That was good of her. Kathyrn, the three children, my mum and my mother-in-law accompanied me. The Queen chatted to me for a few minutes – she knew about my career and my work with Celtic in detail. I don't know whether she is briefed the night before or has an earpiece in place. Afterwards, in the courtyard, people, including some who had been knighted, were queuing to have their photograph taken by the official photographer, but I was able to skip that. Several press snappers were there to get a picture of me because I was a sports star. That was a nice wee bonus. I enjoyed my day and we all repaired to the George Hotel for a magnificent meal afterwards.

It wasn't all posh hotels and palaces for us that day, though. We had been travelling down the Royal Mile in Edinburgh, on the way to the ceremony, when Kathryn asked me to stop the car so that she could change. She had worn everyday clothes for the journey to the capital to prevent the smarter gear being crushed. Her good dress was in the boot. So we stopped on the Royal Mile and Kathryn nipped up a close to change into her rig-out for the palace, while her mother stood guard at the top of the close for a few minutes. I don't suppose too many of those at Holyrood that day prepared by doing the same thing.

Residing on the Ayrshire coast helped me in a professional sense. As I've mentioned, fitness was one aspect of being a footballer in which I took a great interest, and even during the close season, I found it no great hardship to head down to the beach at Saltcoats and get in a bit of hard running. During the season, I would use the soft sand on the beach to begin getting back to fitness if I had picked up an injury. Once the injury was improving, I'd progress on to the hard sand. I'd also go up to the local park during the summer and stay sharp during the close season by organising a bounce game with some schoolboys enjoying the long summer holidays. I'd have four or five boys in my team against ten or twelve in the opposing team. They would ask at the end of our match, 'Will we see you tomorrow, Bobby?' I'd be back the next day for another wee game, which was a great way of combining fun with fitness. Pre-season was so hard that I thought it best to go back in a good state of fitness rather than going back unfit and having to pound your way through training to get back in shape. Jock used to say that when I came back after the close season, I was fit enough to be able to play competitively within a handful of days, which I regarded as a great compliment.

Bringing up the children involved a lot of work – for Kathryn. Most fathers in the 1960s, 1970s and 1980s would not get involved in such nitty-gritty matters as nappy-changing but I was always around for the children. Disciplining them was never much of a problem as far as I was concerned. If they misbehaved, you would just leave them in the garage for a couple of days . . .

My own three children helped to keep me fit. We'd go to the park and I'd give them a start and then we'd race each other to see who could touch a particular tree first. On holiday in Spain, I'd shovel them all into a wee rubber dinghy, pull it out into the water until I was up to my knees and then pull them along to strengthen my legs. It was a lot of fun keeping fit in that way. At home, I'd have a quick session of powering up and down the stairs, two at a time, if I felt I needed it. Sometimes Kathryn and I would be sitting watching television and I'd say, 'I'm away out for a half-hour run.' That was never any trouble and it kept me in trim. I wanted to maintain my fitness so that I could prolong my career for as long as possible. More than anything, I simply liked being fit – it made me feel better.

Gill was a good athlete and captain of the netball team at school. Gary always had a ball in his hand and from his earliest days he would be out the back of the house, playing football. When he wasn't doing that he would talk about players and the game. He was blown slightly off course when he became a professional and went to Dundee – he could maybe have been helped more at that club. Jeff was also good enough to have a chance of making it as a player, but when he reached the age of 16, he became more interested in going dancing and having fun. That's the time when it's crucial to discipline yourself greatly in terms of socialising if you're serious about being a professional footballer.

Although I was keen on keeping in shape, I never paid much attention to my diet. I trained hard, so it would not even occur to me that I might not be able to eat what I wanted. Quite often, by sheer coincidence, we would happen to have our annual family holiday in the same place as John Clark and his family, and John and I would keep in trim by going running together. He was a great lover of cakes. We would go for a run along the front at a Spanish resort so that John could indulge in a cake and I could relax with a pint of lager. The Celtic players of my era could have eaten anything and remained in good shape with the amount of training we did. Jock put us through so much hard work – running, running, running – during pre-season that you could still feel the beneficial effects six months later. It helped that I had a naturally light build. I could indulge in fish and chips or whatever else I might fancy as often as I wanted. It may have been different for other players but, being young and fit athletes, it probably wouldn't have done any of us too much harm. For me, whatever Kathyrn cooked up in the kitchen was the only health food I ever wanted.

CHAPTER 16

HERE AND NOW

The past is never far away for me, even though I like very much to live in the present. Supporters are, understandably, always keen to relive the great Celtic games and occasions. One of the oddest reminders of the past came when I was prodded into recalling a distinctive Fairs Cup tie with Barcelona that took place in December 1964. Celtic lost 3–1 in the Nou Camp and then drew 0–0 at Celtic Park. I didn't play in the first leg but in Glasgow I was up against a really tough opponent, a stocky right-back called Benitez. He was one of the finest footballers I ever faced, and I hardly got a kick against him.

After the match, I dropped off Ian Young, our right-back, in Neilston on the south side of Glasgow and stopped at a chip shop there to buy a bottle of lemonade for the road home. As I was about to get back into my car, a couple of guys, Celtic supporters, came over to talk to me. They weren't aggressive in any way but the most opinionated one of them wasn't going to miss the opportunity of telling me what he thought.

'I've got nothing against you personally,' he said, 'but Celtic won't make any progress and won't win anything until they get rid of guys like you. I don't think you're a good player and you shouldn't be playing for my club.'

The best thing to do in such a situation is to try to defuse it gently.

'Fine,' I said. 'If that's what you think, you're perfectly entitled to your opinion.' With that, I got into the car, closed the door and drove away, saying to myself, 'What a clown!'

Four or five years ago, I was at a Celtic supporters' function in the USA when a guy came up to me and said, 'You'll not remember this but I spoke to you in Neilston one night . . .'

'I'll tell you where it was,' I responded right away. 'It was outside a chip shop and you told me I couldn't play, more or less, and that we would never have a successful team with players like me at Celtic.'

He couldn't believe that I remembered the episode and said, 'Since the year after I said that to you, I've been desperate to apologise. You became a big hero of mine.'

I couldn't be too hard on him. Supporters tend to rush into rash and emotional decisions at times, and if it had not been for the North American Federation of Celtic Supporters' Clubs, to which he belonged, my life in recent years would have been a good deal less colourful and varied. Those transatlantic fans have done much to return the Lisbon Lions to prominence and their appreciation of our achievements all those years ago has led to many memorable experiences for us in the here and now.

Following my dismissal as reserve-team coach, I became disillusioned by the way things had ended up at Celtic and decided to concentrate on running Bobby's Bar, my pub in Countess Street, Saltcoats. Pubs in any town go in and out of fashion but we were fortunate that ours was going through a popular spell in the 1990s, a decade that proved good for business and put us back on an even keel financially. We eventually decided to sell it in 1999 because things were starting to tail off a wee bit and Kathryn and I had lost a bit of our enthusiasm for running it, even though we had always been fortunate in having good staff.

During my final year or two at Celtic, I had not been enjoying my job of reserve-team coach so the disappointment I felt was not so much with football generally or the hard fact of losing my position but more with the way my departure had been handled by Liam Brady. I was not glad to leave Celtic but I was glad no longer to be doing the job in the prevailing circumstances. The club had changed by the early 1990s, and bore little resemblance to the Celtic for which I had played. It did not seem as happy a place to me. It felt as though something needed to be done to get the club's spirit back.

I retained a great fondness for Celtic and followed their fortunes as closely as ever I had done, although sometimes not as closely as I would have wished. I remember phoning for a couple of tickets for a pre-season friendly with Tottenham Hotspur, during the Fergus McCann era, and being charged a considerable price for them, which was fine, but when Kathryn and I got to the ground we discovered that we had been given seats about four rows from the rear of the east stand, way behind the goal. I'm not saying I should automatically be given privileges, and I was happy to pay my way, but when I looked across to the centre of the main stand, I saw lots of empty seats. I felt that, having given a fair amount of service to the club, we could have been allotted a couple of seats there.

That sort of thing, I have to admit, became a bit disheartening during the 1990s. On another occasion, I phoned the club to ask for tickets and was told by an office employee, 'Yes, we can get you tickets but on no account can you come in for a cup of a tea. You must go straight to your seats in the stand.' I hadn't asked for anything other than tickets but I had still been put firmly in my place. I met Fergus a few times and he was fine but he was never much of a conversationalist with us. I got the impression that he was not the greatest fan of the Lisbon Lions. The clear impression given at the club during that era was that we were history and the club was now building for the future. Yet don't the words of the Celtic song go, 'If you know the history . . .'?

Before taking control of Celtic in 1994, Fergus said that he would reconstruct the stadium and put a decent team on the park, and he did it. He kept his promises during the five years in which he was in charge and he has to be given credit for that. The stadium, with its 60,000 seats, is terrific, although sometimes it can be quiet. On European nights and at Old Firm games, the place is jumping, but at other times it maybe needs something to enliven the atmosphere. When the Celtic fans are in full song and are getting behind the team, it really does help the players on the park but I think that nowadays the team has to lift the support, whereas in the 1960s and 1970s the support would lift the team when it was going through a sticky spell during a match. The pitch today is in pristine condition throughout the season, a far cry from our day when it could get churned up like a ploughfield during a match in wintertime.

Off the field, during Fergus McCann's time at Celtic, there was a lot of chopping and changing of manager. Liam Brady had been succeeded by Lou Macari shortly before McCann's arrival but Lou lasted less than a year before being replaced by Tommy Burns, who was succeeded by Wim Jansen, Dr Jozef Venglos and John Barnes. To me, that wasn't Celtic. We were always a big family with someone at the helm. I feel Celtic needs consistency, especially in the position of manager.

Wim Jansen brought Henrik Larsson to the club, which makes Wim a star right away. We had played against Wim in the 1970

European Cup final and whenever he saw any of the Lions, he would say, 'Oh here come the star players now!' He made us feel quite at home inside the club. Dr Jo seemed like the nicest man in the world and on those occasions when I spoke to him, he proved himself to be nothing less. He brought Lubo Moravcik to the club, which was a fantastic piece of business.

It was during the McCann era that the North American Federation of Celtic Supporters' Clubs got in touch with half a dozen of the Lions and asked us to be guests of honour at their annual gathering in Las Vegas. That brought us back into the picture a bit, back into the fold. Tommy Donnelly and Jackie Meechan are the two guys who deserve special mention for organising and running that rally. Initially, we thought it would be a one-off but Stevie Chalmers and I have been back every year since. There were 500 or so people at the first one but now several thousand attend.

At the second convention, half a dozen Texan supporters were noticeable because of their green stetsons and, having played in the state, I went over to their table. John McAloon, one of their number, and I had a good blether. Houston Hurricane, sadly, are no more: they had carried on for another two seasons after I left but went out of business just as the North American soccer boom began to lose momentum and implode.

Soon after returning from that second rally, I received a phonecall from Tommy Hanlon in Cleveland. Tommy is originally from Stevenston, and he asked if the Houston branch could use my name and call it the Bobby Lennox Celtic Supporters' Club. I was delighted and for the past eight years, the committee in Houston have invited Kathryn and me over for their Christmas party. During that week in early December they put us up in style and we are treated magnificently. Twice we've been accompanied by Stevie and Sadie Chalmers, and once by Ronnie and Rosemary Simpson. The hospitality at the golf days, dinners and lunches to which we are invited is wonderful. Traditionally, a bottle of Buckfast wine is there to be auctioned at the Christmas party and it usually fetches around $500. In my opinion, this is the best Celtic supporters' club in the world. It is more than attending a function when we go there; it feels closer to meeting up with a lot of very good friends and Kathryn and I always enjoy ourselves enormously. One small gripe I have with the Houston club is that they don't invite me over for their committee meetings – I only get to go over once a year. They should really do something about that!

The midsummer week with the North American Federation of Celtic Supporters' Clubs is equally enjoyable – a wonderful mixture of hospitality, lounging by the pool and golf. The golf courses are smashing but I'd have to say that some of the Scottish exiles have taken time to adjust to the new conditions. On one trip to Las Vegas, Tommy Donnelly attempted to play an entire round of golf using nothing other than an eight-iron and seemed to think that this was quite normal. Even more disconcertingly, when he hit the ball into a pool of deep water, he insisted on wading in, waist-deep, and scrabbling around with his club to try to retrieve his ball – this despite snakes being known to inhabit standing water in those parts. Tommy, who is based in Toronto, also seems to think that golf courses in Canada have 17 holes. When we played there, he insisted strenuously, for reasons he will know best, that we leave the course after 17 holes, even though we knew we had another hole to go. It seems strange that a Scotsman, from the home of golf, should become so confused by his native land's game simply through switching continents.

The North American Federation re-ignited interest in the Lisbon Lions back in Scotland and soon we were once again being welcomed in and around Celtic Park. We were always a close bunch of players during our playing days but we have recently drawn a lot closer. During the past decade, we have seen each other an awful lot and have attended numerous functions together. A few of us play golf together frequently and we see each other at Celtic games – we are almost like a big, extended family now. The tragedy for us in recent years has been seeing three of our number pass away – Jimmy Johnstone, Bobby Murdoch and Ronnie Simpson. All three of them had their own endearing characteristics.

Out in Houston with Ronnie one time, we had a question and answer session with the supporters. One of the questioners asked me how I had felt on being named as a member of the greatest-ever Celtic team, for which the Celtic support had voted in 2002. 'Surprised and delighted,' I responded. Ronnie, in his own laconic style, piped up, 'Aye, we were all surprised.' He was a witty man. In Ireland, on another occasion, at a supporters' function, we were watching the hurling, where you get points for sending the ball over the bar. 'Lennox,' Ronnie said, drawing out his words slowly and deliberately, 'you would have been a star at this game.' Bobby Murdoch, who was sadly the first of the Lions to pass away, in 2001, was the easiest man in the world to get along with – I don't think I ever saw Bobby Murdoch angry away from the football field. He was such an amiable, pleasant guy and great company.

Jimmy Johnstone was my closest friend in the team during our playing days. The week of his funeral in 2006 was one of the hardest of my life. Bertie Auld phoned me at half past seven on the morning of Monday, 13 March to tell me that Jimmy had died. It was a real shock because Stevie Chalmers and I had been up to see Jimmy at his home in Viewpark, Lanarkshire, only four days previously, and as we had been leaving I had given Jimmy a big kiss on the cheek and had told him we would be back to see him again soon. Jimmy was extremely ill, although mentally he was sharp as a tack and he was perky, as usual. We had a laugh and a bit of fun, although his voice wasn't great by then and it was clear his condition had taken a severe toll on him, physically. He had lost a lot of weight. He had heard that I was to be fitted with a pacemaker the following week and had rapped out the line, 'What do we call you now? Gerry?' That was pretty clever, I thought, and we had a wee laugh about it. So when Bertie rang me with that awful news, I couldn't believe it.

Kathryn and I went straight to Jimmy's house to see Agnes, his wife, and their children, and she told us that the funeral would be on the Friday. I was scheduled to go into hospital on the Tuesday, the day after I heard about Jimmy, to get the pacemaker fitted, but I insisted that I would not have the procedure carried out unless I had a guarantee that I would be able to attend the funeral on the Friday. Dr Hall gave me that guarantee and at teatime on Thursday, I was duly released from hospital and attended the funeral the next morning. I was drained of emotion and strength in the aftermath but I had promised to attend the League Cup final at Hampden Park on the Sunday. Celtic defeated Dunfermline Athletic 3–0, and it turned into something of a Jimmy Johnstone tribute match, with the players all wearing Jimmy's number seven on their shorts and the fans singing 'Dirty Old Town', the song that Jimmy had recorded with Simple Minds. On returning to Saltcoats that Sunday evening, I said to Kathryn, for the first time in my life, 'I'm beat, exhausted, wabbit.' It had been a tough week. The funeral had been incredible – so sad yet so joyous as well, with so many people at the church and on the streets outside wishing to pay their respects to a man who had touched them all.

Jimmy and I roomed up everywhere we went with the team from the mid-1960s onwards, and the two of us would always be at the back of the bus starting the sing-songs. We were always together. Even our pegs in the dressing room – numbers 17 and 18 – were side by side. It was so sad to see Jimmy pass away. He had been suffering from motor neurone disease for five years, but we still expected him to remain with us a bit longer than he did. His passing means that we have now lost the oldest – Ronnie Simpson – and the two youngest of the Lisbon Lions.

We never became millionaires as footballers but we have memories that money cannot buy. Occasionally, though, it is brought home to us how modest our earnings were. A few years ago, the Lisbon Lions were invited to a joint dinner in London with the Manchester United players who had won the European Cup in 1968. We flew down, found ourselves in a big, swanky hotel in central London and on the night on which we arrived decided to head out to Soho for a meal. We chose an inviting restaurant, ambled in, sat down, took a look at the menu and left. It was far too dear for us – we decided to go somewhere cheaper. To me, that was quite embarrassing for a bunch of guys who were the champions of Europe at one time – any one of the current European champions could have bought the restaurant without noticing a dent in his bank balance.

These days I'm back at Celtic Park, working as a match-day host. At home games, I meet the other hosts at noon inside the ground and we then go our separate ways to meet and greet supporters in the hospitality lounges. It's very enjoyable to trade banter with the fans, meet a lot of nice people and get to see the matches. I know a lot of people at Celtic nowadays and we are welcomed heartily wherever we go. Most people are pleased to see us. Celtic Park, I would say, is back to being a happy place and Peter Lawwell, who became chief executive in 2003, has helped to nurture a good spirit inside the club. Martin O'Neill, who came to the club as manager in 2000, also helped to return Celtic to being a bit more of a family club. When Martin arrived, one of the first things he did was to take all the Lisbon Lions out to dinner and he did the same the following year, which was great. If you met him inside Celtic Park, he would always take the time to stop and have a good chat with you.

When we went to Seville with Celtic for the 2003 UEFA Cup final, we discovered that our hotel had no swimming pool. Martin found out about this and insisted that we come up to the team hotel and use the facilities there. We told him we didn't want to get in the way when the players were preparing for the match but it was nice of him to make the offer. We always felt comfortable in the company of Martin and John Robertson, his assistant, and I enjoyed going to watch their team. That was a big, strong team and people said they played the long ball, which was not entirely true. They could play that way if they wished but they also passed the ball very well. Against Olympique Lyon in the Champions League in 2003, on a night when Celtic Park really did roar, they scored a goal that must have involved around 30 passes and you don't do that if you are long-ball merchants. Gordon Strachan, who became manager in 2005 after Martin left the club, is another nice guy and I was pleased to see him achieve success in his opening year as manager, when Celtic won the 2005–06 League championship title.

The club has had a lot of good players in recent years, most notably Henrik Larsson. Lubo Moravcik was also quite exceptional. Stilian Petrov and Jorge Cadete are others who have particularly impressed me. Henrik's exceptional work-rate ensured that his ability would shine through and as a striker he was close to flawless. I was also a great fan of Jorge Cadete during the year or so he was at the club, towards the end of Tommy Burns' time as manager. Cadete was a 6-yard-box scorer but he wasn't there long enough to establish himself fully with

Celtic. Of the Gordon Strachan team, Shunsuke Nakamura, the Japan international, is my favourite for his tremendous skill and flair.

It was a big thrill for me to be named alongside players such as Henrik, Paul McStay, Kenny Dalglish, Danny McGrain and several other Lisbon Lions in the 'greatest-ever Celtic team', as voted for by the Celtic supporters in 2002. We didn't know before we arrived at the Clyde Auditorium that night whom they had selected so it was a genuine surprise to be called up to the podium. Celtic has been going for 120 years now and I got picked as one of the best 11 so it can't get any better than that, especially when you look at the guys who were named with me in that team and, perhaps even more significantly, at the guys who were not chosen for it. It was a real honour and I'm extremely proud of it.

Being the highest living goalscorer in Celtic's history and the second-highest overall, second only to Jimmy McGrory, also makes me immensely proud. When I look at the guys who are close to my record, such as Henrik Larsson and Stevie Chalmers, and at my goalscoring contemporaries at Celtic, such as Willie Wallace, Joe McBride and Dixie Deans, plus the great scorers from Celtic's early years, such as Patsy Gallacher and Jimmy Quinn, it is clear that there have been numerous great strikers in Celtic's history. It is extra special to me that I have attained that record even though I played an awful lot of games for Celtic in a wide position. When I scored the hat-trick against Rangers at Ibrox in 1966, Mr McGrory came into the dressing room and said, 'I would have loved to have scored your first goal.' I was really pleased and thrilled when he said that.

During my career, I was never sure of exactly how many goals I had scored at any given point. One day in November 1973, down at Dumbarton, I scored with a penalty and in the dressing room afterwards, Kenny Dalglish said, 'Well done. You've just passed Stevie's record.' I hadn't been aware of it. Even though I was one of the top scorers at the club almost every season, I think I'd actually have scored more goals if I had been played through the middle. It was late on in my career before I got to wear the number nine and I enjoyed that, just being the number nine. It's an instinctive thing, scoring goals. It's about knowing where to be, when to be there, where the ball is likely to fall and having the quick reactions to stick it away.

It would not have bothered me if Henrik had surpassed my goalscoring record for Celtic because, if he had done so, it would have been in the process of winning another championship or another cup for Celtic and that would have delighted me. It will be hard for anyone else to score more than 200 goals because players tend not to stay at clubs for so long nowadays. If anyone does get past us, it will be because they have helped Celtic to success and that can only be a good thing. I'd be fine with that.

I was also proud to be inaugurated into the Scottish Football Museum Hall of Fame at Hampden Park early in 2006. On the same night, John White, the magical Tottenham Hotspur and Scotland player who died at a tragically young age, was inaugurated along with the late Willie Waddell, as was Lawrie Reilly, the great Hibernian and Scotland striker, and Joe Jordan, who scored for Scotland in three successive World Cup finals.

My children have grown into fine people and are all happy and doing well in life. Gill is a number-one air hostess with easyJet, which means that she is in charge of the team of hostesses on her allotted flight. Gary drives a fire engine and Jeff has his own window-cleaning business. My grandchildren are smashing too. Calvin, who is 12, is Gary's son. Nicole, who is ten, and Zack, nine, are Gill's children. Gill, her husband Colin, Nicole and Zack live down the road from us in Saltcoats. Gary, his wife Elaine and Calvin live in Ardrossan, while Jeff and Lisa, who were married in June 2006, live in Kilmarnock. It's good to have the family all living close to our home. The children are all seriously interested in the game of football and Nicole and Zack play with TASS (Towns Ardrossan, Saltcoats, Stevenston) Thistle. I go to watch them every time they play and am always impressed. Calvin joined Stevenston Thistle in 2006 and we enjoy going to watch him play as well. All of our children and grandchildren are committed Celtic supporters. They know the shirt numbers of every player and have their own favourites in the side. The grandchildren also have second-favourite teams, as children of that age tend to do. Zack likes Manchester United, Nicole Chelsea and Calvin has become a fan of Hearts, whose Paul Hartley when he was with the Tynecastle club, was kind enough to provide Calvin with an autographed strip that he had worn, within minutes of a Celtic–Hearts match concluding. I was really pleased to see Paul join Celtic in January 2007.

As often as I can, I go golfing with Stevie Chalmers, although that activity was suspended for a while after I began having severe trouble with my knee, and that, rather oddly, led to me having my pacemaker installed. Nowadays my ankles, which gave me problems throughout my career, are absolutely fine but my knees give me frequent trouble even though, as a player, I never once suffered a knee injury. I had been due to be fitted with a replacement knee in early 2006 but when they carried out the various tests, prior to the planned operation, they discovered that my pulse was too low for me to go under anaesthetic and the only way to increase it was by fitting a pacemaker. The knee operation was duly carried out on 29 August 2006, the day before my birthday, and although there was a bit of initial discomfort, it was well worthwhile having it done because it gave me greater mobility. Stevie Chalmers was also pleased. I don't think he had won a golf match since

I had to stop playing because of my dodgy knee and he was desperate to see me back on the course to help him out . . .

It's so strange that I have become a golfer. As I mentioned before, Jimmy and I were the two Celtic players in the 1960s who never played the game. I started by playing with a friend of mine, Pat McGlynn, and had a set of clubs for years, but I footered around with the game and, really, for a long time could make neither head nor tail of it. Eventually, I began playing in a foursome at Routenburn Golf Club on Sundays with Pat, Martin Brodie and John Brady, and looked forward to it and enjoyed it so much that I joined Largs Golf Club.

It is such a hard game. You can go home after a round and reflect on doing well on the course but the next time you play it can be as if you have never held a golf club in your hand. I'm fortunate that Stevie has always been a great golfer and had a lot of patience with me when I started playing. We've now golfed all over the world and the two of us are invited frequently, as a pair, to attend golf days and tournaments, which is most enjoyable. I have now played on a lot of superb golf courses. I'm not the world's greatest golfer – my handicap is 15 – but I'm a happy golfer. I never let the frustrations that the game throws up get to me. I reason that if I'm playing badly it's because I'm a mediocre golfer so I should not expect things to go perfectly all the time.

Stevie Chalmers and I enjoy regular matches against Billy McNeill and Bertie Auld. Billy and Bertie have picked up numerous second prizes in that contest, because of Stevie. He and I also enjoy our games with our two good friends Michael Church and Chris Currie. Another good friend, but one who doesn't play golf, is my lifelong pal Tommy Burns, with whom I attended primary and secondary school, and who was on the milk run with me when we were boys.

Reading is another pastime that I enjoy greatly. I can spend an entire afternoon relaxing with a book. On a long aeroplane journey, I'll read a book from cover to cover, barely looking up from it. Lynda La Plante and James Patterson are among my favourite authors. The plots of their books always have lots of twists and turns. I'm a bit of a television enthusiast as well. I watch a lot of films and sport on the small screen, and on Champions League evenings, I cannot be budged from in front of the box. It is the greatest competition in the world, I believe. The World Cup is a great spectacle with great players but for concentrated quality, the Champions League tops it. It was a big thrill to see Celtic progress past Christmas in that tournament in late 2006 when, on a very special November night, they defeated Manchester United 1–0 through a stunning Shunsuke Nakamura free-kick, executed with magnificent technique. It had taken time for them to qualify from the group stage but the club is too big for that not to have happened eventually, and it was terrific to see that promise come to fruition. Gordon Strachan must have been delighted with that – and he's entitled to be.

It is a different tournament from the one in which we played. You can have a bad night in the Champions League group stage but remain in the competition but it was very difficult to have a bad night in the old knockout European Cup and survive. It is still a great tournament with fine teams and wonderful players, and extremely difficult to win, although I feel that a Champions League should be for champions. When Liverpool won it in 2005, they had qualified by finishing fourth in their League, 30 points behind Arsenal, the 2004 FA Premier League champions. Money talks and the clubs from the bigger Leagues in Europe seem over-represented in the Champions League. It should maybe be renamed 'The Champions League, plus the runners-up and the team that trailed in after them plus the one that clawed their way into fourth position before the door slammed behind them . . .' It is a magnificent spectacle, though, and I love watching it, and when Richard Keys, the Sky Sports presenter, says, on a Champions League evening, that we will see every goal in Europe before the end of the programme, it is poetry to me. 'Good for you, Richard,' I always say at that point. It is a more commercial competition than it was in our time and that may have killed some of the romance of the European Cup – but it is great to watch.

The Lisbon Lions, as has often been noted, were all born within 30 miles of Celtic Park, a statistic that in today's footballing world I don't think will ever be repeated. I was at the outer extremity of that distance, since that's the number of miles from the East End of Glasgow to Saltcoats. It is a different Saltcoats now from the one in which I was born. All three of the local towns – Ardrossan, Saltcoats and Stevenston – have expanded considerably since the days of my youth. There always seems to be housebuilding going on at some new site. The three cinemas that I attended as a boy have long since gone and a lot of pubs have disappeared. When I was wee, you knew everybody and their family but now, in Saltcoats, many people have their homes here but commute to work in Glasgow, Kilmarnock, Irvine and elsewhere. The work at ICI dwindled away down the years and it is now only a minor employer in the area. Quay Street, where I lived during my earliest years, is barely recognisable to me now. A lot of the small, family-owned shops have succumbed to the pressures of competing with supermarkets and gone out of business. The police now patrol in cars rather than on foot, when you knew who they were. Despite all that, I would still say that Saltcoats is a good place in which to live. The beach and the promenade provide the town with an impressive frontage and there remains a core sense of community. It is no longer the holiday destination that it was – almost everybody goes abroad now – but for those of us who live here, the fresh air and relaxed atmosphere that are intrinsic to a seaside town make it, at times, idyllic.

On a really nice summer's night, I will still go to watch Junior football at Saltcoats, Ardeer or wherever it is being played, just as I used to do with my father when I was a very young boy. I suppose my life has now turned full circle. They say that once you have left, you can't go home again – I wouldn't know because I have never moved away from Saltcoats. I've still had a journey through life that could not have been bettered and I'm looking forward to seeing how the next few chapters will unfold.

CAREER STATISTICS

Bobby Lennox, born Saltcoats, 30 August 1943.
Career: St Michael's School, Irvine; Star of the Sea Amateurs 1959, Ardeer Recreation 1959, Celtic 5 September 1961. Debut 3 March 1962 v Dundee. Houston Hurricane 29 March 1978. Celtic 19 September 1978. Retired and appointed Celtic coach 8 November 1980. Dismissed 10 June 1993. Awarded MBE 1981 New Year's Honours List.

Honours:
11 Scottish League championships, 1965–66 to 1973–74, 1976–77, 1978–79. 8 Scottish Cup honours 1964–65, 1966–67, 1968–69, 1970–71, 1971–72, 1973–74, 1974–75, 1979–80. 4 Scottish League Cup winners 1965–66, 1966–67, 1967–68, 1968–69. European Cup winners 1966–67. European Cup runners-up 1969–70.

Scotland 10 caps, 3 goals.
1966 v Northern Ireland (1 goal)
1967 v England (1), USSR, Wales
1968 v England, Denmark (1), Austria, Cyprus (sub)
1969 v West Germany
1970 v Wales (sub)

Scottish League 3 matches, 2 goals.
1966 v League of Ireland (2 goals)
1968 v Football League, League of Ireland

Season	League		Scottish Cup		SL Cups		Euro Cup		Glasgow Cups		Other	
	Apps	Goals	Apps	Goals	Apps	Goals	Apps	Goals	Apps	Goals	Apps	Goals
CELTIC												
1961–62	1	–	–	–	–	–	–	–	1	–	–	–
1962–63	4	–	–	–	5	–	–	–	–	–	–	–
1963–64	7	1	–	–	–	–	1+	1	–	–	–	–
1964–65	22	9	6	6	6	1	3#	–	3	3	–	–
1965–66	24	15	2	1	11	5	6+	4	–	–	–	–
1966–67	27	13	5	5	7	5	7*	2	3	7	–	–
1967–68	28	32	–	–	9	7	2*	2	2	3	3	–
1968–69	28	12	6	3	9	14	4*	1	–	–	–	–
1969–70	20	14	4	3	8	2	7*	–	–	–	–	–
1970–71	24	10	6	4	8	6	6*	1	–	–	–	–
1971–72	26	12	4	2	9	4	8*	1	–	–	–	–
1972–73	23	11	7	1	7	5	3*	–	–	–	–	–
1973–74	19	12	1	2	8	7	3*	1	–	–	3	5
1974–75	14	5	2	–	7	2	2*	–	1	–	3	1
1975–76	30	10	1	–	9	3	3+	–	1	–	–	–
1976–77	5	2	–	–	6	–	2#	–	1	–	–	–
1977–78	3	–	–	–	4	–	3*	1	–	–	–	–
HOUSTON HURRICANE												
1978	30	3	–	–	–	–	–	–	–	–	–	–
CELTIC												
1978–79	14	4	2	1	2	1	–	–	2	–	1	–
1979–80	29	6	6	3	6	1	6*	–	2	2	1	1
TOTAL	378	171	52	31	121	63	66	14	16	15	11	7

Other cups
1967–68 World Club Championship
1973–74, 1974–75 Drybrough Cup
1978–79 Anglo-Scottish Cup

* European Cup
+ European Cup-Winners' Cup
# Fairs Cup UEFA Cup

INDEX

The abbreviation BL is used to refer to Bobby Lennox in entries such as Lennox, Eric (BL brother)